# *The* Cook's Tales

To Edie —
  Who's taught me more than
I can ever remember —
          Lee Edwards Benning

Other Cookbooks by Lee Edwards Benning

*Oh, Fudge! A Celebration of America's Favorite Candy*
*Make Mine Vanilla*

# *The* Cook's Tales

## Origins of Famous Foods and Recipes

*by*

**Lee Edwards Benning**

The Globe Pequot Press

Old Saybrook, Connecticut

Text credits: P. 26: Recipe for Classic Tomato Soup Spice Cake reprinted courtesy of Campbell Soup Company; Campbell's is a registered trademark of Campbell Soup Company. P. 46: Recipe for Filet of Sole Marguery à la Diamond Jim Brady reprinted by permission of *American Heritage* magazine, a division of Forbes Inc., © 1964 Forbes Inc., 1992. P. 187: Recipe for Perfection Salad courtesy of Knox Gelatine, Inc., Englewood Cliffs, NJ 07632. P. 188: Recipe for Tunnel of Fudge Cake reprinted with permission from Pillsbury. P. 204: Recipe for the Original Lady Baltimore Cake reprinted with permission from the University of South Carolina Press from *Two Hundred Years of Charleston Cooking*, recipes gathered by Blanche S. Rhett, edited by Letti Gay.

Library of Congress Cataloging-in-Publication Data

Benning, Lee Edwards, 1934-
The cook's tales: origins of famous foods and recipes / by Lee Edwards Benning. — 1st ed.
    p.    cm.
Includes bibliographical references and index.
ISBN 0-87106-229-1
1. Cookery—Terminology. 2. Cookery—History. I. Title.
TX349.B415  1992
    641'.03—dc20                          92-14369
                                           CIP
Book design by Nancy Freeborn
Illustrations by Lana Kleinschmidt

Manufactured in the United States of America
First Edition/Second Printing

To

CHARLOTTE LACAZE
Associate Professor of Art History
The American University of Paris

*and*

LARRY FORRY
Research Librarian
Montgomery County–Norristown Public Library

whose interest in the past enriches the present and ensures the future

# Table of Contents

# Acknowledgments

Would you believe some people skip right over this section? Perhaps they equate it to a written version of an Oscar acceptance speech. You know what I mean, the ones that sound as if the acceptor is reading the telephone book. Ahh, but thar's gold in them thar phone books. For example, want to know on what day of the week a certain date occurred, such as your birthday? You'll find the information in the yellow pages of the telephone book.

Similarly, in the acknowledgments section of a cookbook you can find buried treasure. For example, have a question about a recipe? Call the author. Most don't have unlisted phone numbers. To find out where they live, check the acknowledgments for clues. Lots of mentions of one particular town is a dead giveaway. I know. Maida Heatter tracked me down that way. As did a Texas professional confectionist who will probably make a mail order fortune selling one of my candies. More power to her.

If the author's a woman and apt to be listed under her husband's name, check the dedication first, acknowledgments second. Somewhere she's going to acknowledge her debt to him, if for nothing else than his willingness to eat the same recipe a zillion times until she got it right. In my case I owe my husband, Arthur, so much, he almost qualifies as my coauthor.

Are you looking for a literary agent? Most authors, and I'm no exception, acknowledge their agent's help in selling the book. Thank you, Jane Jordan Browne of Multimedia in Chicago. May some reader of this book make you rich.

Do you have a manuscript similar to or better than this one? You may want to send it to the folks at Globe Pequot. Here is also where you'll find acknowledged the contributions of such specific editors as Laura Strom and Mike Urban. May gold come over their transom. But let me warn you; they're whip-crackers, and you rewrite until you get it right. (Mustn't forget Betsy Amster, either, who was there in the beginning and has now moved to the West Coast.) Globe Pequot also has a recipe-rabbit up its sleeve who can turn sixteenth-century recipe gibberish into twentieth-century good eating. Her name? Cary Hull.

Want more information on a product or recipe mentioned in the book? You'll find that here, too. For example, for more of the classic soup recipes, contact Kevin Lowery, Manager of Communications, Campbell Soup Company, Camden, N.J. For Knox gelatin recipes, Maggie Vetildi in Englewood Cliffs, N.J. For Fleischmann information, Shelita Acosta came through for me.

Want information on the Pillsbury Bake-Off? Write or call Marlene Johnson or Joseph Andrews, Product Communications Managers, 27A1 Pillsbury Center, Minneapolis, MN 55402; (800) 328–4730. Looking for a bundt pan? Contact Kari Lee of Northland Aluminum Products, Inc., Minneapolis, Minnesota. If you're lucky, as I was, you might even get to speak to Dave Dalquist, the president.

Think you have a more humane way of killing lobsters? Then Robert Bayer wants to talk to you. He's a professor at the University of Maine in the Department of Animal and Veterinary Sciences and Maine Lobster Institute. Want to learn more about lobsters? Contact Frank Matter, editor-in-chief, Acadia Press, Bar Harbor, Maine; he's published a book on the subject.

Have a question on Italian cuisine? The man with the answers and the magnificent cuisine is Antonio Schiavone of diLullo's Centro in Philadelphia. Delmonico's in New York lives on, thanks to Ed Huber, the latest upholder of the tradition, who is quick to share his knowledge. Want the most accurate information on French cuisine? Take a side-trip to Contres, France, and ask for Jean-Claude Metivier.

Interested in Old and Middle English foods? Contact David Boyd, Ph.D., Chaucerian expert at the University of Pennsylvania in Philadelphia.

And now for the Academy Award portion of this section. (I admire the intestinal fortitude of those writers who simply list first names, thanking every Susie and Sal they know simultaneously. I am not that courageous.)

Many thanks to all the librarians extraordinaire whom I consulted: Denise Gibbons, Rumford Branch, East Providence Public Library, Rhode Island; Loretta Ryder and Pat Kelly, research librarians, Montgomery County–Norristown Library; Trudie Buri, Wissahickon Library; Curtis Kiefer and others at Philadelphia Public Library; and the many helpful hands at the Schlesinger Library at Radcliffe in Boston and the Henry Francis du Pont Winterthur Museum in Delaware.

More thanks to Mario Mele, Chairman of the Montgomery County Board of Commissioners and the force behind the Caterina de' Medici Society; Jeffrey Clova, chef at Philadelphia's Sheraton and the voice at the end of the Chef's Hot Line; Nancy Whitby, lobster connoisseur; Samuel Jackson who makes a mean bouillabaisse; Sally Duff, whose quiche not only delights but freezes; Loretta Sigman Philips, the original Kosher Kid, her husband, Alan, and brother Gary; Ben and Helen Menin, who can *gefilte* my fish any day; Sue Coll, whose madeleines inspire all of us; Jennifer Hoff, my connection with Aidar B. Axmetoby, expert on Russian cuisine; and those others whose recipes made my life tastier and easier.

If this book has piqued your interest in the history of food, especially early American food, by all means visit colonial Williamsburg. Go to the converted Greenhow Lumber Company on Duke of Gloucester Street, and sign up for the two-hour, once-a-week food tour. But get there early. Only through the great kindness of a sympathetic employee, who must remain anonymous, was I squeezed onto the tour. She shall never know what a difference taking that tour made in the writing of this book.

Finally, I must thank the many food historians who came before me and took the time to collect the myths, legends, fables, and facts about food that have enabled me to write this book. You'll find a partial list of their editorial output in the Bibliography at the end of this book.

# Introduction

## *The First*
# Cook's Tale

Some six hundred years ago on a fine April day, Geoffrey Chaucer sent twenty-nine assorted, fictional pilgrims off to visit the shrine of Thomas à Becket at Canterbury.

They halt at the Tabard Inn in Southwark. Its host decides to join the pilgrimage and challenges the group to a storytelling contest that he will judge. Each pilgrim is to tell four tales, two tales on the way to Canterbury and two more on the way back. The teller of the best tale will get a free dinner.

Chaucer never completed the ambitious sixty tales with prologues planned for *The Canterbury Tales*, but the tales he did tell are as diverse a group as one could wish, from biographical to bawdy, folk tale to sermonette. And for the first time in the English language, food was used as simile and metaphor in both the tales and the descriptions of the pilgrims. For example, we know the Prioress is well-bred because she never lets a crumb fall from her mouth nor dips her fingers so deep into the sauce as to get them wet. So fastidious and scrupulous is she at wiping her upper lip that no spot of grease shimmers in her cup after she drinks from it.

About the cook among the pilgrims, we are told by Chaucer,

> *He koude rooste and seethe and boille and frye,*
>
> *Maken mortreux* [a thick soup] *and wel bake a pye.*

We nod our heads and think, sound credentials these. But then the host speaks up. He reminds Roger, the cook, that his tale had better be good because he is a man known to make dry, gravy-less pastries, sell twice-warmed up Jakke of Dover (a pot pie), serve his stubble-fed geese with a cursed parsley stuffing, and run a cookshop full of flies. Immediately, we have taken the man's measure and wonder what sort of tale such a scoundrel might tell. The piece no sooner begins than ends, left undone like a piece of raw dough. Perhaps fittingly so, for the story of cooks and cookery is always ongoing.

I do not pretend to be another Chaucer, but my ambitions are no less than his: to amuse, to edify, to shock but only a little, to expose foibles, to prick myths, to label fables, to fashion facts into tales as interesting as fiction. Hopefully, at the end of our pilgrimage to find the origins of some of the world's most famous foods and dishes, you will be left with a good taste in your mouth. As a writer and lover of food, I can ask for no more.

# A
## is for Apple

Imagine an apple, any apple—bright crimson or dull red, green-skinned or yellow, basically round, yielding to the bite with a satisfying crunch and rewarding you with a flood of juice and a blatantly sweet or slightly tart taste. One mouthful and you know—mmm, perfection!

Yes, of course A is for apple; anything else would be heresy. But just as one bite of apple inevitably leads to another, so, too, does the thought of an apple conjure up still another image, that of America's favorite pie.

At the very thought of apple pie, our collective chests swell with patriotic fervor, for here is the ideal, the synthesis of native American cuisine. No wonder metaphorians have made a truism of the expression "as American as apple pie."

Which it's not. We may have taken it to our hearts, but it is neither our invention nor even indigenous to our country. In fact, the apple pie, in its infinite variations, predates our country's settlement by hundreds of years. What's more, the apple tree is not even native to our country. European settlers brought it with them. (So valuable was it that Governor John Endicott, in 1649, exchanged 500 three-year-old apple seedlings for 200 acres of land.)

Once here, though, we took the apple to our collective cookery bosoms; hence, "as American as apple pie." Exercising typical American ingenuity, we picked our apples, then dried them and fried them, stewed them and sauced them, preserved them and fermented them, baked them and caked them. We combined them with pork and with poultry, added them to cabbage or celery, and mixed them with mayonnaise. But we took particular delight in putting apples and dough together in every conceivable way. When we were finished, we added a slice of sharp cheese, a dribble of hard sauce, a gob of whipped cream, or a scoop of ice cream. Yes, indeed, all of that is *very* American.

But what is *especially* American is the way we accepted into our culinary repertoire all the different European forms of apple pie. In America it can have one crust or two, be latticed or crumb-topped, of shortbread or short-flake dough. In other words, an American apple pie can be Italian, French, German, or British in origin. Not so in Europe where each variation has its own ethnicity—the Italian *torta* and *crostata*, the French *flan* and *tarte*, the German *kuchen* and *torte*, as well as Britain's tart and plate-pie.

You can actually take a world tour by going westward along the apple route. Beginning in southwestern Asia, the apple made its way westward via the Roman Empire. It later traveled further westward in the saddlebags of Crusaders and crossed the channel into England. From there, still going due west, it was brought by Europeans to America's eastern shores. "Johnny Appleseed" Chapman (1775–1847) planted apple trees throughout the Midwest, and gold-rushing westward-ho'ers took it to the Pacific coast. Once there, some anonymous sea captain loaded it on his ship and introduced the apple to Japan and China. All together, the apple went around the world in two thousand years.

If one were to conduct a survey of Americans to determine the typical American pie, chances are it would be a large, deep-dish, two-crusted affair, which is actually an

American combination of two European pies: the tartlet and the "great standing pie," or savoury.

The tartlet, sometimes known as a pasty or saucer pie, is a single-serving dish usually made from two small circles of crust with a spoonful of apple filling placed in the middle of one. The filled circle is then topped with the other crust, the edges pinched together, and the whole tartlet deep-fried or oven-baked. (If the crust is a square folded triangularly over the filling, we know it as a turnover.) Americans took the tartlet and aggrandized it into a multiple-serving dish.

**Dr. Acrelius, a Swedish parson in the colonies, wrote home in 1758, "Apple-pie is used through the whole year, and when fresh apples are no longer to be had, dried ones are used. It is the evening meal of children. House-pie, in country places, is made of apples neither peeled nor freed from their cores, and its crust is not broken if a wagon wheel goes over it."**

We accomplished this by substituting apples for the typical filling of a "great standing pie," or savoury. This large, deep, double-crusted dish was usually made with meats and/or vegetables and served as an entrée. For example, the original mincemeat pie of medieval times combined minced or hashed meat with suet plus a handful of raisins, perhaps nuts, maybe even apple chunks. In the savoury, unlike the American apple pie, the quality of the crust was unimportant. It need not even be edible. Its singular purpose was to act as a casing (or "coffin") for the filling and, optionally, to sop up the excess juices released by the suet. The resulting savoury was thick, solid, and filling.

Not the optimum description of an apple pie. But then, so few apple pies approach the ideal. All too frequently the apples are either overcooked mushy or undercooked crunchy, too sweet or too tart. Perhaps the juices have dried up or overflowed onto the bottom of the oven. Take heart, such are not the faults of the cook but of the apples used, and that, too, is not the fault of the cook but the marketplace. During the three hundred years or so since apples were introduced to our country, we have developed more than 2,500 different varieties, but you're lucky to see as many as a half dozen of these in the typical supermarket.

Getting back to that "ideal" pie, its crust is crucial but sometimes proves disappointing. The bottom crust can easily become soggy; the upper half-raw or half-scorched. Europeans solved the problem of soggy crusts by making their tarts and flans with a single bottom shortdough crust comparable to a rich cookie dough, a method adopted by early American cooks, too. Other cooks used puff pastry with its many layers of buttery dough. Still others simply avoided making piecrusts altogether, in the process inventing still more variations on the basic apple pie.

**Though humans had husbanded apples for centuries, the Roman statesman, Cato, in the third century B.C., recognized in his writings a mere seven varieties. More than 2,000 years later, more than 7,000 varieties exist worldwide. America grows more than 25 percent of the world's crop of eating apples, and all-purpose apples.**

The most goof-proof variation is the pandowdy, a late-eighteenth-century New England dish. It is sometimes known by the very descriptive name of "turn under pie" or, in older cookbooks, by the even more apt label "humbug pie" (as in fake pie). Whatever the name, it is baked in a rectangular pan with a molasses-sweetened, sometimes precooked, apple filling on the bottom and a single crust on top. After baking, the crust is "dowdied," or broken up and stirred into the filling. (*Trivia Question:* Which came first, the cooking term *pandowdy*, or the word *dowdy*, meaning "messy in appearance?" *Answer:* The former.) Actually, dowdying is a typically Yankee, very logical way to serve a large number of people from a single dish. The first spooning of pie would break up the crust anyway.

Another interpretation, called apple slump, is served with a single crust intact and on top. It is an apple version of the mashed potato-topped shepherd's pie that is better known as a cobbler.

The oldest in this family of no-fail, nonconventional apple "pies" dates back to 1723 and is called the *poupeton* or pupton. Both terms mean "mess in a pan." A progenitor of pandowdy and more English than American, it appeared on Virginia tables as late as the early nineteenth century. In this version, the apples were cooked down to the consistency of marmalade, then blended, when cold, with an egg-yolk-enriched bread crumb mixture. The whole was baked in a slow oven until set, then turned out like a cake on a plate, sliced, and served hot, with or without a sauce.

It bears a striking resemblance, ingredient-wise, to the brown Betty, sometimes known as the brown Betsy. This one is all American, owing its name to the Negro minstrel shows common in Virginia during the Christmas season prior to the Civil War. The revelry usually included a mummery (a costumed pantomime), with as large a cast as possible—all amateurs, all residents of the plantation, and, not infrequently, all slaves. The play included two stock characters: Father Christmas and his female counterpart, Old Bett or Mother Christmas, the latter played by a young male slave in women's clothing. After the performance, Father Christmas might hand out gifts, but Old Bett (or Betty) served up a special Christmas treat made from dried apples, molasses, and layers of stale bread crumbs. By 1857 this apple dish was appearing in cookbooks as brown Betty. Some cookbook authors, not finding that particularly descriptive, rechristened it apple brown Betty. I am happy to report that Old Bett's namesake lives on in recent editions of those thick, all-purpose, 1,001-recipe books such as *The Joy of Cooking.*

**Women in early New England gathered together for apple bees, which, like quilting bees, made quick and pleasant work of an annual task—in this case, not quilting but the preparation of apples for drying.**

For all the various ways of combining apples and dough, none can match the apple dumpling. Most of us think of dumplings as spoonfuls of dough, frequently from a biscuit mix, steamed or baked atop a stew. But even when made with chopped apples, this is not a true apple dumpling. The real McCoy for hundreds of years has been a whole apple, peeled and cored, stuffed with sugar or marmalade, wrapped in dough, tied in a cloth, and boiled for nearly an hour like a plum pudding. Modernists bake it, first in a 425° F oven, then in a slower oven for forty-five to ninety minutes, depending on the size of the apples.

Baked apples without benefit of dough anywhere are yet another popular twist on the apple theme. The most illustrious baked apples were those served by David Ogilvy (born June 23, 1911), who claims in *Confessions of an Advertising Man* that he owes his fame and fortune to this delicious treat. Just in case the name doesn't ring a bell with you, Ogilvy was the advertising man who took a $1.50 eye patch, put it on a male model wearing a white dress shirt, and turned the stodgy, century-old Hathaway Shirt Company into a multimillion-dollar business. Ogilvy is also the ad man credited by his peers with having written the best headline for an advertisement: *"At Sixty Miles an Hour the Loudest Noise in the New Rolls-Royce Comes from the Electric Clock."* (When the chief engineer at the Rolls-Royce factory read the ad, he was heard to complain, "It is time we did something about that damned clock.")

**"Hell is an idea first born on an undigested apple dumpling," wrote Herman Melville in *Moby Dick*.**

Before Ogilvy came to this country and founded the ad agency of Ogilvy & Mather, he did a stint as a chef at the Hotel Majestic in Paris. Even with thirty-seven chefs on staff, each put in ten hours a day, six days a week, and worked under such pressure that there was a saying among them that "a cook by the time he is forty is either dead or crazy." This was driven home the night the chef potagier threw forty-seven raw eggs at a dodging Ogilvy, scoring nine direct hits, all because Ogilvy had raided the stock pots for bones for a customer's poodle. Even at that time, Ogilvy was a fervent believer that if you make yourself indispensable to a client, you will never be fired. He likes to tell the story of the baked apple to prove it.

It seems in 1931 that the Majestic's most important client, an American lady, was on a special diet based on a baked apple at every meal. She was not pleased, however, with the apples served her and threatened to move to the Ritz. The challenge was handed to Ogilvy. He developed a technique for baking *two* apples, passing their flesh through a sieve to remove all traces of core, and then replacing the flesh of both apples in one skin. The result was the most voluptuous baked apple the client had ever seen (and more calories than she suspected). Word came down to the kitchen that the chef who was baking those apples must be given tenure. Fortunately for the history of advertising, Ogilvy chose to give up apple-baking and take up copywriting.

If Ogilvy had decided to stay with the Majestic, one can only dream of what he might have done with an apple pie. Would he have used one crust or two? Maybe a shortbread buttery crust on the bottom and puff pastry or meringue on the top? Alas, Ogilvy refuses to say. Americans, being Americans, however, will continue bragging that nothing can match a good old-fashioned American apple pie.

# Apple Pie

*Even home economists approach the making of apple pies with trepidation. What appears simple has many booby traps, for instance, choosing the right variety of apple. Nine out of ten times, if your pie is too sweet or too tart or too watery, it is the fault of the apples used. Then there's the crust. At its best, a piecrust should be light, flaky, and tender. This effect is not always easily achieved, even by experienced cooks. Personally, I think it all boils down to one part the fat used, one part the flour used, one part handling, and one part luck.*

## Crust

Cuisines are often categorized by the fat used in cooking. China and Italy, for instance, have oil-based cuisines, and India's is butter-based (actually a clarified butter called *ghee*). France's in the north is butter-based, in Provence oil-based, and in the south animal fat–based. In the United States until this century, our southern cuisine was mostly butter-based and the northern was lard-based. It was in the north that the flakiest and tenderest piecrusts were found. Lard is tasteless, has a high melting point, and contains protein. Since lard and cold water don't mix, enterprising cooks long ago developed the water-whip method of combining hot water and room-temperature lard. This mixture would then be poured straight into the flour barrel and enough flour worked in with the fingers to make a crust that won raves. Although much the same results can be achieved through the use of a solid, hydrogenated shortening, to my mind, lard is still best. (If using lard, omit the milk and use the entire ⅓ cup of water.)

The antecedent for this recipe is Hannah Glasse's "A Good Crust for Great Pies," found in her *The Art of Cookery, Made Plain and Easy*, seventh edition (London, 1760).

**⅓ cup less 1 tablespoon boiling water**

**⅔ cup hydrogenated shortening**

**1 tablespoon milk**

**½ teaspoon salt**

**2 cups stirred, scooped, and leveled all-purpose flour**

**2 tablespoons melted butter or tasteless oil spray (optional)**

Pour boiling water over shortening and beat with an electric mixer or a fork until creamy. Add milk. Let cook until tepid. Add salt to flour and stir to incorporate. Mix with shortening. Can use immediately, or, if made in advance, wrap in plastic and chill. For a double-crust pie, divide into two pieces, about 60/40. Roll between sheets of wax paper to avoid incorporating more flour. Fit larger piece into pie pan and cut edge even with the outside of the rim. Brush with melted butter or spray with tasteless oil to prevent sogginess by creating an oil-and-water-don't-mix barrier between the apple juices and the crust. Reserve second crust. Makes enough pastry for one 8-inch thick double crust pie. For deep-dish 9-inch pie, increase ingredients by 25 percent.

## Filling

The apple variety you choose has much to do with the success of your pie. *Don't* use Red or Golden Delicious. Use Grannie Smiths or Greenings in the fall, Winesaps or Roman Beauties in winter. Avoid making apple pie in the spring and summer when you would be using remains of the previous year's apple crop.

As you peel and cut your apples, note whether they are mushy or crisp, juicy or dry, sweet or tart. This will affect how thick you slice them (cut mushy ones thick; crisp ones, thin). If the apples are very juicy, add a bit of flour to thicken the juices. If the apples are dry, add water or cream. Pick up a slice and taste it; if it's bland, add larger amounts of spices and lemon juice. If you're adventurous, substitute vanilla for lemon juice—it will maximize the other flavors.

**6 medium or 8 small apples, pared, cored, and sliced**

**½–⅔ cup sugar (or more to taste)**

**¼ teaspoon salt**

**1 tablespoon flour (optional)**

**¼–½ teaspoon cinnamon**

**⅛–¼ teaspoon nutmeg**

**1½ tablespoons butter, cut into small pieces**

**1–2 tablespoons water or cream (optional)**

**1–2 teaspoons lemon juice or ½–1 teaspoon vanilla**

Preheat oven to 350° F. Mix dry ingredients together thoroughly and coat apple slices with them.

Place apples inside the piecrust. Dot with butter. Add additional liquids if necessary. Then top with extra crust. Let crust dangle evenly over edge of pie, then tuck it under lower crust, crimping edges together to seal. Cut wide slits in several places in top crust or make a center hole to allow steam to vent. Bake for approximately 60 minutes.

Many cooks start their pies on the bottom shelf so that the crust gets a blast of heat immediately to set it; then after 10 minutes they move the pie into the middle of the oven. Others begin the baking in a preheated 450° F oven for 10 minutes, then reduce heat to 350° F and cook an additional 45–60 minutes. Either way, cook until the crust is brown and the filling is cooked. (To test for doneness, pierce the filling with a fork or knife through the vents.)

# B
## is for Burnt

O r blackened, as it's now fashionably called. To be honest, my taste buds can't tell the difference. No more than they could in the days of nonautomated bread toasters when, in our house, nonblackened toast was a matter of exact timing and the exception rather than the rule. In those days my father tried to talk us kids out of scraping the toast. He called the black stuff "activated charcoal" and told us it was good for us. I didn't buy his argument then, and I don't buy it now, especially not in restaurants.

So now you know where I stand with burnt food. I make only one exception: marshmallows toasted on the end of a stick over a campfire. Otherwise, any food I serve burnt hasn't been done so on purpose—it's genuinely unintentional. This was true of nearly everybody (except perhaps those who liked "Pittsburgh rare" or "black 'n' blue" steaks: charred on the outside, rare to raw inside)—that is, until 1984.

That's when the "burnt is blackened is delicious" trend began at Paul Prudhomme's K-Paul's Louisiana Restaurant in New Orleans. It began as an outgrowth of an annual family camping trip with his father and twelve siblings. Cooked over an open fire and in an iron skillet, fresh fish developed "a good, smoky taste"—a taste unlike that of any fish he ate at home. When Prudhomme opened his restaurant in 1979, he attempted to duplicate this effect.

**It is impossible to do a steak charred outside, rare inside, with the usual home kitchen broiler, which is not capable of the 800° F heat of a commercial range. To give you an idea of how hot 800° F is, it's the temperature reached by ovens to self-clean.**

The result was and is a dish called blackened redfish, in which fish is cooked in a dry cast-iron skillet that has been heated until "you see white ash in the skillet bottom (the skillet cannot be too hot for this dish). . . ." This instruction was later amended to "just short of the point at which you see white ash or a white spot forming in the skillet bottom." He doesn't explain how one tells one is at that point before one gets to it, but he says that the ideal temperature is 500° F, if that's of any help.

Anyway, the recipe was included in Prudhomme's 1984 cookbook. More than 600,000 readers got the message, as did too many chefs. Blackened fish became a feature of many restaurant menus and a health hazard in many households, the blaring of smoke alarms being the least of the problems. In his sequel, Prudhomme admitted that "blackening should be done either outdoors or in a commercial kitchen." He also said it can't be done over ordinary packaged "charcoal" briquets (which aren't really charcoal, but we won't get into that), only over chunks of hardwood or on a gas or butane grill. My experience with it, both as cook and restaurant-goer, is that it should be done at K-Paul's Restaurant, period.

Sudden popularity aside, blackened isn't new. The novelty was in Prudhomme's blackening *fish*—which is normally treated more gently. Of course, in his sequel he cashed in on the popularity of the fish recipe with blackened chicken, hamburgers, and pork chops.

More interesting than Prudhomme's blackened dishes are the ones created to avoid just such blackening. Louis XIII of France (1755–1824), also known as Louis le Desire, did not like his lamb overcooked, much less blackened. To avoid this the chef prepared *cotelettes d'agneau à la martyre*, in which two lamb chops are martyred to protect a third. Basically, it is a lamb chop sandwich: a lamb chop placed between two other lamb chops. Both outer sides are grilled, then the martyrs are thrown away. The chop in the middle is cooked to perfection—juicy and without a touch of browning (especially if, as was frequently done, the entire sandwich is wrapped in sheets of suet). Of course, at today's lamb prices, this is a dish fit *only* for a king. Who else could afford it?

A variation on this lamb dish was created by the French chef Montmireil in 1882 for the French ambassador to England. Out of necessity it was made of beef, more readily available in England, the land of wool and mutton, not lamb. The ambassador was Vicomte François-Auguste-René de Châteaubriand, writer, statesman, and lover of the famous, infamous Madame de Recamier. Using the large end of the tenderloin, weighing ¼ to 1½ pounds—now known for obvious reasons as the chateaubriand—Montmireil grilled the whole piece, creating a crusty outside shell with all the juices locked inside. To serve, the outside crust was removed, leaving a solid chunk of uniformly rare fillet. The classic and proper garniture for a genuine chateaubriand was, and still is, first, *pommes château*: sautéed pared and blanched new potatoes (or olive-shaped pieces cut from previously boiled potatoes), to which, optionally, small strips of bacon may be added and, second, sauce béarnaise: a reduction of herbs, shallots, and wine or vinegar thickened with egg yolks and butter (it is a member of the hollandaise family of sauces).

**The easiest way to make *pommes château* is to use canned potatoes. Rinse them, dry them thoroughly, roll them in melted butter, and oven-bake at 325–350° F until crusty. Roll them over occasionally and/or baste them with butter. The longer you bake them, the more crusty they become.**

Duplicating the chateaubriand on a commercial basis took ingenuity, but a Parisian restaurant was up to the challenge. In order to stretch the chateaubriand, of which each beef yields but two, the chefs at Champeaux took a slice of the chateaubriand and sandwiched it between two pieces of inferior quality beef—and voilà! Ersatz chateaubriand à la martyred lamb chops.

If one has used generous outside pieces so that the charring can be removed, one can make chateaubriand sauce by extracting the juice from the excess pieces in a press and adding it to the same herbs, vinegar, and butter as in a béarnaise, leaving out the egg yolks.

Other less extreme and expensive methods of cooking a whole filet are to do it *en croute* (in a casing of dough, like Beef Wellington) or to *bard* it, tying a layer of bacon or fatback around the outside of the roast.

The ultimate nonburned meat is steak tartare, or raw steak. As prepared around the turn of the century in a gourmet restaurant, it offered the maitre d'hotel a marvelous piece of showmanship comparable to today's last-minute tableside presentations of Caesar salad or crepes Suzette or steak Diane. Steak tartare is finely minced between the flying blades of two chef's knives. Back and forth across the chopping board the knives fly until the beef is chopped just this side of ground. It is then divided into serving sizes and placed on plates. Using a spoon, the chef makes a small nest in the center of each round of beef and gently spoons a perfect, golden, raw egg yolk into each nest. Sprinkled over that are the condiments: a smattering of salt, a bit of freshly ground pepper, some minced chervil or scallions, and even some capers. Toast points finish the dish, which, by the way, was originally known as *bifteck à l'Americaine*. The reference doesn't seem particularly flattering, nor do I think it was meant to be.

**The practice of barding fillets led to that challenge to home cooks: the bacon-wrapped fillet mignon. If you cook the wrapped fillet only until the meat is rare, the bacon remains raw; cook it until the bacon's well-done, and it will have shrunk so much it no longer provides protection to the fillet. Solution: blanch the bacon first to remove excess fat; it will then be cooked by the time the fillet is rare or medium-rare.**

Somewhere along the line the name was changed, perhaps when tartare sauce was substituted for the egg yolk, or perhaps as a reference to the alleged practice of

Russia's Tartars eating raw meat. In any event, once Tartars were mentioned, legend soon followed, such as the Tartars' purported use of slabs of meat as saddle clothes to be tenderized during the course of a day's ride. According to my Russian authority on cooking, Aidar B. Axmetoby, the description was partially correct. Small strips of partially cooked meat were indeed placed under the saddle's skirt or side flaps—the portion of the saddle gripped by the rider's thighs. The meat was put there simply for convenience's sake—to have food handy so the rider need not stop to take nourishment. A side effect was that the combination of heat from horse and rider, plus friction and pressure, served to tenderize it. (The practice was not confined to the Russians; the French cavalry did it, too.)

The chef de cuisine of the Berlin restaurant Kempinski took *bifteck à l'Americaine* and turned it into *Lucca-Augen* or Lucca-Eyes, not the most appetizing choice of names. But then, the opera singer at the Royal Court Opera for whom it was named—Pauline Lucca (1841–1908)—was noted, one contemporary reviewer wrote, "not so much due to her voice or technique but rather to the fascinating charm of her appearance." I assume this charm must have included beautiful eyes. Instead of serving the dish with the raw egg yolk intact and in the hollow, the yolk and the condiments were blended into the meat first. Then the hollow was made, filled with caviar, and topped with a raw oyster. Talk about avoiding overcooking: raw meat, raw egg, raw fish roe, raw oyster. The only cooked element of the dish was the toast, which brings us back to the subject of burnt.

**Lucca-Augen, if made properly, should have the oyster placed slightly off center, to give "the appearance of an [oyster-eyeball] with an eyebrow" of black caviar. Unfortunately, this sounds even less appetizing than the name, an effect not fair to the dish, which tastes better than it looks or sounds.**

If you racked your brain for dishes containing the term *burnt*, the first and maybe the only one you'd come up with is burnt almond, the ice cream flavor. Although the name for this flavor dates back to 1840, many ice cream makers have found it objec-

Not all caramelized foods are desserts. Glazed carrots, candied sweet potatoes, and pan-fried onions are all examples of caramelizing the vegetables in natural sugar. To make them, simply cook in butter. To be safe, most cooks add a tablespoon or so of sugar just in case.

A staple of how-to kitchen books is how to remove the burnt taste from food by, for example, using pieces of bread or chunks of potato to absorb offensive flavors. Take it from me, they don't work. What does work are some defensive maneuvers. First, do not under any circumstances stir a dish you suspect of being burnt; you will just mix in the bad (*i.e.,* burnt) with the good. Second, do major surgery on burnt areas. Scrape, chop, or lop off the black and camouflage with chopped parsley if a savory and whipped cream or icing if a sweet.

tionable and so have replaced it with butter almond. (Others retain burnt almond and save "butter" for their pecan ice cream.) Regardless of the name, the treatment of the almonds is the same. They're blanched, chopped, and then cooked with sugar and butter. These caramelized (or "burnt") nuts are softer than raw ones, and their flavor is more intense. In the process of caramelizing the almonds, such high heat may be used that the real butter turns nut brown, which is just this side of burnt.

Another near-burnt dish whose name was changed to make it more appetizing is that classic of confectionery, *crème brûlée,* literally "burnt cream." Originating in the seventeenth century, this wonderful custard dessert went under its own good English name or some variation thereof until two centuries ago. James Beard has found it described as "burnt cream" at Christ College at Cambridge and "grilled cream" at King's College, Cambridge. So popular was this dessert that a special heatproof dish about the size and twice the depth of a soup plate was created for it by the Copeland-Spode Company.

Around the turn of the eighteenth century, the name was frenchified into *crème brûlée.* Who did it no one seems to know, but fingers point to Thomas Jefferson, that lover of everything edible and French. The time frame certainly lends credence to the story. Jefferson, however, added his own touch to the dessert—the flavors of lemon and orange. As served at the Hermitage, Andrew Jackson's home in Tennessee, almond was its flavoring. More than 100 years later, White House chefs served it to the Kennedys, as originally made, with real vanilla beans.

When made properly it is a marvelous custard with a thin, crunchy, caramelized sugar topping. It should not be burnt at all, just exposed to heat until it turns dark brown. In fact, it is a test of a home cook's skill to maneuver the dish just so under a broiler so as to caramelize the topping without burning it. Professionals use a "salamander," a special broiling unit to flash-caramelize food.

**Because butterscotch is cooked to such a high tempurature, it often has a hint of burnt flavor. For this reason many people think that the word butterscotch started out as "butter-scorched." Others say it began as "butterscot" from the use of brown sugar and butter as a treat on a Scotsman's porridge.**

Whether you have learned to love your food blackened or have succumbed to sushi, enjoy while you may. Restaurants are running out of cooking extremes, and eventually the middle ground will become fashionable once more.

## Crème Brûlée

*T*his is a dish whose reputation is misleading. It sounds too fancy for anything but gourmet clubs. It's not, though—just a wonderful combination of flavors and textures (and even without the crust, it's one of the best custards you've ever eaten). The preparation sounds trickier than it is. On the other hand, it benefits from being made the day before. Once the caramel top is broken, however, it will get runny, and the dish, although it still will taste great, won't look great.

Before starting, check the configuration of your broiler. If the coils or flames are close together, you can do it classic style, in one large dish and without fear of blackening the top. With wide-spaced coils or flames, it's best to do the crème brûlée in individual dishes set within a baking pan so that each dish can be placed directly under heat.

4 egg yolks, well beaten

⅓ cup sugar

1 pint (16 ounces) heavy cream

2 teaspoons real vanilla

½ pound soft brown sugar (can use granulated)

Butter a shallow, ovenproof 9-inch pie plate or 6 individual dishes. You will also need a much larger pan in which to place the pie plate or ramekins.

Beat egg yolks with sugar with electric mixer until well combined. Scald cream, stirring frequently, in large saucepan. When bubbles appear around the edge, remove from heat and, while running mixer, very slowly dribble about one-fourth of the cream into the egg yolk–sugar mixture. Pour mixture back into the cream in the saucepan and cook over medium-high heat, stirring constantly, for about 10 minutes. Mixture should thicken and coat a spoon (if you draw your finger down the back of it, the two parts should be cleanly separated; if you use a wooden spoon, you will barely be able to make out the grain through the custard). Let cool for 10 minutes, then add vanilla. Pour through a sieve into buttered ovenproof dish(es). When completely cool, refrigerate and chill thoroughly or overnight.

Preheat broiler. Fill larger pan with approximately ½ inch of ice water. Sprinkle custard with a thin layer (¼ to ⅓ inch thick, no more) of brown sugar—just enough so there is no custard show-through. Place baking dish(es) in pan of ice water and run under broiler for 2 to 3 minutes, leaving door open so you can watch. Sugar should become very bubbly and caramelize to a darker brown. Keep moving dish or dishes around so that the sugar melts evenly. Don't let it scorch! For photographic purposes, *crème brûlée* is sometimes pictured almost blackened. This is not the way it should be done. So, unless you're a dedicated blackened-fish fan, you won't like your custard black! Remove from oven and allow to cool undisturbed; then chill until ready to serve. Serves 6.

# C is for Cookbookery

All the novels in the world, say the sages, have among them a total of twenty-six basic plots, and all the cookbooks but twenty-one basic recipes. Why then the hundreds upon hundreds of cookbooks published each year? Good question, when studies show fewer and fewer people are cooking from scratch.

Market researchers tell us that some cookbooks are still bought to be used, especially those that cover advances in basic equipment or the introduction of new techniques. Others satisfy a demand for special recipes such as ethnic, vegetarian, low cholesterol, or whatever. But some cookbooks are bought only to read. Dieters, for example, claim cookbook browsing sublimates their desire for food. (Such willpower! With every new diet, I have to give up reading my cookbooks, too.)

Whatever the reason for buying them, the ability to own more than a handful of cookbooks is a twentieth-century achievement. Centuries after the invention of the printing press, machine-printed books were too expensive for most households.

Therefore, up until the 1800s, most cookbooks were laboriously hand-copied by one generation from another.

The oldest known cookbook, written in 350 B.C. by Archestratus, a Greek, survives in name only: *Gastrology*. Though the cookbook is lost, the entitling is not. Today, "gastronomy" or "*gastronomique*" appears on the title page of many a cookbook.

**How does one go about buying one of those hundreds of cookbooks published each year? If the local bookstore doesn't have enough to satisfy you, join a cookbook book club or dial the 800 number of the only catalog devoted simply and in full color to cookbooks. Called rather intriguingly *Jessica's Biscuit,* its name, according to owner David Stymish, comes partially from his dog, Jessica. The biscuit part? As I understand it, he tackled the creation of the catalog with the same relish Jessica had for her biscuits. Later, the catalog inspired Stymish to name a second dog Biscuit.**

The first complete cookbook to survive was compiled by Marcus Gavius Apicius of the first century A.D. during the rule of the Roman emperor Tiberius. Apicius' book on sauces and another on general recipes were combined around A.D. 400, with fragments of other books into *De Re Coquinaria,* or *The Art of Cookery.* The collection might better have been entitled *The Art of Eating,* for that's what Apicius did. He ate. And ate. And ate some more. And then recorded what he ate in his books.

His nine-word description of how to preserve food would not seem out of place to twentieth-century canners and freezers: *In calidam ferventem merge, et statim leva et suspende.* Translation: "Plunge into boiling water, remove instantly, and hang up."

In other words, blanch and hang. It was also Apicius who gave us our first sweet and sour *minutal Matianum,* or fricassee in the style of Matius. (Matius, a friend of Julius Caesar, had written a book on housewifery based on his observations, not his experiences.) In his honor Apicius created a pork stew to which, halfway through, diced apples were added; it was then served with a vinegary sauce thickened with bread crumbs.

Unfortunately Apicius ran out of money before he ran out of recipes and new dishes to try. In less than a decade, he ate his way through one hundred million sesterces worth of food at a time when 25,000 sesterces could support a noble family for a year. At the ripe old age of twenty-three, his fortune had dwindled to a mere ten million sesterces (the equivalent of almost three-quarters of a ton of gold bullion or over nine million 1990 dollars). Fearing he would be unable to eat in the style to which he had accustomed himself, he ordered his cooks to prepare him a final, poisoned banquet.

Although such gluttony was extreme, historically those who could afford it ate well and ate often. The pleasingly plump, verging on rotund woman was a walking testimonial to the financial success of her father or husband. Not until the twentieth century did thinness surface as the condition of choice for the well-to-do. With food plentiful and everyone capable of being fat, those who wanted to distinguish themselves from the masses became followers of the premise that "one can't be too thin or too rich." These folks also made diet cookbooks best-sellers.

What secures Apicius' book a place in culinary history is not just its "first-ness" and influence on cookery but also its effect on cookbook authors and book-namers. For centuries afterward, imitators of Apicius abounded.

For example, a group of thirteenth-century Sienese noblemen, who called themselves the Spendthrift Brigade, commissioned the writing of *A Book of Cookery*, which, like their lifestyle, was simply an updated version of Apicius. In the fourteenth century an unknown Frenchman tacked on an addendum to create the first known French cookbook. The first professional cooking treatise was commissioned in the 1370s by Charles V and written by Guillaume Tirel, who started as a scullion in the royal kitchens, rose to the position of head cook, and eventually was made Lord Taillevent. The book, *Le Viandier de Guillaume dit Taillevent*, was privately published several times but not publicly printed until 1492. It had an instant, enormous success and influenced other French cooks. If one looks closely, however, the recipes are remarkably similar to those of Apicius. So, too, are the recipes in the first known cookbook written in English. *Forme of Cury, or Art of Cooking*, appeared at the turn of the fifteenth century and is attributed to King Richard II's master cook.

Indeed, besides borrowing heavily from Apicius' recipes and methodology, cooks fervently embraced his choice of book title. *The Art of Cookery* has appeared in many transmutations over the centuries. Even the first cookbook written by a woman for women and published in England in 1747 was titled *The Art of Cookery Made Plain and Easy*. Like most of its predecessors and many of its successors, it contained many borrowed recipes. But at least its author, Hannah Glasse, admitted as much. "Some few of these have been taken from other publications, the Editor does not pretend to deny. . . ." Her honesty did not hurt sales; the book went through twenty editions during the next fifty years.

Glasse's candor was not only admired but copied. In *American Cookery*, published in 1796, Amelia Simmons confessed herself a mere orphan and "without sufficient education to prepare this work." Modesty again proved profitable. Her book, the first ethnic cookbook, contained American recipes using American ingredients and was monumentally successful—so successful, in fact, that many of Simmon's recipes found their way into Englishwoman Susannah Carter's appendix on American cooking for her book, *The Frugal Housewife*. That appendix soon turned up, copied word for word, in a subsequent edition of Hannah Glasse's work meant for American readers. How does that expression go? What goes around . . .

Between 1795 and the present, thousands of cookbooks have been written, and many have sold by the tens of thousands. Like Apicius', some have had more influence on cookbookery than others.

One of these, *L'Art de la Cuisine*, was published in 1833 in five volumes. The masterwork of the founder of France's *grande cuisine*, Marie-Antonin Carême, it included recipes, the theories behind them, and a brand-new philosophy of perfection. Carême's genius led his employer, the statesman Talleyrand, to institute the precursor of the two-martini lunch. He invited foreign diplomats to small, intimate dinners. In

**It is said that on his deathbed, Carême took the preparer of his last meal to task. The quenelles of sole were good, he said, "but prepared too hastily. You must shake the sauce pan lightly—see, like this . . ." And just like that, he was gone.**

this setting adversaries were wined, dined, and surfeited on culinary marvels. In the process they found themselves open to discussions (and agreements) they would otherwise have avoided. Once Carême's genius became well known, he was wooed away first to England and then to Russia and the court of Czar Alexander I. It was there that he discovered *borscht* and other classic Russian dishes, which he introduced into French cuisine.

Another influential volume was *Le Grand Dictionnaire de Cuisine* from the pen of known plagiarist Alexandre Dumas, *père*, author of *The Count of Monte Cristo, The Three Musketeers*, and hundreds more. Of all his works, he felt this dictionary of culinary terms and ingredients was his legacy to the future. Published posthumously in 1873, it focused not on recipes per se, but on ingredients, with the emphasis on food facts and fictions (not always easily distinguishable from one another). As usual, Dumas stole unabashedly from the writings of his culinary predecessors and contemporaries. Still, he can be credited with inventing a new cookbook format: all topics arranged in alphabetical order. From his book have come all the encyclopedic works written, including this one.

A third important work is that of Auguste Escoffier, still considered by professionals to be the greatest chef who ever lived. *La Guide Culinare* or *Escoffier's Cook Book*, published in French in 1902 and in English in 1907, is considered the cookbookery classic of classics, containing recipes for many dishes served today in the most fashionable restaurants. But his *Ma Cuisine* was recognized as more significant in its influence on cookbooks. In it, for the first time, a professional cook wrote not for his fellows but for the home cook!

The fourth of these history-making cookbooks had nothing to do with haute cui-

Sarah Tyson Rorer, author of *Mrs. Rorer's Philadelphia Cook Book,* was responsible for the creation of a product we take for granted today. In 1893 she asked the Charles Knox Company to produce gelatin in a form easier to measure and to dissolve. A year later Knox introduced "Sparkling Granulated Gelatin," and within ten years flavored granulated gelatin had been developed. Hello, Jell-O! ®

sine. Written by Fannie Farmer, a director of the Boston Cooking School, and published in 1896, it was not the first comprehensive book for the home cook, nor was it the first to list ingredients separately from directions. (That had been done a decade before by the founder of the Philadelphia Cooking School, Sarah Tyson Rorer.) *The Boston Cooking School Cookbook* was touted as the first "scientific cookbook," on the basis that it used "leveled out" measurements. With this book American cooks were assured that all guesswork was removed from recipes. Thus every dish, every time, would turn out perfect. To the untrained homemaker, the "leveled out" feature was a winner. Farmer's book went through eleven editions as well as a title change to THE FANNIE FARMER *Boston Cooking School* COOK BOOK. Three million copies were sold before a major revision was done in 1979, at which time the Marion Cunningham version of *The Fannie Farmer Cookbook* became a best-seller all over again.

**Yes, author Fannie Farmer is the same Fannie Farmer whose name appears on candy shops. She was not, however, a candy-maker; she was only doing what so many celebrities do today: licensing her name.**

The fifth cookbookery milestone was not even a cookbook. Instead, it was the first treatise on the art of cooking, entertaining, eating, and even digesting. In other words, it examined the physical act of nourishing oneself and explained the philosophy behind it. Written over a span of nearly thirty years by Jean Anthelme Brillat-Savarin and self-published in 1825, *The Physiology of Taste* is considered by many to be the ultimate book on the subject of food. Though Brillat-Savarin himself considered it simply the meanderings and meditations of an old man, he utilized for the first time a conversational style—an *entre nous*, between-you-and-me idiom, deliberately designed to engage and entertain the reader. As the author himself said, "I myself have yawned, now and then, over other men's works. I have done everything in my power to avoid this danger. . . ."

He was successful. More than a century and a half later, a modern reader still admires such thought-provoking truisms as "the discovery of a new dish does more for the happiness of mankind than the discovery of a star"; "dessert without cheese is like a pretty woman with only one eye"; "the most indispensable quality in a cook is punctuality and no less is required of a guest"; "beasts feed; man eats"; "tell me what you eat; I will tell you what you are"; and more.

But Brillat-Savarin might never have touched a responsive chord in English-speaking hearts if it weren't for M.F.K. (Mary Frances Kennedy) Fisher, who translated his book in 1949. She, too, had perfected the conversational style and is considered by many to be the philosopher-poet of the kitchen. It is she whom her peers consider the most original writer of original cookbooks of our time. Written with humor, wit, and delight in the body sensual and sexual, all of her books make delicious reading.

Two of the five that make up the anthology *The Art of Eating* are especially noteworthy. The first is *How to Cook a Wolf*. Created for the housewife suffering through wartime shortages with the wolf a'whuffing at her door, it managed to combine sound advice with a lighthearted approach, as epitomized by her chapter on How to Be Cheerful while Starving. The second, *Consider the Oyster*, is a tour de force—the first cookbook ever to deal with a single ingredient.

One might well note the absence of certain great cookbooks from this list, including *The Joy of Cooking* by Irma S. Rombauer (recently revised and updated by her daughter) and *Mastering the Art of French Cooking*, Volumes I and II, by Julia Child, et al. Certainly these had tremendous influence on the art of cooking—but not on cookbookery.

In fact, most of today's most influential cooking authorities are not innovators but perfectors. The late James Beard (1903–1985), for example, who died but continues to be published in the persona of the James Beard Foundation, made a life's work out of cookbook writing and specialized in perfecting the single-subject cookbook. Craig Claiborne perfected the art of recipe writing in his newspaper columns in *The New York Times*. Julia Child reduced haute cuisine to the level of the common folks by demystifing it. Along the way she demonstrated that it was okay to make mistakes.

Today's cookbook writers have much in common with those of previous centuries. They work with those twenty-one basic recipes. They are opinionated. They consider nothing and no one sacred but confine their most virulent criticism to others' recipes, proof positive that one cook's poison is another cook's delight—to the delight of those who read cookbooks for pleasure. James Beard, for one, thought Escoffier's candlestick salad (a slice of pineapple, a chunk of upright banana, a cherry topping, and a mayonnaise dressing) was revolting. On the other hand, he had a weakness for Waldorf salad (apples and celery bound with mayonnaise), which the late Michael Field, concert pianist turned cooking instructor and cookbook author, found "appalling." (Escoffier added nuts to the dish and included it in his guide for professional chefs, *Escoffier's Cookbook*.)

**Ever notice how many cookbook authors had the forethought to be born of parents with appropriate names? There's Hannah Glasse; Maida Heatter; Maggie Gin (but alas, she writes on china, not liquor); Waverley Root; Edith de Plata, the Mexican authority; and James Beard (whose name is an anagram for bread). King writes on fish and Reyniere (the fox) on chicken. Somehow vegetable cookery seems to attract more than its share of suitable names: Blanc writes on white potatoes, Spear on broccoli and asparagus, Greene on greens. Then we have such coauthorships as Wolf and Tiger writing on Chinese food and Sales and Sales writing on claypot cookery.**

Beard also liked that gelatin-enriched, contest-winning version of coleslaw known as perfection salad; M.F.K. Fisher condemns all gelatin salads as horrible. But Fisher recommends tomato soup cake as a "pleasant cake" that keeps well. (The Campbell Soup company reports that it is one of six recipes they consider classics and which are requested by the thousands each year.) Needless to say, Craig Claiborne turns thumbs down on a cake made from canned soup. Claiborne, on the other hand, is a fan of ambrosia, that standard Southern dessert with its base of orange slices and shredded coconut topping. Beard didn't even give it cookbook space in what most consider the best and most complete book on American cookery. And I could go on and on, but if you read cookbooks you'll know what I mean.

Reviewing the history of cookbookery, it must be to Apicius that we tip our chef's toque. If he hadn't chosen to eat well, neither would we. Or, as Brillat-Savarin said via M.F.K. Fisher, "the pleasure of eating is the actual and direct sensation of satisfying a need. . . . [it] demands appetite, if not actual hunger; the pleasures of the table are most often independent of either one or the other."

Oh, what Apicius has wrought!

# Classic Tomato Soup Spice Cake

*I*n How to Cook a Wolf, M.F.K. *Fisher notes that this cake has three pleasurable qualities. First, it keeps well; second, it puzzles people who can't quite place it; and third, it bakes sensibly in a moderate oven while you're cooking other things, a small but ennobling pleasure. Enough others agree with her to make this one of Campbell's most requested recipes.*

**2 cups all-purpose flour**

**1⅓ cups sugar**

**4 teaspoons baking powder**

**1½ teaspoons ground allspice**

**1 teaspoon baking soda**

**1 teaspoon ground cinnamon**

**½ teaspoon ground cloves**

**1 can (10¾ ounces) Campbell's® Condensed Tomato Soup**

**½ cup shortening**

**2 eggs**

**¼ cup water**

**cream cheese frosting (optional)**

Preheat oven to 350° F. Grease and flour two 8-inch round cake pans.

In large bowl, combine all ingredients. With mixer at low speed, beat until well mixed, constantly scraping bowl with rubber spatula. At high speed, beat 4 minutes, occasionally scraping bowl. Pour into prepared pans.

Bake 35 to 40 minutes or until wooden toothpick inserted in center comes out clean. Cool in pans on wire racks 10 minutes. Remove from pans; cool completely. Frost with your favorite cream cheese frosting, if desired. Serves 12.

# Waldorf Salad

*T*his is the recipe from the maitre d'hotel of the Waldorf, Oscar Tschirky, as it appeared in *The Cookbook by "Oscar" of the Waldorf (Werner Company, 1896). It is inconceivable that in those days of pretension in cahoots with ostentation the salad would have been presented so simply. Instead, one thinks it would have been served on a lettuce cup and given the proper garniture (perhaps a rose made out of apple peel, soaked in lemon water). And "dressed" would have meant napped or carefully dribbled about rather than the whole thing tossed together willy-nilly.*

Peel two raw apples and cut them into small pieces, say about half an inch square, also cut some celery the same way, and mix it with the apple. Be very careful not to let any seeds of the apples be mixed with it. The salad must be dressed with a good mayonnaise.

Variations—not his—include the addition of nut pieces by Escoffier. And/or raisins and miniature marshmallows. The latter two may have been variations on a popular garnish of the period—raisin-stuffed marshmallows.

# D
## is for de Médicis

G o into any truly good restaurant in France and somewhere on the premises you'll find a portrait of a rather dowdy, decidedly plain, big-nosed woman dressed in black with a ruff around her neck and a black cap on her head. One might easily mistake her for an aging and mourning Queen Victoria, but she is a French queen, the woman chefs consider their patroness, Catherine de Médicis. It is upon her arrival in France that they fix the true beginnings of haute cuisine.

Come to the United States and in Philadelphia you'll find aficionados of Italian cuisine meeting under the banner of the Caterina de'Médici Gastronomic Society. They, too, hail this woman as their patroness, not for her contributions to Italian cuisine but for her foresight in bringing with her to France a retinue of *capi cuochi*, the Italian cooks credited with introducing to the French "the secrets of the most sophisticated cooking of the time."

Who was she, this revered figure in culinary history? The great-granddaughter of

Lorenzo the Magnificent, she was born in 1519 just fifteen days before her mother's death, which was followed within days by the death of her syphilitic father from consumption or an assassin's knife, depending on which authority you consult.

**The Caterina de'Médici Gastronomic Society was originally organized in Manhattan in the 1960s by Jack Rosenthal, president of the world-renowned Culinary Institute. On January 28, 1984, the first official Philadelphia meeting of the society, headed by gourmet/ bon vivant Mario Mele, was held at La Famiglia Restaurant. The group has continued to grow and grow. Mr. Mele spells out the criteria for membership as not just a love and appreciation of Italian food and wines but also "amenability with other members, and a sense of decorum."**

Catherine's dowry was huge and included the city-state of Florence, which greatly pleased her fourteen-year-old bridegroom, Henri, the second son and spare heir to Francis I, King of France. On the minus side she also brought, in her own fourteen-year-old person, a not so pleasing face and figure, neither of which were competition for the beauty of Diane de Poitiers, a widow nineteen years Catherine's senior. Three years after his marriage to Catherine, Henri and Diane began one of the most surprising royal liaisons in history. He wore only her colors, black and white; he signed his letters with an H adjoining a double crescent, the emblem of Diane the mythical huntress; and when he became King Henri II, he gave her the crown jewels and Chenonceau, a chateau known today as the "ladies' castle." It took the taste, work, and money of seven successive chateleines to transform Chenonceau into a veritable fairy castle standing astride the river Cher.

Henry II remained faithful to Diane until the day of his death; Catherine nursed her hatred of Diane just as long. One of her first acts as regent for her son was to oust Diane from Chenonceau. There Catherine's architects built a formal Italian garden alongside the castle, a sixty-meter-long gallery bridging the River Cher, and a modern (for those days) kitchen.

It was in this kitchen that she—actually her cooks—made the greatest contributions to France. Every time you try to balance peas on your fork, think of her. Not only did she introduce the garden pea, she also brought with her the fork, which had been in use in Venice since 1518, a year before her birth. The fork, maybe because of the peas, did not catch on in France nor, seventy years later, in England. As of the beginning of the eighteenth century, most Europeans still ate with their fingers. Eating so was the rule in the British Navy in 1897; the use of knives and forks was considered unmanly.

Catherine's other contributions to the culinary arts are judged differently by various authorities. Most, however, agree it was her chefs who taught the French to cook the most famous duck dish in the French repertoire—*canard à l'orange*, which the Italians call *Anitra all'arancia*. The duck is stuffed with herbs, garlic, vinegar, and sometimes a whole orange, then spit-roasted (the spits are still there in the kitchen at Chenonceau) and sauced with the zest and/or juice of oranges cooked in wine.

As wife of the dauphin, Catherine was known as "the pill-maker's daughter" or "shop-keeper's daughter." As queen-dowager, she was called "Le Serpent" or "Madame Snake." So secretive was she that her cabinet at the Château Blois had 257 carved panels, concealing almost as many secret chambers to house her poisoned daggers, poisoned rings, and poisoned goblets. In need of spies, she enlisted the services of her maids of honor, who were chosen for their beauty and retained for their loyalty and willingness to seduce potential informants.

In addition, that stickler for food accuracy, Waverley Root, credits Catherine with introducing savoy cabbages, haricots verts, and that well-known aphrodisiac, the globe artichoke. Others add to the list grated Parmesan cheese, macaroons, and poultry quenelles, as well as *lumache* (snails made with puréed peas, the predecessor of our oysters Rockefeller). Include also zabaglione or sabayon—both the creamy wine-enriched dessert and the sauce made with Marsala—as well as frangipane tarts. Her greatest achievement, both French and Italians agree, was the introduction of sorbets, which approximated today's ice milk. Working with Sicily's Arab-derived *sorbetti*, milk- or honey-based frozen drinks, the artist-inventor Bernardo Buontalenti in 1565 learned how to freeze them to make sorbets. His pupils went to France to supply the queen with this newest delicacy.

Despite all that good food and lots of artichokes, none of Catherine's sons produced an heir. Instead they were succeeded by Catherine's son-in-law, Henry Navarre, the first of the Bourbon kings. When he was served chicken at his coronation as Henry IV, he is reported to have said, "Je veux que le dimanche chaque paysan ait sa poule au pot." Translation: "I wish that on Sunday every peasant had his own chicken in a pot." When widowered, Henry IV took as his second wife another de Médicis queen, Marie (1573–1642), daughter of the duke of Tuscany and a cousin of Catherine.

**In addition to her culinary contributions to her adopted country, Catherine introduced the sidesaddle, freeing women from confinement to carriages or riding pillion. She also made ballet history on October 15, 1581, when, in the style of Italian banquet extravaganzas, her household put on the *Ballet Comique de la Reine,* her own version of the legend of Circe.**

Besides his chicken-in-every-pot fame, Henry IV can be credited with at least one other culinary achievement. At his court was served, for the first time, the second most popular duck dish of all time, right behind Catherine's *canard à l'orange: caneton à la Montmorency* in which a roasted young drake is served with a sauce of Montmorency cherries similar to the morello bitter cherry. But it is to Queen Marie that cuisine owes the greater debt—one that was at least on a par with Catherine's contributions—for without her, there would be no French patisserie as we know it.

**Henri IV may have been the first to wish the peasants a chicken in every pot, but he wasn't the last. In 1928 Herbert Hoover's campaign slogan was "A Chicken in Every Pot, a Car in Every Garage." He won the election, but the Great Depression thwarted his plan.**

As a bride Marie de Médicis of Tuscany brought another retinue of *capi cuochi* with her, and they knew the secret of true puff pastry. Without Marie de Médicis there would be no *napoleons*, no *palmiers*, no *Pithviers*, no *gateau St. Honoré* (the traditional French birthday cake). No, there would not even exist that staple of the banquet circuit, chicken à la king in a pastry shell.

Puff pastry or, more accurately, the French *pâté feuilletée* and the Italian *pasta sfoglia* (both of which mean "leafed") had been in use for centuries in the Mediterranean in the form of tissue-thin pastry sheets, which we know as phyllo, or filo, leaves. What made the Tuscan invention different was the interleaving of animal fat (butter or lard) among the layers of dough; this made the finished pastry rise dramatically when baked yet remain in separate layers.

Long after Marie de Médicis's death, French historians were crediting the invention of puff or leafed pastry to Claude Gelee, better known as Claude Lorrain, a famous seventeenth-century landscape painter and amateur cook. Others, such as Joseph Favre, author of *Dictionnaire Universel de Cuisine*, say Feuillet, chief pastry cook to the house of Conde, was the inventor of puff pastry.

Italian authorities, however, are unanimous in naming Florence as its birthplace, noting it was specifically mentioned in a 1525 decree issued by the Council of Ten in Venice condemning it and other dishes as overly ostentatious and that batches of it were served at Marie and Henry's totally overly ostentatious wedding.

Nothing personified the extravagance and even vulgarity of a de Médicis banquet more than Marie's wedding to Henri IV. Tables were bedecked with sugar sculptures; sideboards disappeared via complicated mechanisms only to reappear freshly laid with different food; and puff pastry, poultry, meats, and sweets appeared in dozens of forms as the chefs raised the ordinary to the extraordinary. Cockerels were formed out of prosciutti, quails came *en croute,* capons were covered with ravioli, wild boar was sauced in wine, and piglets were served whole.

Whatever their faults (extravagance perhaps being the least of them) the de Médicis's influence on the world of cookery is inarguable. Without their prodigal insistence on the best and most, who knows what we might have missed.

# Canard à l'Orange

*I*n France a delicately flavored Nantes duckling is preferred for this dish. It is smaller than other ducks, weighing less than four pounds when fully developed, at four months.

**4 tablespoons bacon fat or 2 tablespoons olive oil and 2 tablespoons butter**

**1 duckling, no larger than 4 pounds**

**oranges for stuffing in cavity (optional)**

**1 carrot, coarsely chopped**

**1 medium onion, coarsely sliced**

**1 bouquet garni of parsley, thyme, and bay leaf**

**¾ cup white wine**

**2 cups chicken stock**

Remove any giblets from duck cavity. Rinse duck. Put optional oranges in cavity and truss the duckling like a turkey.

Melt bacon fat (or oil and butter) in bottom of ovenproof casserole. Brown duckling very lightly on all sides. Add carrot, onion, bouquet garni, and white wine. Cover casserole, bring to a boil over medium heat, and reduce wine to a small amount. Add stock, bring back to boil, and place in preheated 350° F oven for 60–90 minutes or until juices run clear. Transfer duck to serving plate, remove trussing and oranges, and keep warm while making sauce.

## Sauce

2 tablespoons sugar

2 tablespoons wine or cider vinegar

1 orange

½ lemon

2 tablespoons orange liqueur such as curaçao or Grand Marnier (optional)

Degrease the liquid remaining in the roasting pan and strain. Caramelize the sugar and vinegar in a small saucepan. Add cooking liquid to caramelized mixture and boil down until very thick. Remove the rind from the orange and lemon half; blanch, drain, and cut into julienne strips. Set aside. Squeeze juice of orange and lemon half into sauce and reduce again. Strain. At the last moment, add the julienned rind and optional liqueur. Pour sauce over duckling and serve immediately.

# Puff Pastry

*T*he easiest way to make puff pastry is to buy it ready-made. But it doesn't taste the same. And the following method is easier and faster than the usual classic method. According to Escoffier, the secret of a perfect puff pastry is always to have the dough and the butter of exactly the same consistency, which isn't easy. To accomplish this, bakers have always chilled the dough, then tried to work miracles to get the butter right. Some recipes, for example, suggest kneading the butter under cold running water to make it malleable. Others suggest whacking it over and over again with a rolling pin. Escoffier would have you put the butter in the middle of a floured tea towel and work it with the palm of your hand.

There is another way—starting with butter at room temperature and a soft, barely chilled dough. The two then harden simultaneously in the refrigerator.

2¼ cups stirred, scooped, and leveled all-purpose flour

¾ cup cake flour

1–1¼ cups cold water

1 pound butter

Place both kinds of flour in large bowl of your electric mixer. With a flat whip, if you have one, and the mixer running on slow, gradually add 1 cup water, plus enough more to form a soft, stringy dough. (If done in food processor, dough will form a ball.) Chill, covered, in refrigerator for about an hour. While dough is chilling, allow butter to come to room temperature. (It should not be weepy, just soft enough to work easily.)

On a lightly floured board, roll dough into a rectangle about 12 by 18 inches, with the long side parallel to you. Spread one third of the butter, using your hands, over the right-hand two-thirds of the dough. Then, as if folding a business letter, fold the unbuttered third to your left over onto the buttered middle third. Now bring the buttered right-hand third over onto the middle. The folds should now be perpendicular to you. (Here's where the method begins to depart from the normal.) Wrap dough in plastic wrap and chill in refrigerator for 30–60 minutes.

Unwrap dough and roll across the folds into another rectangle, again 12 by 18 inches, but this time the short side should be closest to you. Fold as before, letter fashion, top third over middle third, bottom third up over both portions. Now turn so folds are again perpendicular to you. Roll it out another time and fold it again. Roll it one more time and spread half of the remaining butter over two-thirds of it as you did before. Fold into thirds and chill again. This is considered one "turn." (Chefs who have multiple packages of puff pastry chilling mark each with indents to denote the number of turns done.)

Roll it out again and fold again. Repeat the folding and turning and rerolling for a total of three times. The third time spread the last of the butter on it and refold. Chill once more. This is the second "turn."

One last time, roll and fold three times for the third "turn," and chill.

The pastry is now ready to be worked but will keep, plastic-wrapped, for several days in the refrigerator or can be frozen. Keep chilled until ready to roll out. Roll out and rechill for 15–30 minutes just before baking.

When cutting the finished puff pastry, dip a knife in flour and press down, rocking the knife back and forth. Don't drag the knife through the dough, as it will stretch it. And handle the cut edges as little as possible.

# E
## is for Epicure

The earliest mention of an epicure is found in the *Republic* by Plato (427–348 B.C.) in which he likens himself to "an epicure who snatches a taste of every dish which is successively brought to table before he has fairly enjoyed the one before."

That was at least thirty-eight years before the birth of Epicurus from whom the term *epicure* is derived. He, according to scholars, practiced asceticism. Frugal, plain, and water-drinking, he once said, "Send me a little pot of cheese, that, when I like, I may fare sumptuously." By the time of Diogenes, however, 600 years later, in the third century A.D., legend had transformed Epicurus into the epitome of sensuality. Accused of being a pimp, advocating homosexuality, and vomiting twice a day due to overindulgence, he represented the very opposite of an ascetic.

By A.D. 1350, *epicure* again referred to one with refined tastes, especially in food and wine. Two hundred years later, another transformation: *Epicure* described one dedicated to sensual enjoyment of food and drink.

Today an epicure remains as defined by the late Albert James Alroy Symons, Englishman and founder, in 1933, of the Food and Wine Society.

*One who cultivates a refined taste for the pleasures of the table . . . he is not a man who thinks of, and lives for, his belly alone; he is not a sensualist for whom dinner is merely an elaborate prelude to sexual passion; he is not a hedonist who sees life as a succession of pleasurable sensations to be obtained by hook, crook or levitation; he is not a table-bore who rams his one subject down your throat; he is not a pride-starved victim of insufficiency striving to assert a false superiority by making undue fuss over wine and food.*

Besides which, he is not very interesting compared to his less refined fellows, or so time has decided. Even culinary histories ignore the epicure, with the exception of Brillat-Savarin, while savoring every unsavory folly and foible of gluttons, gourmands, and sybarites.

One of the earliest of these, although he considered himself an epicure, was Lucius Licinius Lucullus (117–56 B.C.), whose name still appears on modern menus in conjunction with dishes of extraordinary richness.

Living at the time of Pompey and Cato, he had successful careers as both consul and general, but it is his retirement from politics and war that interests food historians. At his country villa in Naples, he built pleasure-houses, then diverted the sea to surround them with moats and to form stocked fish-ponds. To supply his table with fowl, he built fattening coops. He equipped his home with baths and porticoes, tunneled into the hills for food and wine storage, and insisted on not one or two but many dining rooms.

**Current culinary definitions:**

**glutton:** one who eats and drinks excessively or voraciously

**gourmand:** one who is fond of good eating, often indiscriminatingly and to excess

**gourmet:** one who is a connoisseur of good food and drink; an epicure.

To dine with him was to sit upon rare purple coverlets, to have one's wine and water poured from bejeweled beakers, to taste the rarest foods served on plates decorated with precious stones. Between courses the stomach luxuriated as other senses were beguiled with song and dance. But it is the monies spent on these meals, particularly the foods, that provides the stuff of legends—legends that frequently bear little resemblance to one another yet are all based on a single source, *Parallel Lives* by Plutarch (circa A.D. 46–120).

**Besides his interest in dining, Lucullus was a great gardener; at one point his gardens were said to rival the emperor's. In them grew seedlings of a then-unknown fruit that he had brought to Rome from Armenia in 74 B.C. The fruit was the kerusus, which we know as the cherry.**

According to Plutarch, Lucullus enjoyed his retirement and gloried in entertaining. Once, when several Greeks had accepted his hospitality day after day, they began to decline his invitations because they felt he was spending too much on them. To this he replied, "Some of this, indeed, my Grecian friends, is for your sakes, but more for that of Lucullus."

The most legendary of the Lucullan anecdotes centers around the rare occasion when he supped alone. To his surprise, only one course was served, and that was but moderately furnished. He sent for his steward and reproved him. The steward explained that he assumed there would be no need of any great entertainment when nobody was invited. Lucullus replied, "What, did not you know, then, that today Lucullus dines with Lucullus?"

When this story became known about the city (and it was certainly not retold by the steward), Cicero and Pompey stopped Lucullus in the forum one day and asked a favor of him.

"We should like," said Cicero, "to dine with you today, just on the dinner that is prepared for yourself."

Lucullus, surprised, agreed but requested a day's delay, which they refused to grant. Nor did they allow him to talk to his servants for fear he would order more than had been appointed before. This much they did allow—that, in their presence, he might send word to his steward that he would sup that night in the Apollo dining room.

Unknown to the other two, he had outwitted them. Each of his dining rooms had its own rate of expenditure. Thus, by knowing where he would dine, the servants knew also how much was to be expended and in what style and form dinner was to be served. The expense for the Apollo was fifty thousand drachmas, or 6,250 ounces of silver. The resulting, supposedly everyday meal left Cicero and Pompey suitably impressed.

Centuries later, commonfolk who visited Versailles at mealtimes to watch Louis XIV (1638–1715) dine with other royals also saw a mighty good show. But then, King Louis ate ostentatiously even at intimate dinners, such as that given for the pope's legate to France, which only the queen and her entourage were allowed to observe. According to one onlooker, the table was set with but two knives and forks, according to protocol: the king's at the proper place, the legate's four seats down on the same side. The first course of ten potages was already on the serving board when, preceded by ten house stewards and the chief house steward, the king entered, the legate on his left. When the king reached the top of the table, the duke of Enghien, as the great master of ceremonies, offered him a napkin to wipe his hands while the chief steward presented another to the legate. After the king and then the legate were seated, three men stood before each to serve them. Serving the king were a marquis as chief cup-bearer, a count as chief of the buttery, and the chief carver, who was also the king's taster. Three lesser officials served the legate. At every course the eleven stewards left the hall and then, preceded by the usher of the hall, returned two by two, each carrying one or more dishes, with the chief steward bringing up the rear. When the diners had made their choices, the plates were served and then cleared by footmen.

In all there were four courses of no less than ten choices each, followed by dessert, which consisted of four pyramids of twenty-four porcelain plates of fresh fruits, fourteen plates of preserved fruit, plus other dishes. What most impressed the onlooker was not the staggering amount of food served to two men nor the fact that it took eighteen people to serve each course. No, it was that the king was so restrained and epicurean in his drinking. He drank only twice from the hand of his chief cup-bearer as compared to the legate who drank four times!

No courtier at any court in Europe would have seen anything extravagant about the service of this meal or the number of dishes. Quite the contrary—they would have considered a mere five-course meal to be quite frugal, as did Grimod de La Reynière (1758–1837), who was notorious for his extravagance. Even he, however, may well have been outdone in the area of sheer ostentation by his son. According to Alexandre Dumas, *père*, La Reynière was overtaken on a business trip by night or bad weather or some such obstacle so insurmountable that it forced him, an epicure, to stop at a village inn and ask the host to give him

**The contemporary meal most reminiscent of Louis XIV's was that of Craig Claiborne in 1975 at the Chez Denis in Paris. It cost 17,600 francs ($4,000) and was denounced by the Vatican as scandalous.**

supper. The innkeeper confessed that his larder was bare, but La Reynière could see seven turkeys turning on a spit. Indignantly, he accused the innkeeper of lying, but the innkeeper held his ground, stating that all seven had been reserved by a newly arrived guest from Paris for his own dinner.

**The *sot-l'y-laisse* (literally, "fool he who leaves it") is what we know as the "oyster" of the bird, or the two pockets of flesh to either side of the spine. On occasion the turkey oyster is mistakenly called the pope's nose or the parson's nose, but these are slang terms for the turkey's tail.**

"He must be a giant then," said La Reynière.

"No, sir. He is scarcely taller than you."

The guest turned out to be Grimod's own son. The young man explained his apparent gluttony in ordering seven turkeys by saying, "Sir, I have always heard you tell your friends that there is nothing edible about a turkey cooked without truffles except the *sot-l'y-laisses*. I had seven turkeys put on the spit to get fourteen *sot-l'y-laisses*."

To which the father replied, "It seems to me a bit spendthrift for a boy of eighteen, but I cannot say it is unreasonable."

It is unknown whether the father shared the fourteen morsels of flesh or had to make do with other lesser portions of the birds.

America has had many followers in the footsteps of Lucullus, but none has been better documented than that larger-than-life pair, Lillian Russell (1861–1922) and "Diamond Jim" Brady (1856–1917). The former, born Helen Louise Leonard, became the queen of the music hall, the variety show, and burlesque. Her forte was comic-opera or operettas, and her show-stopping tunes were "Fiddle-dee-dee" and "Whoop-dee-doo." She went through five husbands and countless lovers and was the fantasy of every red–blooded American male for thirty-five years. She was a big star both figuratively and literally. Although not especially tall, she tipped the scales at more than 200 pounds and made Dolly Parton and Jane Russell look underdeveloped.

From 1804 to 1812, Grimod de La Reynière wrote a series of anecdotal and practical guides to Paris called *Almanach des Gourmands*. Among his words of wisdom were: "Soup must be eaten boiling hot and coffee drunk piping hot—happy are those with a delicate palate and a cast-iron throat"; and, "the local wine, a dinner at your friend's house, and music performed by amateurs are three things to be equally dreaded."

In the area of eating, Lillian Russell shattered all conceptions of feminine delicacy, according to one tut-tutter. She matched Diamond Jim Brady, her usual dinner companion, oyster for oyster, steak for steak, chocolate for chocolate. Some restaurateurs say on occasion she was known to eat more than he did—no mean feat.

Diamond Jim, so named for his habit of wearing diamond jewelry worth half a million dollars, was the original expense-account king. He made his fortune selling equipment to the railroads; he spent his fortune on food. A typical daily ration, which looks more like a restaurant's bill of fare, included a breakfast of pancakes, hominy, eggs, cornbread, muffins, steak, chops, fried potatoes, and four glasses of freshly squeezed orange juice; a mid-morning snack of two or three dozen shellfish and more orange juice; a lunch of oysters, clams, deviled crabs, a couple of lobsters, roast beef, salad, two or three servings of pie, and still more orange juice; and an afternoon tea of two or three dozen shellfish and lemon sole washed down with more orange juice or lemon soda pop. All this and Diamond Jim hasn't had dinner yet.

Even when Brady dined alone, dinner (either at Delmonico's or the Waldorf or, as on one particular day, at Rector's) included two or three dozen 6-inch Maryland oysters, half a dozen crabs, two bowls of green turtle soup, half a dozen lobsters, a double portion of terrapin, two canvasback ducks, a large sirloin steak with appropriate vegetables, one of everything on the dessert tray, two pounds of chocolates, and yet more orange juice. After that, a visit to the theater with snacks and lemon soda pop at every intermission, and, après-theatre, several game birds and more citrus drinks. Diamond Jim's dinner checks, back in the early 1900s, frequently topped $500 for food alone (he didn't drink liquor), to which he added a $100 tip.

**Diamond Jim was the human version of the French force-fed goose, the source of foie gras, only no one forced Brady to eat six meals a day. When he died, an autopsy revealed his stomach was six times normal size.**

So greatly was he appreciated as a patron that George Rector once remarked, "Jim Brady is the best twenty-five customers we have." When Diamond Jim, therefore, described the fact that sole Marguery could only be had in the Paris restaurant of its creation, George Rector promptly pulled his son out of college, gave him a ticket on a boat bound for Paris, instructed him to seek work in the Marguery's kitchen—and to steal the recipe.

What happened next is a matter of dispute. According to one version, young Rector charmed the recipe out of Nicolas Marguery in less than six months. Another has the lad taking more than eighteen months to ferret it out. Still another says Rector's efforts came to naught and in desperation he created a facsimile of the original. (This may be borne out by the fact that when, in the 1930s, Prosper Montagne assembled the original *Larousse Gastronomique*, the recipe given him by Nicolas Marguery for sole Marguery differed in many respects from that published by the Rectors.)

Whatever really happened, upon young Rector's return, he was supposedly greeted at the pier by Diamond Jim yelling, "Did you get the recipe?" To which the lad waved a piece of paper. That very evening the first American-made sole Marguery was served to Diamond Jim, who declared it just the way he remembered it and ordered eight more servings before going on to the next course.

As you may have noticed, all of the foregoing are essentially of the Lucullus-dines-alone variety of epicureanism. But history is replete with feasts where gluttony rules and epicureanism is left behind in the kitchen.

Petronius (died A.D. 66), so-called *Arbiter Elegantiae* of Rome, summed up all the excesses of his time and centuries to come in one satirical piece about Trimalchio's dinner. Initially part of *The Satyricon*, some 1,800 years later it was the subject of an entire book written in 1898 by Harry Thurston Peck.

Using the device of a single meal, Petronius described every conceivable excess then appearing on the tables of Rome—several of which are with us still. The familiar divided relish/olive bowl, for example, made its appearance at Trimalchio's dinner in the form of a miniature bronze ass fitted with a sort of packsaddle containing pale green olives on one side, dark ones on the other.

From first course to last, the entire dinner featured dishes with deceptive appearances. For example, sausages were "smoked" on a silver grill over black coals that turned out to be dark Syrian plums; the red-hot coals were scarlet pomegranate seeds. A wooden bird nested atop dough eggs that, when split open, contained a whole, plump, cooked reed bird surrounded with the yolk of egg well seasoned with pepper.

**One of the dishes served as dessert at Trimalchio's feast was a quince stuck with thorns to imitate a hedgehog. Centuries later, one could find on Williamsburg tables a special treat: an almond-studded porcupine. The difference between them? Although the latter was by far the more edible, it was also by far the more costly.**

So went the feast, with every course appearing as one delicacy, then revealed to be another. Live birds flew out of a cooked whole boar, and a selection of pigs was trotted out for the guests to select which they would have that night. Shortly thereafter, in less time than a chicken could be cooked, the pig was served, but it had been cooked whole and not drawn; inside it a vast array of cooked sausages surprised the guests. (Trimalchio boasted that his chef was a master of pork: "He could make you fish out of a sow's paunch, and pigeon out of bacon, a turtle-dove out of ham.")

But Trimalchio himself would have been jealous of a feast given on March 28, 1903, by Cornelius Kingsley Garrison Billings, the American millionaire horseman.

Louis XIV would not have been impressed by the versatility of Trimalchio's cook with pork. One day Louis boasted that his chef was so great an artist he could cook a pair of old shoes and render them appetizing. When one of the courtiers scoffed at this, Louis sent for the chef, presented with him some old slippers, and ordered him to turn them into a ragôut for the following day. According to legend, on October 30, 1651, a mammoth silver tureen was placed before the king. When the chamberlain removed the cover, there sat the slippers, boiled to a pulp, together with various vegetables, the whole made harmonious by the addition of spice and herbs and suitable garniture. The royal family ate this unique course and declared it was the best dish they had ever tasted. There is no record either of the recipe or whether the dish was ever made again.

For thirty-six guests, all members of New York's Equestrian Club, the ballroom of Sherry's (Fifth Avenue and Forty-fourth Street) had been transformed into a woodland scene. Real sod covered the floor. The walls bore scenic backdrops. Live birds perched on potted trees. But the pièce de résistance was the table service. Up the freight elevator came a horse for each guest. Sipping champagne from tubes connected to saddlebags, the horsemen dined from miniature tables attached to the pommels of the saddles. Waiters dressed as grooms used mounting blocks to serve and clear each course. Toward the end of the banquet, the waiter-grooms brought in elaborate feeding troughs filled with oats so that the animals dined with their riders. After the meal had been served and cigars lit, the riders dismounted and were entertained by a vaudeville show while the horses were taken back down to the street in the freight elevators. This novel Lucullan feast must rank as epicurean compared to the more recent debutante party that concluded with the release over the dining tables of more than a million dead butterflies.

Although no menus exist for either feast, dozens exist for banquets from 1865 to 1892, and all are mind-boggling in the quantity of dishes and number of courses included. A dinner for nine, for example, given in

February, 1892, began with an oyster bar, included a choice of a shrimp bisque or *consommé condorcet*, a selection of hors d'oeuvres, a fish course of bass with *pommes dauphine*, a game course of venison with fried eggplant, a choice of terrapin Baltimore or filets of chicken Toulouse, followed by a palate-clearing *sorbet au champagne*, then duck with a lettuce salad, three desserts (including plum pudding with rum sauce), and coffee. Purists will note there was no cheese served.

Where will you find the menu for this and dozens of other multicourse Lucullan feasts? In the 1893 treatise on the culinary arts written by Charles Ranhofer, former chef of Delmonico's. It was entitled *The Epicurean*.

# Filet of Sole Marguery à la Diamond Jim Brady

*T*his is the recipe that Diamond Jim declared perfect. At current prices, satisfying Diamond Jim's gargantuan appetite would cost you more than $115. This covers just the fish and shellfish, not the leeks, carrots, parsley, and other ingredients.

"Have 2 flounders filleted. [Set fillets aside.] Place bones, skin, and heads in stewpan. Add 1 pound inexpensive fish cleaned and cut into small pieces, ½ cup thinly sliced young carrots, and 1 small chopped leek, 3 sprigs of parsley, 10 whole peppercorns, 1 small bay leaf, 1 sprig of thyme, 1½ quarts cold water [add the pint first and note how high it comes on the side of the saucepan]. Bring to boiling point very slowly and simmer until liquid is reduced to 1 pint, then strain through fine cheesecloth. Place fillets in buttered baking pan and pour over 1 cup [of the] fish stock. Season with sprinkling of salt and pepper, and place in moderate [preheated] oven (325° F) 15 to 20 minutes. Carefully lift fillets from pan and arrange on hot ovenproof serving platter. Garnish with 1 dozen poached oysters and 1 dozen boiled shrimps, which have been shelled and cleaned. Pour remaining fish stock into baking pan in which fillets were poached and simmer gently until quantity is reduced to 3 or 4 tablespoons, no more. Strain into top part of double boiler and add 4 tablespoons dry white wine, ¼ pound butter. Cook over hot water, stirring until butter is melted. (Have very little water in lower part of double boiler, just enough to create a gentle steam.) Add 4 egg yolks that have been well beaten. Stir constantly until sauce is the consistency of a medium cream sauce. Pour this creamy sauce over fish fillets, oysters, and shrimps, and place under broiler flame until nicely glazed or lightly browned. Allow 1 fillet per serving."

# Pancakes Lillian Russell

*Such a pedestrian name, pancakes, for what is in truth an extraordinary dessert. Breaking with a tradition followed by Escoffier and Carême, Henri Charpentier shows his creativity in Food and Finesse, the Bride's Bible (1947) by not blithely poaching the pear but using it au naturel. Thus it is imperative that one use a very ripe pear.*

## *Filling*

1 very ripe pear

1 tablespoon currant jelly

1 tablespoon butter, melted

½ lemon, juiced, or 4 teaspoons lemon juice

1 tablespoon granulated sugar

¼ teaspoon vanilla

¼ teaspoon grated lemon peel

¼ teaspoon grated orange peel

1 tablespoon white curaçao

Peel and core pear, removing any brown spots, then mash with fork. Add other ingredients and mix well. Set aside in plastic-wrapped bowl.

## *Pancakes*

**2 tablespoons butter, melted**

**1 tablespoon flour**

**1 tablespoon milk**

**1 whole egg, beaten**

**⅛ teaspoon salt**

**1 teaspoon granulated sugar**

**6 tablespoons (3 ounces) brandy**

Put melted butter into bottom of low, heatproof serving dish [can use 8-inch pie plate]. Heat crepe or small frying pan until drop of butter bounces across pan. Add flour to milk and stir until lump-free. Add egg and salt. Brush preheated frying pan with melted butter from serving dish. Make first of four small, very thin pancakes or crepes by pouring one-fourth of batter into pan and swiftly swirling batter about. When it begins to puff in middle, turn over momentarily.

Remove pancake from pan and spread with one-fourth of the filling, roll, and place in serving dish. Keep hot while you make the other three. Sprinkle rolled pancakes with granulated sugar. Warm brandy, then ignite and pour over pancakes. Serves two normal people. Triple the recipe for one Lillian Russell.

# F
## is for Flops

According to Webster's, a flop is a complete failure—a dud. It's also what you and I call our cooking disasters. Television cooks call them "oops" and pretend they're a rare occurrence. Doyennes of cooking schools advise the neophyte cook to look upon culinary misadventures as "happy accidents" and recipe opportunities. They also suggest camouflaging disasters with generous sprinklings of parsley or paprika or even a layer of frosting. Entire cookbooks exist to help the home cook cope with such problems as the addition of too much salt, lumpy gravy and curdled sauces, cakes that never rise or, contrarywise, that overflow the pan, and a hundred other vicissitudes to which cooking is prey.

If helpful advice doesn't help and you've become gun-shy, the food producers of America have been quick to offer ready-made substitutes for those dishes that most often cause cooks problems. Packaged cake and pudding mixes, canned gravies and sauces, frozen pie crusts and pastry are convenient and goof-proof. For ease and peace of mind, many cooks are willing to sacrifice optimum taste and pride of "authorship."

But don't be too quick to blame yourself for flops. Many cooks' goofs are due to mistakes in the original recipe. For example, there's the caramel sauce recipe that's been around for years. Usually it appears in a spiral-bound, locally issued recipe book, but recently it made the big time when it appeared in a famous author's "author-tested" hardbound book. It calls for the cook to submerge cans of sweetened condensed milk in boiling water for several hours. The resulting sauce melts in your mouth. Unfortunately, on occasion the cans explode in the pan. As a result Carnation has taken the extraordinary precaution of labeling their cans, "Caution—never heat unopened can."

Another example. This one recently appeared in the Sunday magazine section of a major metropolitan newspaper. It was a marvelous piece, nostalgically written by a bachelor, telling in two full pages about finding, in his late mother's desk drawer, a slice of cake from his father's favorite and secret recipe. The name of the recipe? The Never-Fail Cake. Several weeks later, in a letter to the editor, a reader wrote, "What emerged from my 350° F oven 30 minutes later were what appeared to be two nine-inch tortillas." She went on to cite three possible reasons for such a result. One, that the author "may be carrying on his father's grand tradition of not dealing the full deck when he shares recipes. Two, [his father] wants [the author] to remain a bachelor. Or, three, his mother knew what she was doing when she put her slice of cake in the desk drawer."

Two weeks after that, another reader wrote in and said she'd made the cake with success by changing the recipe slightly. First, she used eight-inch, not nine-inch cake pans and, second, she cooked the cake for twenty-three minutes not thirty. Oh, yes, and she had to make changes in the icing, too. "Never-Fail" indeed!

**Credo of the cooking schools as expounded by John Keats: "Don't be discouraged by a failure. It can be a positive experience. Failure is, in a sense, the highway to success, inasmuch as every discovery of what is false leads us to seek earnestly after what is true, and every fresh experience points out some form of error which we shall afterwards carefully avoid."**

The brownie is the perfect example of making the best of a cake gone wrong. Adding too much liquid, mismeasuring the flour, omitting the baking powder, using the wrong size pan, having the oven too hot (or too cold), baking for too long or too short—any one of these can turn a cake into a brownie.

**Maida Heatter, author of those "Great Dessert" books, is held in the highest regard by cookbook reviewers, not just for her truly great recipes but for her dedication to author-testing. For example, she had no sooner completed her first book on desserts when she discovered her oven was off by twenty-five degrees. She rolled up her sleeves and remade every dessert that called for oven-baking.**

Actually, the first brownie was an Australian sweet bread made in 1883 with brown sugar and currants. Fourteen years later it showed up in all its chocolate glory in, of all places, a Sears Roebuck Catalog. Sometime in between, according to the aptly named *Bull Cookbook*, it was invented in Russia and named for the Russian brown bear. The earliest recipe I know of (courtesy of Maida Heatter) was for Bangor Brownies, which originally appeared in a cookbook published by the local YWCA in 1914 according to Mrs. "Brownie" Schrumpf, a member of the Maine Historical Society. Personally, I prefer the far more fanciful and totally inaccurate version that begins at the long-vanished Hotel Touraine in Boston in the 1920s. It seems a brave or perhaps foolhardy new chef was simultaneously making butter cookies and melting chocolate for pudding when a fire broke out in the kitchen. With smoke billowing about him and blinding his eyes, he rescued the about-to-scorch chocolate by pouring it into the nearest bowl, which contained the cookie batter. Did he run for his life or help dowse the fire? Apparently not. He was more intent on rescuing the cookie-chocolate mixture, which he calmly poured into a pan, baked, and served in the smoke-free dining room as Boston Brown Bars.

**This secret for making either chewy or cakelike brownies from the same recipe was found in a spiral-bound community cookbook: "For soft-type brownies bake at 325° F for 40 minutes; for chewy ones, bake at 350° F for 25 minutes." It is in error, however. Follow those directions and you'll get the opposite results.**

Although the Hotel Touraine account wouldn't hold up in a court of law, there have been many other bona fide delicious accidents. One of our favorite candy bars (it has a nougat center) was not initially a great success. One day, by accident, extra egg whites were added to a batch. The company that capitalized on that mistake is worth billions today.

Even fudge, America's favorite sweet (which I wrote about in my book, *Oh, Fudge*), was created by mistake in Baltimore in 1886, either the result of overcooking fondant or overmixing and undercooking caramel (nobody knows which). Sold at forty cents a pound, it was discovered by a student at Vassar, Emelyn Hartridge, class of '92, who took the recipe to school with her. So popular was it that eventually Vassar installed fudge kitchens in every dorm. (From Vassar it spread to Smith and Wellesley, each of which came up with its own variation.)

Even the most glorious version of a caramel-apple pie—the *tarte Tatin*, or more accurately, *la tarte des demoiselles Tatin* (the tart of the two unmarried Tatin ladies)—was made by accident. The story has been embellished and reembellished by food writers, but it boils down to a few simple facts. It took place in a little town just south of Orleans, Lamotte-Beuvron, Loir-et-Cher, France. Sisters Caroline and Stephanie Tatin, forced to earn their living by running a hotel, chose as one of their dessert selections their father's favorite caramel-topped apple pie. As is the custom in France, this pie is made in a flan ring on a cookie sheet. It is usually a simple matter to remove the pie or tarte from the ring to serve it, but one day the pie fell, literally, landing caramel-side down. In no position financially to simply discard it and unable to get it back into the pan without breaking it up, they slid a baker's board, like a pizza paddle, beneath it and served it as is with the caramel on the bottom, the pastry on top. The result was such a success, they continued to make it that way—without the dropping, of course.

Another happy accident: the Toll House Cookie. In August of 1930 Ruth and Kenneth Wakefield mortgaged themselves to the hilt and realized a dream when they bought a 1709 former tollhouse on the outskirts of Whitman, Massachusetts. Calling it the Toll House Inn, they went into business with a male assistant, a waitress, and seven tables seating about thirty-five guests. Within three years they'd expanded to a staff of ninety, sixty-four tables, and up to 2,000 guests a day.

One day Ruth Wakefield decided to make some chocolate cookies from a butter cookie recipe. As a shortcut, instead of melting a pound of Nestlé's yellow-label semisweet chocolate, she cut it into pieces the size of a pea and added them to the batter. To her surprise, they didn't melt during the cooking. Instead of a chocolate cookie, she'd discovered a vanilla cookie with a chocolate crunch.

Soon Nestlé discovered the cookie, too, and began printing the recipe on their semisweet chocolate bar wrappers. In 1939 Nestlé began marketing uniformly shaped chocolate chips, again with the cookie recipe on the wrapper. The recipe you find on today's package is not the original, however. Under the terms of the 1939 licensing agreement, Nestlé had to run Ruth Wakefield's recipe as it was for forty years. When the agreement expired in 1979, Nestlé changed the recipe. They eliminated sifting the flour, left out the water used to dissolve the baking soda, reduced the baking time, and said you didn't need to grease the baking sheet. Many old-time Toll House cookie-lovers do not find the changes an improvement.

**You will not find a recipe for Toll House Cookies or even Chocolate Chip Cookies in the 1936 edition of Ruth Wakefield's Toll House cookbook, which went to twenty-five printings by 1948. Instead, the cookies are called Chocolate Crunch, as they still are in the facsimile edition published in 1991.**

*Beurre blanc* is another accident, circa 1900. Apparently an assistant to the cook of the marquis de Goulaine was making a béarnaise sauce and forgot to add the egg yolks. The marquis tasted it, liked it, and named it—surprisingly enough, not after himself. The cook made a note of the recipe, and when she opened her inn at Saint-Julien-de-Concelles near Nantes, she began serving it with fish. There it was discovered by Mere Michel before she opened her famous restaurant in the Rue Rennequin in Paris. From there *beurre blanc* was disseminated all over the world, not as a mistake, but as an original recipe.

You will note that all of these dishes are comparatively new in culinary history and are well documented. We shall never know how many errata occurred in the days before mass-produced cookbooks and were simply absorbed into the mainstream of cookery.

As far as errata are concerned, they are, said one wise person, "the price we pay to have at our fingertips the culinary knowledge of the ages. We must count ourselves fortunate," continued she, "that we don't have to hand-copy each and every recipe as our great-grandmothers did."

Failures test not only one's own soul but also the good manners of guests. My nominee for such a dish is the one I prepared for a young man upon whom I had matrimonial designs. On paper the combination seemed a natural: onions, pork, peanut butter, and a little nutty sherry. The directions said it would emerge from the oven beautifully sauced. One look at the finished casserole and I wished I were. Those lovely ingredients hadn't come together at all. Instead, there was a layer of sherry and a layer of peanut butter. On the bottom, a layer of pork, and, floating on top, a film of the bacon drippings in which I'd fried the onions. My guest's face turned the same yellow-green of my cheap cooking sherry, but, gallant soul that he was, he pulled up his chair and prepared to eat it.

I was the one who yelled stop. Try as we might—scraping and washing—we couldn't salvage those chops and so ate vegetarian that night. It turned out to be one of the more memorable meals of my life—and the perfect test of his devotion and intentions, not to mention his sense of humor. I have to report that in the thirty years we've been married, he has never again taken me up on my offer to attempt pork chops and peanut butter.

# Chocolate Crunch Cookies

*T*his is the recipe that originally appeared in Ruth Wakefield's Toll House Tried and True Recipes *by Ruth Graves Wakefield, Dietitian-Lecturer, in 1936. Note that it is written in a transitional style, with the directions merged into the list of ingredients. Previously recipes were written in paragraph form with quantities buried within the recipe itself. Modern recipes segregate the ingredients so that the cook can work more efficiently by gathering together and measuring everything prior to final assembly.*

*Cream*

1 cup butter, add

¾ cup brown sugar

¾ cup granulated sugar and

2 eggs beaten whole. Dissolve

1 tsp. soda in

1 tsp. hot water, and mix alternately with

2¼ cups flour sifted with

1 tsp. salt. Last add

1 cup chopped nuts and

1 lb. Nestlé's yellow label chocolate, semi-sweet, which has been cut in pieces the size of a pea.

*Flavor with*

1 tsp. vanilla and drop half teaspoons on a greased cookie sheet. Bake 10 to 12 minutes in 375° F oven.

*Makes 100 cookies.*

# Vassar Fudge

*T*his is Emelyn Hartridge's own recipe, according to a 1921 letter in the Vassar archives. *The fudge would have been made over a "spirit" lamp, or chafing dish, and thus cooked very slowly. Immediate stirring after removing it from the heat results in a grainy fudge. You will note that although ingredients are segregated, they are not given in any particular order.*

**2 cups granulated white sugar**

**1 tablespoon butter**

**1 cup of cream**

**¼ of a cake [8 ounces] of Baker's Premium No. 1 [unsweetened] chocolate**

*Original method:* Put in the sugar and cream, and when this becomes hot, put in the chocolate, broken up into fine pieces. Stir vigorously and constantly. Put in butter when it begins to boil. Stir until it creams when beaten in a saucer. Then remove and beat until quite cool and pour into buttered tins. When cold, cut into diamond-shaped pieces.

*Modern method:* Butter a dish or small broiler-oven–size pan. Over low heat, melt sugar in cream until thoroughly dissolved. Add chocolate and [optionally] butter. Continue cooking and stirring until mixture thickens and comes to a large, lazy, noisy boil. Drop a bit into ice-cold water in a small cup to check if it holds together in a soft ball. Remove from heat and, for grainy fudge, begin stirring immediately—you do not need to beat but you must not stop stirring until mixture thickens and becomes lighter in color.

For creamier fudge, remove from heat and place saucepan in dish or sink filled ½ inch deep with cold water. Add butter now. Don't stir until mixture has cooled (you should feel little or no heat if you hold your palm directly above mixture) and "skin" forms on top. Then stir, no need to beat.

For both grainy and creamy fudge, keep stirring until mixture thickens, loses its sheen, and becomes lighter in color. Pour into pan, score, and chill until firm. Makes 1 pound.

# Beurre Blanc

O r *"white butter."* Beurre blanc *is simply a* béarnaise *that has lost its egg yolks. Strictly speaking, unless you strain it, it is not even a monochromatic one. And even with straining, it's still not white but a creamy color. Here are a classic method and a modern method using an electric mixer, which is faster, easier, and failure-proof!*

1 tablespoon finely chopped shallot

2 tablespoons tarragon (optional)

sprig of thyme

small piece of bay leaf

¼ cup cider vinegar (or, if omitting tarragon, use tarragon vinegar)

¼ cup white wine

⅛ teaspoon or pinch of salt

⅛ teaspoon or pinch of pepper, preferably white

4 ounces (1 stick) unsweetened butter, soft but not melted

squeeze of lemon (optional)

Put everything but butter and lemon in saucepan and bring to a boil. Continue boiling until reduced by two-thirds.

*Classic method:* Remove from heat and let cool until lukewarm or room temperature. Add butter, a little bit at a time, until you have incorporated all of it. Continue beating until mixture becomes thick and creamy. Put through a sieve. Taste for seasoning, adding a little lemon juice to sharpen the flavor or if serving it with fish. Serve at room temperature.

*Modern method:* Make your reduction and let it cool. Then either chop finely in a food processor or strain or even let it be. Cream butter with electric mixer. Incorporate the reduction, a tablespoon at a time. Taste for seasoning, and add lemon juice if you wish.

# G is for Gingerbread

This is cookery's fragrant version of fraternal twins, each with a different texture but essentially the same spicy taste and exactly the same name (though neither is a bread as you and I know it). One, the elder culinary-wise, I call gingerbread-hard. It is dense and cookielike—perfect for making little men with raisin eyes and coats of pastel-colored frosting. At Christmastime this same gingerbread forms the walls of wondrous miniature houses with wafer roofs or tiles of peppermint, thick icing-snow dangling from the eaves, and candy canes guarding the door. It is truly the stuff of fairy tales, as in "Hansel and Gretel." The other, which I call gingerbread-soft, is moist and cakelike and so rich and spicy it can be served plain. Some aficionados of this cake demand a dollop of whipped cream to top it off nicely. Others dress theirs with a ladling of sauce—maybe a brandied hard sauce or a tangy lemon one.

Between them, the origins of these two fabulously aromatic gingerbreads encompass the evolution of bread into cakes.

Even before the gingerroot arrived in Rome in the first or second century A.D., bread had evolved considerably from its beginnings in Egypt as a crisp flat-bread very like the Jewish *matzo* or Mexican *tortilla*. The production of beer had yielded yeast, which, when added to the flat-bread dough, resulted in a thicker, almost solid loaf.

**The word bread comes from the Old English word, *brēowan*, "to brew."** The further addition of honey to the dough paid still more dividends. The natural sugars in honey—fructose, glucose, and a small amount of sucrose—quickened the action of the yeast and increased its potency. The bread raised a bit higher, coming somewhat closer in texture to today's gingerbread-hard. To please the epicure's desire for the new and different, Roman bakers began to spice up their breads with cumin.

Then in rode ginger on the backs of camels driven by Arab traders traveling the spice route from China. The Romans, who seemed to despise the status quo on principle, were quick to see in this curiously shaped root another source of variety. Again, as had happened with honey, adding ginger to bread dough proved doubly beneficial. Not only did it add zest to the flavor, but the oil in ginger acted as a natural preservative. This gingerbread was for all intents and purposes the first gingerbread-hard. All it needed was a little refinement.

For gingerbread to make the very short journey from Rome to the center of Europe took, depending on whom you consult, anywhere from a century to better than eight hundred years. Some authorities credit its spread to a Greek baker from Rhodes; some claim it was an enterprising crusader; others say it was introduced during the visit of Harunal-Raschid, of *Arabian Nights* fame, to the court of Charlemagne in A.D. 800. An eleventh-century manuscript from the Abbey of Micy says the hermit bishop, Saint Gregory, brought it with him from Armenia when he took refuge in a cavern outside Pithiviers, France, in A.D. 992. According to that manuscript, Saint Gregory made the bread himself using honey and spices in the manner of his country from a sourdoughlike starter instead of beer yeast. His guests, tasting it, thought it a bit of paradise on earth. They weren't the only ones. Everyone who tasted it was conquered. The making of gingerbread spread like butter on hot bread to Holland, England, Germany, Belgium, and back down to Italy.

Rich and poor, highborn and lowborn, everyone wanted more of this pastry. So great was the demand, in fact, that a German guild of bakers sprang up in the fourteenth century to do nothing but bake the honey-based thin gingerbread. This effort was the beginning of the German sweet bakings, or *sussgeback*. (Later, when they added candy to their line, the guild became what we now recognize as the first confectioners.)

Competition provided incentive. The problem with yeast dough is that it has a tendency to rise every which way. Rolling it thin helped, but during baking it persisted in bubbling up. A different type of leavening was needed. The solution was found in the antlers of deer: powdered hartshorn. This is a natural form of the carbonate found in carbonated soda (baking soda). The use of hartshorn allowed the bread to rise uniformly but not a great deal. This was just enough to enable the bakers to roll out their dough, cut it into shapes or press it into molds, and decorate and ice the baked pieces. The results were very similar to today's *lebkuchen,* or gingerbread-hard. More than just eat-me-quick cookies, they were special, festival treats—ones that served as ceremonial gifts or lovers' tokens.

The molds became more and more complicated until it took the skill of a sculptor to carve one. Some molds were ceramic; others were cast in metal. Decorations also became more elaborate and extravagant. From piped-on icings and simple sayings, they grew to include entire verses or paintings in icing: portraits, pastorals, and religious scenes in full color. The results were so beautiful and the product so pop-

**In Germany gingerbread men were called gingerbread "husbands." To this day, German gingerbread molds are preserved in museums and are surprisingly diverse, depicting not just "husbands" but roosters and other animals, religious motifs, and actual scenes from the harvest or court.**

**Queen Elizabeth I employed a full-time gingerbread baker; more than 400 years later, some of his molds are still in use today in Queen Elizabeth II's kitchen.**

ular that the gingerbread makers monopolized food sales from their stalls at fairs, markets, and festivals.

At some point—no one knows exactly when —the Germans began to do with their gingerbread what the French and English did with sugar: They sculpted it into fantasies, specifically, into cottagelike gingerbread houses. Eventually these houses grew to enormous proportions; some required up to four sturdy servants to carry them into the banquet halls, where they were paraded around, not as food, but as entertainments over which to ooh and ahh. (The largest gingerbread baked prior to the seventeenth century weighed a reported 150 pounds.)

**In Paris in the eleventh century, a group of monks began holding a Gingerbread Fair on the site of what is now the Saint-Antoine Hospital. At this fair the monks sold their own little gingerbreads in the shape of a pig.**

Though by then ubiquitous, gingerbread still enjoyed a reputation as a food perfectly fit for any king. Thus, many a banquet throughout Europe during the fourteenth to sixteenth centuries ended with a gingerbread course. Still of the hard variety, these royal gingerbreads, too, were carried in on the shoulders of servants, but they often were gilded with real gold and studded with gold-dipped cloves.

**To preserve a gingerbread house, spray it inside and out with a good hair spray. Repeat annually.**

It was the French who developed the first real ginger-*bread*. Neither a wafer nor a flat-bread, and definitely not a cake, it was a true bread—a hearty rye, very chewy and pumpernickel-like, and similar to Sweden's cardamom-flavored *limpa*. Since the French, like the Romans, were never content to leave well enough alone, they made their bread with all sorts of spices. Cloves, cinnamon, mace, nutmeg, coriander, anise, pepper, and allspice (all or some) went into the bread along with the ginger.

Soon the French went even further, leaving out the ginger altogether and calling their version not gingerbread but *pain d'épice*, or spice bread. Like the Germans before them, a French guild of *boulangers de pain d'épice* was franchised or recognized by chicken-in-every-pot Henry IV in 1596 at Reims. Officially the guild maintained their monopoly on spice bread made with rye flour for nearly two centuries. But this, like trying to transport water in a sieve, was doomed to failure. For example, since the fourteenth century, the Burgundians had been making their own spice bread, the *boichet*, out of wheat flour, honey, and leaven. Other regions had their own versions. Some added red wine to darken the color; others replaced the honey with cane sugar. The British replaced the honey with treacle or molasses.

But the most significant changes occurred when the millers began producing different types of flour from the same grain. These different grades of flour yielded different breads. In the fifteenth century, one miller working with one harvest of wheat could provide the flour for white hall bread for guests, bran for hull bread for servants, and the finest, softest white flour for queen's bread for the royals and those nobles who could afford it.

Thus was the stage set for the conversion of bread dough into cake dough. The process began with a white flour yeast dough that was enriched with eggs and butter. Into this mixture was worked fruit, sweetening, spices (including ginger), and maybe even some spirits. The result was no longer gingerbread-hard but the more cakelike gingerbread-soft, much like today's dense, heavy fruitcake. It was different enough for Amelia Simmons to make a distinction among the ginger-flavored doughs and include recipes for gingerbread, gingerbread-hard, and gingerbread-soft in her 1796 cookbook entitled *American Cookery*.

Today an American recipe for gingerbread usually means the cake; one has to look under "cookies" to find the equivalent of gingerbread-hard. As for Europe, in the Germanic countries you'll still find recipes for both gingerbreads: hard, which they call thin (*dunner lebkuchen*), and soft, which they call thick (*dicker lebkuchen*). Only in France will you find real ginger *bread*, under the

**A recipe for gingerbread-hard came over on the Mayflower, and William Penn's wife brought her own "receipt" for *ginger breed*. It calls for lightening the bread by beating it, then dipping it in water, and returning it to the oven to use steam to further lighten it.**

name *pain d'épice*. But hurry. The French have begun converting to the cakelike gingerbread-soft.

It took some 8,000 years to develop bread and 3,500 years for bread to become cake. In the past century or so, cakes, cookies, and breads have continued to change, and not always for the better, as the sad state of our plastic-wrapped white sandwich bread will attest. Evolution has led to revolution.

# Gingerbread

These recipes come from Amelia Simmons's *American Cookery* (1796). Note that in the first recipe, which she calls molasses gingerbread, she is really referring to a *pain d'épice*, or spice bread. The second, which she calls gingerbread cakes and subtitles butter and sugar gingerbread, is the equivalent of gingerbread-hard, the usual gingerbread of the time in America. It would have been this gingerbread that was served as a treat to troops on mustering day and the one a seventeen-year-old Benjamin Franklin would have bought on his way to Philadelphia to become a "printer's devil." The third recipe is for gingerbread-soft and is probably the first appearance of a recipe for such a cake in America.

## *Molasses Gingerbread*

One tablespoon of cinnamon, some coriander or allspice, put to [added to] pearl ash [a.k.a. potash. Like baking soda, it forms carbon dioxide in the presence of an acidic liquid], dissolved in half a pint of water, four pounds flour, one quart molasses, four ounces butter (if in summer rub in the butter, if in winter, warm the butter and molasses and pour to the spiced flour), knead well 'till fluff, the more the better, the lighter and whiter it will be;

*bake brisk [in hot oven] fifteen minutes; don't scorch; before it is put in, wash it with [egg] whites and sugar beat together.*

## Gingerbread Cakes

No. 1: Three pounds of flour, a grated nutmeg, two ounces ginger, one pound sugar [most likely a dark brown sugar], three small spoons pearl ash dissolved in cream, one pound butter, four eggs, knead it stiff, shape it to your fancy, bake 15 minutes.

## Soft Gingerbread to Be Baked in Pans

Rub [literally, with the hand—comparable to today's "creaming"] three pounds of sugar, two pounds of butter into four pounds of flour. Add 20 eggs, 4 ounces ginger, 4 spoons rose water, bake as No. 1.

# H is for Hodgepodge

The dictionary defines hodgepodge as "a heterogeneous mixture," which sounds suspiciously like a teenage get-together but isn't. Actually, it's a medieval, circa 1350, English rhyming variation on *hotchpotch*, a meat stew. By the late 1500s in Britain, the word *hodgepodge* had completely replaced hotchpotch and was used to describe other mixtures than strictly culinary ones. For example, the Earl of Spenser denounced the Irish because "They have made our English tongue a gallimaufrey or hodgepodge of all other speeches."

Both *hotchpotch* and *hodgepodge* come from the Scottish *hotch*, the German *hotzen*, the French *hocher*, the old French *hocier*, and the Dutch *hotsen*—all of which have essentially the same meaning: to shake or jolt. In the tradition of James Bond's famed shaken but not stirred martini, a hotchpotch must be shaken, never stirred. (Professional chefs still use the technique to keep food from sticking. Much preferable the quick shake of a pan in comparison to the slower stirring method: get out a spoon, uncover the pan, let the steam escape, stir, re-cover, clean the spoon.)

For centuries hodgepodges were cooked suspended in a covered pot over a fire. Today they are done in an oven, but still covered. Not all dishes cooked in casseroles, pots, and braising pans, however, are hodgepodges—only those that utilize contained steam to cook the dish and condensation to keep it liquid. Also ruled out, by definition, are dishes cooked uncovered for any length of time and those that come into direct contact with heat, needing stirring to avoid burning. Uncovering a hodgepodge defeats one's purpose, slowing down the cooking. Since they must remain covered, these are dishes that *should* be shaken.

> Circa 1545 *gallimaufry* was a fairly new French word at court, derived from *galer,* to amuse oneself, and, in the Picard dialect, *mafrer,* to gorge oneself. By the mid-1800s, it had become a term of derision used to describe a stew made from scraps.

Today the most common hodgepodge is that stew so delicate that stirring would break up the ingredients and turn the stew into a soup, such as one made of seafood. (There is some controversy as to whether a bouillabaisse meets all definitions of hodgepodge.) In the past most hodgepodges were made from tough cuts of meat such as stew beef, stewing chicken, capons, mutton, or any combination thereof. A classic French *hoche poche* is made from pigs' ears and tails, salt bacon, beef, and mutton, plus sliced winter vegetables. Another is made from pickled oxtail, although gourmets prefer their oxtail stew flambéed with brandy, which some wags would say was just another form of pickling.

> Generations of Yankee cooks have been taught that at some time during the cooking, a stew should "catch on" (stick to the pot just enough to brown), thereby giving the gravy richness and savor.

Every country has at least one version of stew; Great Britain has three: the Lancashire hot pot, the Irish stew, and a Scottish soupy stew made with mutton and beef. Only the Dutch have made a stew their national dish.

As is too often the case, the dish had its origins in war. In 1567 the Protestant Netherlanders rebelled against their Catholic absentee ruler, Philip II, who was king of Spain, much of Italy, all of the Netherlands, and temporarily England (he co-ruled with his wife, Henry VIII's daughter, Queen Mary Tudor).

Philip's well-armed, well-supplied armies were commanded by the ruthless Duke of Alba. Facing him was a small makeshift force led by William the Silent, Prince of Orange. It was no contest. Although William eluded capture, by 1574 Alba was in control of all the Netherlands with the exception of the maritime provinces. The greatest resistance came from the ancient Dutch city of Leiden, near the Hague. Rather than a direct assault, Alba chose to starve her out. The siege would have succeeded except that at the beginning of October, William the Silent opened the dikes, flooded the surrounding countryside, and sailed a small fleet of flat-bottomed gunboats up to the walls of the city. According to a proud Dutchman, the Spaniards took one look at the boats and fled. More likely they took one look at the encroaching water and, preferring running to swimming, abandoned ship, so to speak. They weren't even out of sight when the city gates burst open and starving Leideners stormed the deserted camp. There they found, simmering on the fire, an enormous black iron pot filled to its brim with a beef-and-vegetable stew. Like the bread and fishes, it stretched magnificently to feed the multitudes.

**From the making of the *hutspot* came our modern Dutch oven, a large, heavily constructed pot with a close-fitting lid and two handles on the sides to make for easier shaking.**

Since then, October 3 has been a Dutch national holiday when, as the British eat goose at Christmas and Americans eat turkey at Thanksgiving, almost everyone eats a traditional beef stew called *hutspot me klapstuck*. *Hutspot*, as you might have guessed, means a dish shaken during cooking, and *klapstuck* refers to the particular cut of meat.

Despite the obvious etymological relationship between hodgepodge, *hoche poche*, and *hutspot*, not all such dishes bear similar names. For example, the Spanish stew that saved Leiden was the *cocido*. *Mishmash* is a Yiddish version. A medieval English dish of chicken or mutton stew is a *gallimaufry*. In the northeastern United States we call our hodgepodge a New England boiled dinner (or simply "boiled dinner"), which traditionally was served once a week, usually Monday or Wednesday, from early fall until late spring, and made with cabbage.

The synonym of choice for hodgepodge in most dictionaries is *jumble*, but from a cookery point of view this synonym is inaccurate. A jumble is a small, flat, sweet, little cake, the Dutch *koekje*. Take the jumble batter and add yeast, then drop by spoonfuls into hot oil, and you get an *olie-koecken*, a fritter. Take the dough for the *olie-koecken*, roll it out, shape it into a wreath or bow or knot, and deep fry it, and you have the traditional Dutch Christmas treat, the dough-knot or dow-knot. Instead of shaping it, cut it into a round solid circle and you get a doughnut.

**Jumbles get their name from a "gimbel," a curious two-finger ring popular in the sixteenth century. Today, the name refers strictly to cookies with holes in the middle; originally, a jumble could be any small flat cake, twisted and knotted and/or shaped into rings.**

Since all bread-eating peoples eventually learned to make something resembling a doughnut, all do and can claim credit for inventing it. Most such creations, however, on examination turn out to be more like the fritter—for example, the French *beignet* and the Italian *fritole*. Americans, staking their own claim to the doughnut, cite first the Native American fried bread and reinforce that claim with tales of the Pilgrims making it. (To which the Dutch might reply, "And in what country did the Pilgrims live for eleven years before sailing for America?")

Doughnuts have traditionally played an important role in pre-Lenten festivities, especially on the day before Ash Wednesday. On Shrove Tuesday, often called Fat Tuesday because it is your last chance to fatten up before beginning forty days of fasting, most Germanic peoples eat potato-based doughnuts called *fastnachtkuches*, or fasting-night cakes. Also on this one day women were not only freed from work but forbidden to work. Of course, first they had to break their backs preparing the foods that would be eaten. In any event, the last person out of bed that day was the "Fastnacht" and to him fell all the daily chores usually done by the women.

How the fastnacht or the doughnut got its hole in the middle seems a matter of some confusion. Food historians claim it was a logical evolution from the jumble. Folks in Rockport, Maine, say no. They credit Mason Crockett Gregory with inventing the doughnut hole in 1847; a plaque hanging on his house says as much. One version of the story avers that as a youngster he poked holes in his mother's cakes before she fried them. Another asserts that as an adult he disliked the uncooked centers often found in doughnuts and suggested removing the centers prior to cooking. (It might also be that on his travels as a sea captain he had seen dow-knots elsewhere and wanted to replicate them.) Regardless, he was beaten to the patent office by John Blondell who in 1872 came up with the first doughnut cutter that simultaneously punched out a hole in the center.

**Just as the English eat pancakes on Shrove Tuesday and hot cross buns on Good Friday, cookies and dow-knots were served by the Dutch and Germans at Christmastime. For example, in Germany a hot doughnut was eaten for luck at the first stroke of New Year's Day.**

Whether or not the Pilgrims brought the doughnut to this country from their years in Holland, we owe the Dutch much for their contributions to our culinary traditions. The French owe the Dutch even more but are loath to admit it. During the French persecutions of the Huguenots, for example (in the time of Catherine de Médicis and later), many fled to Holland. There they learned to enjoy an egg-rich sauce similar to mayonnaise but made with melted butter. Upon their return to France, they brought with them what is now known as a master sauce, that warm mayonnaise that the French grudgingly call hollandaise.

Although hollandaise sauce enrobes dozens of famous dishes, the most famous dish to be laved lavishly with that thick, yellow, slightly lemony sauce is eggs Benedict. It is one of three marvelously sauced dishes to trace their origins to Delmonico's Restaurant in New York City. Unlike the other two, there is no mystery about the beginnings of eggs Benedict. It seems—and her grandniece confirms—that a Mrs.

LeGrand Benedict was in the habit of lunching at Delmonico's. One day she expressed ennui and complained about the same old menu. She and the maitre d'hotel came up with something new: a rusk topped with ham topped with a poached egg topped with a soupçon of hollandaise topped with chopped truffles. Today's incarnation offers half a toasted English muffin, a thin slice of Canadian bacon, a poached egg, a slathering of hollandaise, and no truffles. Of the two original components that survive, the hollandaise clearly makes the dish.

The second of the famed Delmonico dishes is lobster Newburg—a dish not usually identified as a stew but very similar to a hodgepodge, especially those of the shake-don't-stir seafood variety. A delicious blend of lobster, egg yolks, cream, and Madeira, it has a story a mile long to go with it. For the entire tale, see "L is for Lobster."

The third Delmonico's dish was chicken à la King, which has nothing to do with the crowned heads of Europe but much in common with

**Chicken à la King achieved its greatest acceptance and popularity during the Depression, a time when, like King Henri IV of France, politicians were promising a chicken in every pot on Sunday.**

hodgepodges. There are three versions of its origins. The first, the Delmonico's version, is set in the 1880s, when it was named chicken à la Keene after Foxhall Keene, a free-spending son of a successful Wall Street speculator. (The dish appears in the 1893 book of Delmonico chef Ranhofer as chicken fricassee à la Favorite.) A second tale attributes the dish to Foxhall's father, James R. Keene, asserting that it was made in his honor at the Claridge Hotel in England after his horse won the 1881 Grand Prix. In neither Keene case does a rational explanation exist to explain the change from Keene to King. The third tale dates also from the 1880s. This time the dish was made at the Brighton Beach Hotel for the proprietor, E. Clark King III. Escoffier, whose connections with English hotels covers that same period, includes a similar recipe in his cookbook that he names neither Keene or King but "old-fashioned fricassee."

In any case, both lobster à la Newburg and chicken à la King are best shaken, not stirred. Like the hodgepodges of yesteryear, an old-fashioned stew, whatever its origins or ingredients, is a richly satisfying meal. Next time you make one, cover it tightly and give it a good shake now and then. See what a delicious difference shaking, not stirring, makes.

# Hodgepodge

*T*he Dutch make their Hutspot *with beef, the Scots with mutton; the Belgians throw in a couple pigs' ears and feet. The French have been known to use all of the above.*

11 ounces (1½ cups) navy (pea) beans (optional)
2 pounds fresh beef brisket
1 bay leaf
1 rib celery, finely diced
1 small onion, finely diced
1 turnip or parsnip, finely diced
4 cups water
½ teaspoon salt

1 pound carrots (2 cups), sliced
3 pounds potatoes (6 medium), peeled and quartered
3 medium onions (1½ cups), coarsely chopped
8 tablespoons (4 ounces or 1 stick) butter, melted and browned
minced fresh parsley
⅓ cup cold water
3 tablespoons all-purpose flour

If using beans: Put beans in a large saucepan and cover with water. Bring to a boil and let boil for two minutes. Remove from heat, cover, and set aside to soak 1 hour. Then return to boil, lower heat, and simmer for an additional hour or until partially cooked. Reserve.

Put meat (whole) in a pot along with bay leaf and finely diced celery, onion, and turnip or parsnip. Add water and salt. Cover and simmer 2½ hours, shaking pot occasionally to make sure meat does not stick.

Add carrots, potatoes, and onions (plus optional beans) to meat, adding just enough of bean-water or plain water so there are at least 2 cups of liquid in pan. Cover and cook until meat and vegetables are tender. Remove meat and slice. Discard bay leaf. Drain vegetables, reserving 1⅔ cups liquid (add water if necessary). Mash vegetables and spoon into shallow serving dish. Pour browned butter over vegetables. Overlap meat slices down the center and garnish with parsley.

To make gravy: Blend cold water slowly into flour, then stir into reserved liquid. Cook and stir until thickened and bubbly. Season to taste.

# Chicken à la King

*T*he closest thing to a chicken à la King recipe in The Epicurean (1893) by Charles Ranhofer, former chef of Delmonico's, is Fricassee de Poulet à la Favorite. *What you find on the banquet circuit is chunked chicken in a cream sauce with mixed vegetables (diced carrots and potatoes plus peas), frequently served in a puff pastry shell. If you want no part of that, try this version of Ranhofer's recipe.*

2½-pound chicken, cut into pieces

4 cups chicken stock

5 cups white sauce

2 large or 3 medium egg yolks

2–3 tablespoons butter

carrot balls, ½ inch in diameter, poached in slightly sweetened chicken stock

small white onions, canned or poached in chicken stock

crawfish for garnish

Soak chicken in cold water for half an hour, then drain and put in a saucepan with chicken stock. Cook chicken, drain in a colander, and run the liquid through an extra-fine sieve. Put it back on the burner and reduce it by half. Add white sauce, then reduce once more until the sauce adheres to the spoon. Add hot sauce to egg yolks and butter. Strain through a sieve, and keep hot in a double boiler.

Wash the pieces of cooked chicken in cold water; debone, and place pieces in the sauce. When they are well heated, pour mixture onto a serving platter. Garnish with a cluster of carrot balls and small white onions. Use crawfish for ornamentation.

# Eggs Benedict

*R*educed to its simplest form, this is a poached egg atop a slice of ham atop a toasted, but not browned, English muffin. Ranhofer calls it "eggs Benedick" and gives the following advice.

Cut some muffins in halves crosswise, toast them without allowing to brown, then place a round of cooked ham an eighth of an inch thick and of the same diameter as the muffins on each half. Heat in a moderate oven and put a poached egg on each toast. Cover the whole with hollandaise sauce.

## *Hollandaise*

Of course, the clinker is the hollandaise sauce, which gives so many cooks trouble that they buy the packaged mixes and put up with the chemical taste just so they don't have to watch good butter and eggs curdle. The secret of making hollandaise is to:
1) Clarify the butter, using only the clear golden liquid, discarding the white solids. 2) Make it in a round-bottomed metal bowl, not your typical double boiler. (3) Use an electric hand-mixer.

**3 egg yolks**

**2 ounces of water**

**½ pound butter, clarified and kept warm**

**juice of 1 lemon**

Put egg yolks and water in a *round-bottomed* heatproof stainless steel bowl that will fit over a saucepan of hot, not boiling, water. Beat sauce over low heat until yolks begin to thicken. Remove bowl from heat and dribble the clarified butter into mixture, beating constantly, until mixture thickens. (If using an electric hand-beater, it will go together quickly and easily.) Add the lemon juice and continue beating until mixture holds together. Return bowl to top of saucepan and keep sauce warm over warm water until ready to serve.

# I

## is for Ice Cream

Mention ice cream, and what names immediately come to mind? Ben and Jerry? Howard Johnson? How about Marco Polo? Why? Because he is said to have brought the Chinese formula for ice cream back to Europe after his 24-year journey. The details of Polo's journey do not clearly support this claim, but we now know—no thanks to Marco Polo—that the Chinese indeed knew the art of making iced drinks and desserts long before the Christian era. They taught this art to the Arabs, who began making syrups chilled with snow, called *sharbets,* from which comes our sherbet. The Arabs taught the Italians. The Italians taught the French, and so it goes. But non of these were ice *creams*.

We know also that at the court of Alexander the Great and, later, of Nero, emperor of Rome in A.D. 57–68, sherbets made from fruit purées mixed with honey and snow were served regularly. So fond of this cold dessert was Nero that he had special cold rooms built beneath his palace. Some were just for the ice used for food preservation during the hot months. One, however, was just for snow. The snow was mixed with fruit juices and flavorings to produce a vintage version of today's water ice.

With the fall of the Roman Empire also fell the habit of having two types of cold rooms. It was revived in America over a thousand years later at Thomas Jefferson's Monticello. Jefferson had two underground wells—one for snow (used in frozen desserts) and the other for ice. Each was approximately 16 feet deep, lined with stone that extended 4 feet above the ground, with an interior 8 feet in diameter. The aboveground section made it possible to put a roof over the structure and insulate the roof with a layer of dirt. Access was through a short door in the side. At the bottom of the ice well was a lattice of boards covered with a bed of straw. As the ice, cut in blocks from the river, was added, the walls were lined with straw and the ice tamped to form a solid mass. The top of the ice was then covered with more straw or wood shavings. A well-managed ice well would last long enough to preserve food through the entire summer.

According to legend, whenever Nero yearned for a snow dessert, he'd order a slave to run to the mountains, gather up snow, and rush it back to the palace. Another version of the story states that slaves would fill baskets with snow and pass them hand to hand over the miles to be dumped into the snow room. Physics forbid! It took an army of wagons to transport the stuff. Jefferson's miniature (by Roman emperor standards) snow room held fourteen wagonloads of snow collected from fields preferably less than 5 miles from Monticello.

Snow preservation presented a greater problem. First, you needed a heavy snowfall to guarantee shoveling clean snow. But such snowfalls also made transporting the snow difficult. Second, once collected, the snow could not be stored in direct contact with either straw or wood shavings, so burlap or other fabric also lined the snow well.

To go back in time and across the Atlantic again, after the fall of the Roman Empire the Italians continued collecting and storing snow for drinking and eating and making *granitas*, coarse, granular versions of sherbets. In the north, the French had their ice rooms for preservation of food, but no sherbet. That came with their acquisition of an Italian queen, Catherine de Médicis, in the sixteenth century. She and her chefs introduced the custom of cooling drinks with ice or snow, which in France was only adopted by persons of great refinement. The next step was Catherine's introduction of *sorbetto*, or ice flavored with fruit juices. Although the French to this day eschew iced drinks, they love *sorbets*, and it was they who began the practice of serving sherbet between courses as *entremets*.

**The major problem with ice houses, wells, or rooms was the melted ice water that accumulated on the bottom. This had to be bailed by hand until 1806 when Jefferson had the first sump pump built. The water removed was so dirty that it had to be strained even to be used to mix plaster for the walls.**

By 1660 variously flavored water ices were available to the French commonfolk courtesy of a Sicilian named Francisco Procopio. To increase his sales, Procopio changed his name to the more Gallic-sounding Procope, and some ten years later he opened a café in Paris in what is now la rue de l'Ancienne-Comédie.

**The most popular ice cream in Paris in the 1990s is Häagen-Dazs, owned by America's Pillsbury Corporation.**

Other Parisians followed his example, and by 1676 it was necessary to give statutory recognition to this corporation of vendors and to authorize its members officially to sell ice creams and water ices. It is said that there were in Paris at that time 250 limonadiers who were selling ices—but only during the summer.

Procope's successor, a man named Buisson, attempted in 1750 to sell ices year-round, but he flopped—his product was of too poor a quality.

The seasonal nature of these ice-based refreshments changed in 1775 with the appearance of two new products, first, a custard-based ice cream made with milk, cream, and eggs. It was so delicious that it was destined to catch on as a year-round treat. The other was the forerunner of today's ice cream machine, which manually whipped air into the product while breaking up large ice granules. In 1798 two more Italians—Paratti and Tortoni—arrived on the scene in France with fine ice creams; Tortoni launched the iced sponge cake that year.

By the late 1770s ice cream, still known then as cream ice, had crossed the Atlantic to America. The first written recipe for ice cream was in the hand of Thomas Jefferson. It was made in much the same way homemade ice cream is made today, from a custard mixture packed in ice and salt. George Washington imported one of the newfangled ice cream machines that became available in the last part of the eighteenth century, but ice cream was still such a rare treat in 1809 that Dolly Madison delighted her dinner guests at the White House with ice cream as the grand finale.

It is claimed that custard-based ice creams (which are known as French ice creams) were introduced in 1650 in England by the chef of Charles I of England, who paid him to keep his method secret. Research shows, however, that King Henry V (1387–1422) of England was served an ice cream-like dish at his coronation banquet.

The first ice cream factory in the United States was established in Baltimore in 1851 by Jacob Fussell. Shortly thereafter came the ice cream soda, invented when a scoop of ice cream was accidentally dropped into some flavored soda water by a counter clerk at James W. Tuff's soda fountain. That was followed by the invention of the ice cream sundae. The average American, however, was still making homemade ice cream from snow. Snow, after all, was free. The ice needed to make ice cream wasn't. (In 1868 the delivered price of ice in ten-pound blocks from ice plants was one dollar a cake or ten cents a pound at a time when top-quality beefsteak in parts of the United States cost two cents a pound.) Not until the 1900s did the ice cream craze sweep the country, helped immeasurably by the appearance of the ice cream cone at the Louisiana Purchase Exposition in 1904 in St. Louis.

In the meantime, back in Europe, two great desserts based on ice cream had made their appearance. One, rarely served these days, demonstrated the ultimate superiority of simplicity. The other, complicated beyond the grasp of the average cook, is the dessert of choice at banquets designed to impress.

In the nineteenth century, chefs were expected to create upon demand special desserts to commemorate special occasions. In this case the demand was made on August Escoffier (1847–1935) in the year 1887. The occasion was Queen Victoria's golden jubilee, and the dish was a simple (but simply magnificent) combination of poached cherries and flaming cherry brandy. It was called jubilee cherries. It did not catch on, however, until a scoop of vanilla ice cream was added and then it became all the rage.

The second dish has been around even longer but remains a matter of Franco-American controversy. For example, it bears one name in France, another in America, and has at least half a dozen claimants to the credit of creating it.

According to the French it was invented in China and introduced in France in June 1866 when it was taught to Chef Balzaac, the confectionaire of the Grand-Hotel, by the master cook of the Chinese Mission in Paris. The secret was to bake vanilla ice cream in the oven inside a pastry crust and have the crust come out brown, the ice cream frozen solid. For obvious reasons it was called the Surprise Omelette.

Leap forward to 1895 and the Hotel de Paris in Monte Carlo. There the Surprise Omelette was being served by Jean Giroix, who attributed its creation to an American physicist by the name of Benjamin Thompson, Count Rumford (1753–1814). But this was no ordinary pastry-encrusted block of ice cream such as the one served at the Grand-Hotel nearly three decades before. This was the offspring of a wonderful marriage of science and culinary art. Now the ice cream sat upon a base of sponge cake and all about it was, not a crust, but a coating of thick, golden-brown meringue. Experiments in thermal conductivity, based on those done by Count Rumford, had proved that egg whites were such superb insulators that even while browning, they could keep ice cream frozen.

Reportedly, just such a dish had already been served at Delmonico's in New York in celebration of America's purchase of Alaska in 1868, hence the dish's most famous name, Baked Alaska. It was also called the Alaska and the Florida, probably to dramatize the contrast of hot and cold. European chefs also knew the dish as *Omelette à la Norvegienne*, because in the 1860s most of the blocks of ice used in Europe came from Norway.

One good clue to its American origin appears in the 1886 version of *Mrs. Rorer's Philadelphia Cookbook*, which contains a recipe for Alaska Bake. It advises the cook that "the meringue acts as a non-conductor and prevents the heat from melting the ice-cream." (It also recommends browning the meringue with a heated fireplace shovel.)

Today, it is our meringue-coated *chaudfroid* confection that European gourmets mean when speaking of the Surprise Omelette or the *Omelet à la Norvegienne*. The 1991 translation of the 1961 *Larousse Gastronomique* even lists the dish under Baked Alaska. Of course, it also credits the dish to "an American doctor called Rumford."

Ice creams, sherbets, and flavored ices are taken for granted in modern times, but they are no less a taste sensation today than when first invented. America's passion for these cold and/or creamy confections is evidenced in the continuing evolution of the product.

# Alaska Bake

*T*his is Mrs. S. T. Rorer's recipe from The Philadelphia Cookbook (1886). Note that it does not include the normal base of sponge or pound cake.

Cover thickly a two-quart (half-gallon) brick mould of ice cream with a meringue made from the whites of six eggs and six [heaping] tablespoonfuls of powdered sugar. Stand the dish on a board, and place it in a very quick oven to brown. The meringue acts as a nonconductor, and prevents the heat from melting the ice cream. It may also be browned with a salamander or a heated fire-shovel.

Some thoughts on the subject: Be sure the ice cream is frozen hard. Make your meringue by beating egg whites with an electric mixer until they form soft peaks. Add sugar, one tablespoon at a time, being sure to beat long enough for it to dissolve and the meringue to stop being gritty. Spread the meringue quickly and make sure there are no gaps anywhere. Bake at 450° F for 3–5 minutes. The top will be browner than the sides.

# Jubilee Cherries

*T*his is based on Escoffier's recipe for professional cooks, to which, for home cooks, he added red currant jelly. But nowhere does he include that essential ingredient, vanilla ice cream, which turns this recipe into cherries jubilee.

Pit a pound of Queen Anne, but not Bing, cherries. While pitting them, bring 2 cups water and ½ cup sugar to a boil and cook until slightly thickened. Add the cherries (and more water if necessary to cover). Poach until soft (6–8 minutes); drain and return to pan. Add approximately half of a small (10-ounce) jar of red currant jelly to the cherries, stirring until jelly is melted.

For jubilee cherries, set the cherries in small silver timbales. Reduce the syrup to 1 cup and thicken it with one tablespoon arrowroot or cornstarch diluted with cold water. Cover the cherries with the thickened syrup; pour a teaspoonful of heated Kirsch into each timbale and light each one when serving.

For cherries jubilee, put a scoop of vanilla ice cream in the timbales first and then proceed with the recipe.

# J
## is for Junk Food

For every American that eats and cooks gourmet, there are dozens that prefer "junk food"—an expression that first appeared in print in *Time* magazine on December 18, 1972. An anonymous customer of a Los Angeles natural food store is quoted as saying, "It upsets me to see people eating junk. It's just an escape, like drugs or alcohol." A year later the *Journal of Nutrition* was more specific: "Students eat what they refer to as 'Junk'—French fries, pretzels, chips, ice cream, candy, hot dogs." (Note that it was the students, not the editors, who used the term "junk.")

What makes food "junk"? *The Oxford Dictionary* defines it as "food that appeals to popular, especially juvenile, taste but has little nutritional value," which is a pretty broad condemnation of the eating habits and tastes of our young people. But is it fair or even accurate? Not according to that nutritional bible *Food Values of Portions Commonly Used*. Providing the food is traditionally prepared and not laced with additives or ersatz substitutions, all of our kids' favorite foods contribute something worthwhile to their diets, even if it is nothing more than a source of quick energy.

Potatoes, for example, are doubly condemned, first as fries and then as chips. Yet, potatoes are high in vitamin C, supply all the essential amino acids plus twice as much protein as the same amount of wheat, and provide more energy, in the form of complex carbohydrates, per acre than the same acre planted in cereal grains. In their natural state they are 99.9 percent fat free, and, if cooked properly, in very hot fat, the fat seals the potato and prevents fat absorption. Even when commercially prepared, an average serving of French fries contains half the fat of a single pat of butter.

French fries and potato chips are essentially the same entity, differing only in shape and thickness. Interestingly enough, what Americans call a French fry, the English call a chip, and the French call *pomme de terre paille* (julienned and of the very narrow, matchstick size), *pomme frites chip, en liards* (a thin crisp), or *pomme [de terre] Pont-Neuf* (thick-cut). With the opening of American fast-food restaurants on the Champs-Elysées, the French seem to have accepted the inevitable: *pommes frites* now mean America's French fries.

**Pommes de terre means "apples of the earth," and Pont-Neuf means "new bridge." The combination describes an early round (like the arch of a bridge) French fry. It may be, too, that these forerunners of the potato chip took their name from the vendors that sold packets of hot, thick fries near the bridges of Paris centuries ago.**

The principle behind fries and chips is the same: pieces of potato are fried in deep fat and then, optionally, sprinkled with salt. Because the addition of any quantity of raw potatoes to the fryer instantly lowers the temperature of the fat and lengthens the cooking time, fat-soaked potatoes seem inevitable, unless you have professional equipment that quickly heats fat back up to proper temperature. For more healthy fries without professional equipment, use the French method of cooking *pommes frites chip en liards*: double-fry them. First, immerse the batch in very hot fat just until hardened but not brown, then remove and drain. Reheat the fat, and immerse the potatoes again until crisp and brown. (For quantity cooking, use two pans of hot fat and move the chips or fries from one to the hotter other.)

This practice of double-cooking potato slices led to one of the most famous and impossible to duplicate dishes in culinary history: *pommes soufflé.*

It originated in France in 1837, when the Paris railroad line was extended westward to Saint-Germain-en-Laye. Typical of all French official events, the occasion demanded a reception complete with band and flags and a grandiose banquet for the official and royal passengers. Aboard the train were Queen Marie Amélie and two of her sons—the duc d'Orleans and the duc de Montpensier. King Louis Philippe, who would not expose his invaluable person to the perilous adventure of the train ride, came by carriage. Politicians—who feared for their lives aboard the train and their reputations if not aboard—were noticeably absent.

The banquet was to be held at the restaurant Le Pavillon Henri IV, and *pommes de terre Pont-Neuf* were on the menu. At the first wisp of smoke and the first faint whistle, the potato slices were immersed in deep fat. The chef knew that the official ceremonies would be brief—shortened by a lack of politicians and a hungry king. Some music, a few words, then off to the banquet they would go. Therefore, for the Pont-Neuf to be double-cooked, the first batch had to be done as soon as possible. The potatoes had been cooking for but a few minutes in the second fat bath when a messenger burst into the kitchen to warn, "Stop! Hold everything! The train is having difficulty climbing the hill!" Maitre Colinet, the chef, had no choice but to remove the potatoes and set his helpers to peeling fresh ones. Before the new batch of potatoes was pared, another messenger announced, "The train has come, and the king and queen are on their way." A frustrated Colinet dumped the first batch back into the hot fat; his desperation soon changed to amazement. The slices began to balloon. Bigger and bigger they swelled. And, when golden brown and removed from the fat, they kept their expand-

> Louis-Philippe of Orleans is the king with the pear-shaped head who is credited with such deep philosophical insights as, "Salad is a boon to the insides."

ed shape. Needless to say, the crisp pillows of potatoes, *pommes soufflés* were the hit of the banquet. The chef was called forth from the kitchen to receive the royal congratulations. The restaurant owner began dreaming up menus created around *pommes soufflés*, and everyone went to bed dreaming of riches.

Unfortunately, retellings of this true story rarely include the fact that like so many accidents *pommes soufflés* are difficult to duplicate. Even Colinet had trouble recreating his potato pillows. If you have no luck with them, you are in good company and may well be able to blame your potato. To get potatoes to puff, you need a very starchy, loosely textured, mealy potato—not your regular supermarket baker.

The potato chip, on the other hand, calls for a very dry potato. It, too, started life as a *pomme de terre Pont-Neuf*. One day, Chef Crum at Moon's Lake House at the fashionable nineteenth-century resort, Saratoga Springs, New York, had French fries (a.k.a. *pommes Pont-Neuf*) on the menu. Commodore Cornelius Vanderbilt, who fancied himself quite a gourmet, stopped by one day for lunch. Served his French-fried potatoes, he took one bite, found them too soggy, and sent them back as unsuitable, uncrisp, and unfit for eating. Crum wasn't about to take that criticism. He sliced another potato so thin you could see the knife through it, plunged the slices into hot deep fat, sprinkled them with salt, and sent them back out to the dining room. Suspicious, Vanderbilt nibbled on one. Delicious, he declared, devouring the rest. For the balance of the season, he was wont to stop in with friends to sample Crum's Saratoga Chips.

Today, potato chips come thin and thick and rippled, flavored with barbecue sauce and sour cream and onions. Millions of them are eaten each year in this country and abroad—even in Japan, where they are flavored with seaweed.

Another "junk food" snack, which has been around since Roman times, is the pretzel. It began life as a bread. Prayer is the common thread that runs through the many explanations for its name: that it is German, a variation of *brezel* derived from the root word for "prayer"; or that *pretzel* is from the Latin *precprex*, meaning "reward," and that the pretzel was a traditional reward for children's learning their prayers; or that the Latin was *brachium*, or "arm," referring to its crossed-arm shape. In any event, most agree it began with a monk who around A.D. 610 first shaped bread into a long roll, then crossed the ends into the form of two arms piously touching their opposite "shoulders."

**In Copenhagen, the sign of a bake shop is a regal crown atop a golden pretzel.**

Others say nonsense. The shape represents a cross encircled by a ring, which makes it a non-Christian symbol of the cult of the sun. There's more than a little truth to that since the pretzel has always had much to do with superstition. Traditionally, a loaf of bread, pretzel-shaped, worn around one's neck warded off evil spirits. When safe from such spirits or just plain hungry, the wearer removed the bread and ate it.

The pretzel was brought to this country by the Dutch and immediately became popular with Native Americans. In fact, a settler in 1652 was arrested for using good flour to make pretzels to sell to the local natives at a time when his colonial neighbors were eating bran. By the turn of the century, the American pretzel had grown smaller than its forebears but was still doughlike—similar in both size and shape to today's soft pretzel. It was also generously coated with salt. Tavern keepers quickly saw that free, salty pretzels whetted their customers' thirst for beverages. A patron of a German restaurant in the Bowery, circa 1867, described the free lunch counter as looking like "a breastwork thrown up by a regiment of gourmands to oppose the march

**Ever make a wish on a pretzel? It works as well as a poultry wishbone. Simply make a wish and, at the count of three, break a pretzel with someone else. The wish will come true for the person who gets the bigger part. As someone who ends up with turkey wishbones, forgotten and a'drying in cupboards, I recommend the pretzel method.**

of famine." Among its temptations were . . . "baskets full of those queer twisted briny cakes which go variously, I believe, by the names of Pretzel and of Wunder."

Of all the junk foods, candy gets the lowest marks, nutritionally speaking, even though scientists say our desire for sweets is a biological drive present from birth. Sweetness is one of our first recognized taste sensations, and we humans prove we're human with startling frequency.

~~~~~~~~~~~~~~~~~~~~~~~~~~~~~~~~~~~~~~~~~~~~~~~~~~~~~~~~~~~~

According to the candy industry, even during a recession the consumption of candy has increased (twenty-one pounds per person in 1990, up a pound from 1989). The price of candy has also increased. Fancy chocolates and imported toffees sell for up to $75 a pound.

For centuries humans have devoted time and effort to satisfying their desire for sweets. Written and pictorial records of candy were left on tomb walls by the Egyptians. These earliest "candies" were sticky, sugary concoctions made from dried fruit, nut meats, sesame or poppy seeds, and spices mixed and held together with honey. This mixture was cut into pieces and rolled in flour, chopped nut meats, and poppy or sesame seeds.

Some sweets were pressed into crudely carved and shaped molds, then highly colored to attract attention. Unfortunately, such early sweetmeats were beyond the financial means of any but the rich, though the poor could look, making the sweet-shop an early tourist attraction.

So long as honey was the sweetener, sweets remained even too expensive for the middle class. When sugar made its way to Venice from the Far East about the middle of the fourteenth century, things were about to change. The introduction of sugar cane into the Caribbean in the early sixteenth century revolutionized candy-making. Sugar cookery, however, proved to be a temperamental procedure that took centuries to conquer. During this time it was sold by spice sellers or dispensed by pharmacists, who made small batches by hand and used the sweeteners to disguise foul-tasting medicinal compounds.

**Chocolate is a flavoring (made from cocoa) and not a true candy category since it crosses all classes: it can be creamy, hard, crunchy, or chewy.**

Of the more than 2,000 different kinds of candy, all fall into a few general classes: hard candy, such as lozenges, lollipops, and brittles; chewies, such as caramels, toffees, nougats, marshmallows, licorices, jellies, and gums; creams—kneaded or fondant candies that are often chocolate-coated; and finally, America's own invention—fudge. It is the quintessential American sweet, loved by everybody, from

First Lady Barbara Bush to the youngster working on a Boy Scout badge in cooking.

In the process of satisfying America's sweet tooth, confectionery manufacturers have made their products available to the consumer in more retail outlets than has any other producer of any product. Junk food or not, candy seems here to stay.

Also here to stay is the hot dog, eaten regularly by ninety-five percent of American families. In fact, according to the Hot Dog Council, each and every one of us each year eats an average of eighty hot dogs/wieners/red hots/frankfurters or just plain franks.

Although the sausage is one of the oldest forms of processed meat, dating back to Homer's time, Frankfurt am Main, Germany, is considered the birthplace of the frankfurter, and in 1987 the city celebrated the famed sausage's 500th birthday. Other Germans disagree on both counts, saying the sausage was created in the late 1600s by Johann George Lahner, a butcher living in Coburg, Germany. Eventually Lahner traveled to Frankfurt to promote his new product and prudently named it after the city. Another tale has a group of German butchers developing the sausage in 1852, spiced, smoked, and packed in a casing, only they lived in Vienna and called theirs a wiener (pronounced *vee*-ner).

The frankfurter made its way to this country some time in the mid-1800s. H. L. Mencken, famed editor and word maven, claimed in his book *Happy Days* to have eaten a frankfurter in Baltimore in 1886. Mencken said his was encased in a crisp bread and "not the soggy rolls prevailing today, of ground acorns, plaster-of-Paris, flecks of bath-sponge and atmospheric air all compact." Unfortunately, the former never caught on, while the latter obviously did. But not at the 1893 Colombian Exposition in Chicago, when the frankfurter was the food sensation. Visitors found it easy to eat, convenient, and inexpensive even though it was served in a paper wrapping.

**One recipe for fudge raised more than a million dollars for the Allied war effort during World War II. Devised by First Lady Mamie Eisenhower and named "Million Dollar Fudge" by her husband, it is one of the few fudge recipes to call for two kinds of chocolate: semisweet and sweet.**

~~~~~~~~~~~~~~~~~~~~~~~~~~~~~~~~~~~~~~~~~~~~~~~~~~~~~~~~~~~~~~~~~~~~

At the St. Louis Louisiana Purchase Exposition in 1904, a Bavarian concession-aire, Anton Feuchtwanger, disdained paper wrappings and lent white gloves to his patrons to hold the piping-hot sausages he jocularly referred to as dachshunds. When most of the gloves disappeared into the pockets of Anton's customers, he asked his brother-in-law, a baker, for help. The baker improvised long soft rolls that fit the meat, thus inventing Mencken's decried frankfurter bun. The bun caught on but not the name dachshund.

Frankfurter—the name and the sausage—remained a mouthful until one cold April day at the New York Polo Grounds when concessionaire Harry Stevens was los-ing money peddling ice cream and cold soda. Inspired, he sent his salesmen outside the park to buy all the dachshund sausages they could find and an equal number of rolls. In less than an hour his vendors were hawking dachshund sausages from portable hot water tanks, crying "They're red hot! Get your sausages while they're red hot!" And get them they did. From then on, Stevens pushed cold sodas and "red hots."

**The topping of hot dogs with sauerkraut, again according to Mencken, dates back to the 1860s when a German immigrant so sold them, along with milk rolls (not a typo), from a pushcart in New York City's Bowery.**

In 1906, in the press box, sports cartoonist T. A. (Tad) Dorgan was nearing his deadline and desperate for an idea. Hearing the vendors, he hastily drew a cartoon of a barking dachshund sausage nestled warmly in a roll. Not sure how to spell dachshund, he simply wrote "hot dog." The cartoon was a sensation, and the term "hot dog" was born.

Purists maintain that a hot dog isn't a hot dog unless placed inside a roll, slathered with mustard, and topped with slippery relish. Unadorned, it is simply a frankfurter or a wiener or, if you insist, a dachshund.

Today most people would say that the hamburger has replaced the hot dog as the most popular junk food. Certainly those who eat out at fast-food places would have to agree—the hamburger is ubiquitous there and loaded with so much stuff that sometimes it's hard to see the meat, much less taste it, which might be the general idea.

How has junk food progressed in the twenty years since it was first mentioned in print? It depends on whom you ask. For example, to actress Jill Eikenberry of *L.A. Law*, it's oatmeal cookies. Of course, the fiber-conscious may quibble with that. To her husband, Michael Tucker, it's a steak and cheese sub (a.k.a. hoagie/po'boy) with onions and peppers. Of course, proponents of high-protein diets will defend this. To many youngsters it's pizza, but with low-fat cheese, tomato sauce, and a meat and/or veggie topping, even that is a close approximation of a well-balanced meal.

Quincy Jones, the music-producer and genius behind Michael Jackson's mega-hit albums, may have defined it best when he called junk food just-for-fun food.

# Philadelphia Soft Pretzels

*T*he secret of making pretzels (besides having the manual dexterity to twist them into shape) is immersing them in a water bath before baking them, which makes them glossy, crusty, and chewy. When professionally made, the water bath contains lye, or "caustic soda" (sodium hydroxide), that burns off during the baking. Since caustic soda is extremely corrosive and hazardous to handle, it is almost impossible for a homemaker to obtain. A good but not perfect substitute is baking soda. Without such a bath, the pretzel bakes up white and soft all over, not just inside. Some cooks skip the water bath and use an egg wash before baking the pretzels to get that brown crust. (You can use your favorite bread dough recipe, if you wish, instead of this one.)

> 1 package active dry yeast
> ¼ cup lukewarm (110° F) water
> 1 cup warm water
> 5 cups all-purpose flour
> 2 teaspoons salt
> 1–2 tablespoons margarine, softened
> 4 teaspoons baking soda
> kosher or sea salt

Proof the yeast by dissolving it in the lukewarm water. When it bubbles, add the additional warm water. Mix 4 cups of the flour and salt in a large bowl and add dissolved yeast. Mix well (can use dough hook on electric mixer). Add enough of the extra cup of flour to make a stiff dough. Knead for approximately 10 minutes or until smooth and elastic. Form into ball.

Use margarine to lavishly grease a large bowl. Place dough in bowl, turning dough to coat top. Cover with a towel. Turn oven on high for 3 minutes, then turn off. Put bowl in oven and let rise until doubled in bulk, approximately 45 minutes.

Punch dough down and divide into 16 small balls. Working on a floured surface, roll each ball into a narrow coil 18–20 inches long. With coil parallel to you, bring ends toward you and cross them over each other twice; return ends to coil and press into place, thus forming a pretzel shape (like a sideways capital J in script). As you get more dexterous, try to make them in the air as professional pretzel makers do.

To make a soft pretzel, pinch together the two circles formed on each. (To duplicate the soft pretzels sold on Philadelphia street corners, join 4 pretzels together, side by side.)

Preheat oven to 375° F. Dissolve baking soda in 4 cups of water in large skillet (do not use an aluminum one) and bring to a boil. Drop individual pretzels or quartet of pretzels into water and let boil for 1 minute or until pretzel floats. Transfer to cake rack and drain while you make the next batch, then transfer drained pretzels to a greased baking sheet. Sprinkle with coarse salt. Bake 12 minutes or until golden brown. Cool on rack.

To eat Philadelphia style, spread prepared mustard on pretzel.

# Pommes Soufflé

*These are temperamental things. One day they'll puff, the next they won't. But when they do, they are spectacular. When they don't, you end up with a glorified potato chip. Either way you really can't lose. You can do the first frying (actually a double frying) hours in advance. It is wise to make a test batch first to be sure the potatoes contain enough moisture to puff up.*

**1 gallon (approximately) vegetable oil**

**1 large baking potato per person plus 1 test potato**

Divide oil into 2 electric deep-fat fryers or skillets with temperature controls. Heat oil in one pan to 285° F, the other to 400° F.

Peel test potato and cut it into a rectangle, approximately 2 by 4 inches. Traditionally one cuts each corner off, making an octagonal shape. Slice lengthwise into ⅛-inch-thick pieces and dry between paper towels.

Slip about one-third of the test potato slices into the cooler pan of oil. They should sink to the bottom but then rise to the top. Gently turn and stir so that they cook evenly without sticking to one another. They should not brown, but after 6–7 minutes, blisters should form on some of the slices. Using a slotted spoon, transfer slices one by one into the hot oil. It should puff up immediately. Turn it over for a few seconds, then transfer to a tray lined with paper towels. The puff will immediately collapse. Now you can proceed with frying the rest of the potato slices. If test potatoes don't puff, try soaking balance of slices in cold water for 10–15 minutes; then try again. As long as some puff, you're okay. Don't discard the unpuffed, as they may puff during the final frying.

When ready to serve, heat both batches of oil to 400° F. Fry 10–12 potato slices in one batch of oil. They should repuff. Continue frying, turning them over, until golden brown (2–3 minutes). Transfer to paper towels and salt them. While the oil in that pan comes back up to temperature, cook more slices in the other batch..Continue alternating pans until all slices are done. Serve as soon as possible.

# K
## is for Kosher

osher is one of the few Yiddish words most gentiles know, thanks to encounters with delicious kosher foods. Take, for instance, those big, fat pickles, bobbing in a barrel of brine, that manage somehow to be soft on the inside, crunchy on the outside. And the coarse salt one sprinkles on pretzels or uses in a sea salt grinder. Or how about the inch-thick sandwiches of hot pastrami on rye, coleslaw on the side, that one buys in a Jewish delicatessen?

But if that deli is in the Crown Heights section of Brooklyn and non-Jewish-you wants to wash that sandwich down with coffee, you'll have to drink it black. No cream allowed. Delis there observe the dietary laws of Judaism, which forbid the mixing of meat and dairy foods. In fact, the truly orthodox won't have both on the same premises, so you'll buy your pastrami sandwich in a "meat" deli, get your coffee with cream in a "dairy" deli. In neither will you bet a BLT on toast; Jews are forbidden the meat of an animal with cloven hooves that does not chew its cud.

Those meats they can eat must be as close as possible to blood-free, therefore, no steak, charred on the outside, blood-red near-raw inside, for the kosher observer.

**A kosher home only needs one range and one dishwasher. The heat from the former automatically kashers everything it touches. The water used in the latter is considered by scholars to be so hot that the machine automatically cleanses or kashers itself. Therefore, the machine can be used for both dairy and meat dishes as long as each set is washed separately and separate trays are reserved for each category.**

According to Leviticus 3:17 and Deuteronomy 13:23–25, blood symbolizes the very essence and distinctiveness of man and is thus forbidden to the Jew. Furthermore, an animal killed for food must be ritually slaughtered, the jugular vein severed, and as much blood as possible drained off. More blood is drawn off during the act of broiling, a preferred method of cooking in kosher homes. Meat not to be broiled must be soaked and salted and drained and rinsed to rid it of blood before it can be cooked.

The cooking will be done, in a kosher Jewish restaurant, in one of two kitchens: one for meat, the other for dairy. Most kosher homes settle for using duplicate sets of pots and dishes and flatware. Again, one is for cooking, serving, and eating dairy, the other for meat products.

If, by any chance, a dairy dish or pot or knife is used for meat (or vice-versa), into the trash it goes. Especially if made of plastic or earthenware to which, it is believed, unseen particles and/or odors of the food may cling. If nonporous and made of metal, the defiled piece can be *kashered* (made kosher) by immersing it in a pot filled to the brim with boiling water or subjecting it to an open fire until it becomes red-hot or buying it in the earth for up to seventy-two hours.

Some foods, like vegetables and fruits, are *pareve,* or neutral, neither dairy or meat. Interestingly enough, eggs are considered pareve although produced by meat-bearing fowl and sold in dairy departments. If a speck of blood, however, is seen in a freshly broken egg, the egg is considered unclean and must be thrown out.

Of all the foods a Jew eats, bread is the most important. It is bread (*challa,* literally "cake") that is placed on the altar in the Tabernacle, and bread that is an important part, symbolically decorated, of the many Jewish festivals. For example, bread for the last meal prior to the Yom Kippur fast has birds upon it in the hope that prayers will soar heavenward on the Day of Atonement. For the seventh day of Sukkot when the judgment of God, passed on Yom Kippur, is sealed by a written verdict, the bread wears an extended hand.

**Pickles, salt, sugar, and coffee, like vegetables and fruit, may be certified as kosher but they need not be. They are *pareve,* or neutral (neither meat or dairy).**

Although most commercially made *challa* in America today is made of braided dough, once upon a time that was reserved for the Festival of Purim, the commemoration of the deliverance of the Jews of Persia from a massacre. According to the Bible, Haman, prime minister to King Ahasueros, plotted to slaughter all of the nation's Jews. He cast lots, or "purim," to determine the day of the massacre but was foiled by the Jewish Queen Esther, a Jewess.

Instead of the Jews dying, Haman was sentenced to hang by the neck until dead—along with his ten sons. To remind Jews of their deliverance, the *challa* for Purim is braided to represent the hangman's rope, which changed a day of sadness into a day of celebration.

Of all the Jewish festivals, Purim is the most fun-filled and therefore a favorite of children. One reason is the *Hamantaschen,* the triangular Jewish pastry filled with fruit, cheese, or poppy seeds. A German word meaning "Haman's pockets," *Hamantaschen* symbolize the minister's money bags, used to pay for the assassins of the

**Other names for *Hamantaschen* include the more mundane *mohn taschem* ("poppy seed pockets") and the much more colorful *oznay Haman,* or "Haman's ears." The latter derived from the custom of cutting off criminals' ears before they were hanged.**

Jews. Why the triangular shape? Two explanations are given. The first is that Haman removed his three-cornered hat before he was hanged; the second says the three corners serve as a reminder that Esther's strength was derived from her antecedents, the three patriarchs of Judaism: Abraham, Isaac, and Jacob.

Also part of the Purim meal is *kreplach*, also triangular and filled, but this time with chopped meat and onions and seasonings. It came about as a result of the custom of reading the book of Esther aloud. Whenever Haman's name is mentioned listeners clap hands, stomp feet, turn groggers (a type of noisemaker), hiss and boo and generally make a great to-do, slapping or beating whatever object happens to be handy. (You can see why children love Purim.) Once during the reading in the house of a kosher butcher, the butcher, knife in hand, attacked a piece of beef with such fervor that he reduced it to finely chopped pieces. Wondering what to do with it later, he decided to wrap it in pieces of dough, which his wife cooked that night for the Feast of Purim, thus creating *kreplach*.

Once created, *kreplach* became a natural choice, along with specially decorated *challa*, for the pre-fast meals of Yom Kippur and Hoshana Rabba. Both holidays incorporate symbolic beatings—which weren't always symbolic. Back in the eleventh century, on Yom Kippur members of the congregation submitted themselves to a flogging of thirty-nine strokes with leather thongs, during which they confessed their sins. Again, on the seventh and last day of Sukkot, the Festival of Booths, a holiday commemorating the forty-year trek of the Israelites through the desert to the Promised Land, flogging served as punishment for the sins of the previous year. Today, willow branches are ceremonially beaten against the floor or a chair.

The only time the eating of *challa* is forbidden to Jews is during the celebration of the Exodus. The Jews escaping from Egypt had no time to make leavened bread; therefore, during Passover, the first of the major Jewish festivals mentioned in the Bible and the best observed of all Jewish holidays, Jews eat *matzo*, an unleavened bread, according to the directive in Exodus 13:7: "Unleavened bread shall be eaten for seven days, and there shall be no leaven seen with you in all your borders."

Passover may be the most religiously observed, but Chanukah, the Festival of Lights, which takes place in midwinter, is the best-loved by children. It marks the rededication by the Jews of the holy temple in Jerusalem after its desecration by the Greeks. At the time there was only enough oil to keep the lamp burning for one night, but miraculously the oil burned for eight days. And so in honor of this miracle and to celebrate this festival, one candle is lit in a special eight-armed candelabra—the menorah—on the first night, and on each succeeding night an additional candle is lit until all eight are lit on the last night. For children, the best part of this festival is receiving Chanukah "gelt" or a present every single night. Instead of *challa*, the kosher cook prepares fried starches such as doughnuts or potato *latkes*. The smell of cooking oil should permeate the house to remind one of the miracle of the oil.

Another comparatively new tradition—it originated during the Middle Ages—is the eating of cheese pancakes on Chanukah. Its origins are, of course, Biblical and can be traced to the story of Judith who, according to legend, tempted one of Nebuchadnezzar's generals with very salty cheese delicacies. These made him so thirsty that he guzzled much wine, became falling down drunk, and lost his head, literally, to Judith, which led to the defeat of Nebuchadnezzar's army.

Of much greater duration is the tradition of eating fish at least once on all holy days as well as on the Sabbath in remembrance that during the Creation, fish were created on the fifth day, man on the sixth, and the Sabbath on the seventh. For those families who could not afford an expensive whole fish, a more economical, acceptable fish was needed. Enter *gefilte* ("filled" or "stuffed") fish. Traditionally two or three cheap, boned fish were ground up, seasoned with onions and condiments, stuffed into the skin of a fish, and cooked for an hour or so. It looked like a whole fish, but neither cost nor tasted like one. Today one can buy ready-made *gefilte* fish, but its acceptance is not universal. Of all the Jewish foods, *gefilte* fish and particularly ready-made *gefilte* fish arouse the strongest opinion, mostly negative. Today's cook can spend as much time trying to render the ready-made product palatable as the kosher cooks took in the old days in making it from scratch. An acceptable alternative for some is *gehakte* ("chopped") herring, which is made by mixing chopped skinned herrings, hard-boiled eggs, and onions with apples, then seasoning the mixture with sugar and pepper and moistening it with a bit of vinegar.

In addition to serving fish on the Sabbath (the hours between dusk on Friday evening and the appearance of the first three stars on Saturday evening), the kosher cook cannot do any cooking. Still, she must serve three meals, including one hot, must be served during that time: Friday night dinner, Saturday lunch, and *shalosh se'uda,* or third meal (in England the equivalent of a high tea, in America a light Sunday supper).

Friday night dinner presents no problem since cooking can be completed before dusk. Many households take the opportunity to set a table symbolic of the whole of Judaism, including candlesticks, wine goblets, two loaves of challa covered with an embroidered cloth, salt in which to dip the *challa,* and kosher wine. (For wine, either red or white, to be kosher, all work in the preparation of it, from the time of the crushing of the grapes to the bottling, must be done by observant Jews. Other kosher foods may be prepared by non-Jews under the supervision of an observant Jew.)

Since no cooking is permitted for the kosher-observant on the Sabbath, any food necessary for Saturday lunch has to be prepared on Friday afternoon and its cooking commenced before dusk.

In America, the quest for a solution to feeding one's family without cooking on the Sabbath led to such recipes as Boston baked beans. In this country, staunch Protestants in Boston would no more profane their Sabbath by cooking than would a Lubavitcher today. The local baker collected the bean pots (seventeenth-century pot-bellied crocks with a small mouth to ensure little evaporation) of the community's Protestant families and took them off to be baked in the community oven, often situated in the cellar of a nearby tavern. When bread-baking was over, in went the beans, to be finished and returned home before the Protestant Sabbath began at sundown on Saturday. Frequently, the bean pot arrived home with a bonus in the shape of a slab of brown bread. The beans would be served hot for Saturday night supper, and the leftovers would be eaten cold on Sunday morning. (If you've never eaten cold baked beans, you're in for a treat.)

The kosher version of Boston baked beans is the *cholent.* Traditionally, it is made from butter beans, potatoes, onions, seasoning, and a little expensive meat; sometimes a large dumpling is baked over it. It is put on to cook before the Sabbath starts and continues cooking overnight.

The third meal of the Jewish Sabbath takes place early on Saturday evening and precedes the evening prayer. It is usually a cold meal. Remember, no cooking allowed.

At one of these meals, fish will be served but not simultaneously with meat. For that reason, in many traditional homes, at Sabbath and holiday meals, soup (usually chicken) is served between the fish and the meat courses to cleanse the palate. Originally this was done for reasons of health because it was believed that combining meat and fish disposed one to leprosy.

Jewish scholars point out that there is no scholarly tradition ascribing health benefits to observing kosher. They simply quote the Biblical injunction in Leviticus (11:44–45) for the people to keep themselves holy by obeying the mandates in that same book as to the foods that are acceptable or not. Some say the keeping of kosher instills self-discipline. Others say it encourages the avoidance of gluttony. The most controversial explanation is that observance of kosher sets the Jews apart and keeps them separate from their idol-worshiping neighbors. These theorists contend that the dietary laws were instituted as one means of making the Jewish life-style different from that of their neighbors. The thinking goes that if Jews are not permitted to eat with their neighbors, they will not socialize with them. If they do not socialize, they won't intermarry, thus guaranteeing the survival of the Jewish people.

**The dietary laws may not have been meant to promulgate good health, but that doesn't mean that Jews didn't ascribe certain health benefits to different foods. For example eggs, fish, wine, milk, cheese, and fat meat are supposed to increase sexual potency, while salt and barley are said to diminish it. Garlic is credited in the old tales with increasing seminal fluid volume. It also is supposed to warm the body, make the face shine, and cure tapeworms.**

Contentions aside, the kosher tradition lives on in more Jewish homes today than at any other time since World War II. Half of the world's estimated twelve million Jews observe some form of kosher, if only keeping pork out of their homes, while three to four million maintain strictly kosher kitchens. Thus, a four-thousand-year-old tradition remains alive and vigorous.

# Hamantaschen

My kosher guru tells me that the filling and shaping are most important in making Hamantaschen. Therefore, you could substitute any favorite, plain cookie recipe or a mix or refrigerated dough. And, to make life even easier, use a canned prune filling. But if you want the real thing, Thelma Greenbaum to the rescue with a pareve recipe!

## *Filling*

1 lemon, quartered

1½ pound lekvar (available at Jewish delis)

1 box pitted prunes

¾ cup raisins

1 cup walnut haves

sugar to taste

It's more time consuming to make, but the filling is better tasting if you first carefully remove just the zest of the lemon. Cut off white pith and discard, then quarter and seed the fruit. Put lemon zest, lemon, and balance of ingredients, except sugar, individually through grinder or food processor. Mix together and then add sugar to taste.

## Dough

½ cup sugar

½ cup mild vegetable oil

2 eggs

3 cups stirred, scooped, and leveled all-purpose flour

2 teaspoons baking powder

½ teaspoon salt

1 teaspoon vanilla

¼ cup water

Preheat oven to 350° F. In large bowl, combine sugar, oil, and eggs. Stir dry ingredients together and add in the sugar mixture, alternating with the combined vanilla and water. If you can, chill dough before rolling out, as it will roll out thinner. Roll out on floured surface and cut into 5- or 6-inch circles. Place spoonful of filling on center of each circle. Bring up edges in three places to form triangle. Pinch edges together. Bake on ungreased cookie sheet 20 to 25 minutes. Makes 18–24, depending on size of cookies.

# Latkes

Y*ou don't have to be kosher or even Jewish to enjoy potato pancakes, especially these.*

**2 medium potatoes, peeled**

**water**

**2 eggs**

**½ teaspoon salt**

**⅛ teaspoon pepper**

**2 tablespoons matzo meal**

**mild vegetable oil**

Cut up potatoes, just barely covered with water, and process in blender for a couple of minutes. (Or do in food processor, adding water sparingly and as necessary through food tube.) Put potatoes in sieve over a bowl, and press out water, reserving liquid. To potatoes add eggs, seasonings, and matzo meal, plus enough reserved water to make a smooth dough. Heat oil in large skillet. Drop by spoonfuls and flatten. Fry on both sides until brown and crisp. Drain on paper towels. Serves 6–8.

# Cholent

Basically a hodgepodge, this is the forerunner of our baked beans. In a kosher home, it would be put on to cook before the Sabbath begins. In different parts of Europe, some cooks omit the potatoes, others the beans, while others insist on both.

1½ cups navy beans
¾ cup medium white pearl barley
2 medium onions, diced
2 cloves garlic, peeled and chopped
3 medium potatoes, peeled and cut into ½-inch dice
¾ tablespoon salt, or to taste
1 teaspoon pepper
1 teaspoon paprika (optional)
1 pound flanken (or other fatty meat with bones)
½ pound kishke (optional—don't ask what it is)

Soak beans overnight (do not use quick-cook method). Rinse several times, then place with barley in ovenproof casserole that can be used on top or range. Add onions, garlic, potatoes, and seasonings. Cover with water and bring to boil. Lower heat to simmer. Continue to cook for several hours, adding more water as needed. About half an hour before *Shabbat*, add the meat(s) and more water to cover. Place in 200–250°F oven to cook overnight. By morning, it should have crusted over. Serves 8–10.

# L

is for Lobster

ity the poor lobster, especially that Friday night one-and-one-quarter-pound
restaurant special from Maine. Lying there baked, boiled, or broiled, plain or
stuffed, it is totally defenseless except for the occasional spurt or squirt that gets
you in the eye, while you, enveloped neck to lap in lobster-bib, take claw-cracker and
fork to hand and prepare to attack. Will you begin with the legs, one at a time, scraping
out the sweet threads of meat with your teeth as if eating artichoke leaves? Or do the
claws beckon you with enticing nuggets of firm flesh? Or are you one of those who, like
some impatient readers of detective tales, begin with the end—in this case, the tail?

As you dip each gobbet into drawn butter and lick each drip from your lip, do
you once spare a thought for the life of that lovely but lowly decapod? You should. He
or she comes not to this feast at the end of a carefree life. The poor lobster has spent
much of its life in reverse, scurrying backward away from predators and swimming
frenziedly tail first out of danger. In fact, 'tis said that with its tail it can accelerate

from zero to 30 miles in one second and in reverse. Legend has it that it is also capable of using its tail to do somersaults—from which may have come Lewis Carroll's Lobster Quadrille in *Alice in Wonderland.*

Despite the dangers of its undersea life, in its short lifetime your lobster has dined as well or better than you on a diet of clams and crabs, mussels and urchins, starfish and small fish—and even other lobsters. When the lobster has eaten enough to be kept on the boat that takes him to sure death, he is only one-and-a-quarter pounds of the more than twenty million pounds harvested in Maine each year and every year for the past twenty years. His claws are disarmed with rubber bands or pegs and he is off to arrive at the market, antennae waving and tail springing back indignantly when pulled. In other words, this lobster is very much alive.

**How to buy a lobster? Take the advice of a Greek poet, written some 2,500 years ago:**
**"... buy a lobster.**
**Which has long hands and heavy, too, but feet**
**Of delicate smallness, and which slowly walks**
**Over the earth's face."**

At home in your kitchen comes the moment of truth. Be prepared—the lobster meets death kicking and shrieking, antennae flailing. You will find it no surprise that much has been written in cookbooks about the killing of lobsters. Whatever method you choose to perform this unpleasant task, it may help if you hypnotize the lobster first. No, this is not a parlor trick but an honest-to-goodness technique that one practitioner with the Lobster Institute insists works 100 percent of the time. To hypnotize a lobster gently rub its back with a fingertip—back and forth, nice and easy, not too much pressure. You can also rub the poor fellow right between its two gruesome, bulging eyes. Shortly, the lobster should stand stock-still so you can take its life without being pinched in the process.

Still another method, admittedly French, is to forget this gentle business and clobber the bloke with a blow to the head that at least momentarily immobilizes the creature. After that, as Pellaprat advises, "Les decouper sans hesitation ni attendrissement en morceaux." Translation: "Cut them into pieces without hesitation and compassion." This boldness surely kills a lobster quicker than any other way.

In 1930 in Berlin a German colonel who had been a war hero spotted a lobster in a shop window with its claws tied. Outraged by this apparent cruelty, the colonel made a complaint against the fish merchant. When the case came to trial, three expert witnesses testified for the merchant, including a professor of biology who argued that only a lobster could know whether he was suffering. "I am the possessor of the highest German medal for lifesaving," said the colonel, explaining why he was troubling himself with the fate of a crustacean. "But it is of equal concern to me whether I come to the rescue of a human being or an animal that is suffering."

The appeal was enough to convince the judge. He ruled that lobsters do indeed have feelings, that the fish merchant had violated those feelings, and that, accordingly, he must pay a fine of ten dollars.

Another humane ploy, one recommended by the British Universities Federation for Animal Welfare, is to place lobsters in a plastic bag for a minimum of two hours in the freezer at a temperature at least as low as –10° C (14° F). (That's higher than the optimum temperature of 0–5° F that Whirlpool, for example, recommends for its freezers.) If the cold doesn't get him, the plastic bag will. In either case, the lobster gradually loses consciousness and dies and can then be plunged into boiling water to be cooked. This method will not work, however, for recipes calling for raw lobster pieces. In these cases, cut the chilling time back to the point where the lobster is not frozen solid—leave it in for just a half hour or so. If the cold doesn't kill him, he'll come out too stiff to put up a fight.

Now, in any case, you're ready to cook. Boiling is the method of choice for most lobsters, and you have your choice of approaches. You can use the James Beard method for the tenderhearted and squeamish: Put it in cold water, cover the pot, and bring the water to a full boil so the lobster just wafts away in a dreamy state.

Those cooks without sentimentality can just

set one gallon of salted water per lobster to a hard boil; grasp the lobster behind the head so it can't fight back; plunge it in headfirst (watch out for the splash and be sure to let go); then hold it under water with wooden spoons for at least one minute. If an antenna waves frantically for help, push it under. If the lobster shrieks, pretend you're hard of hearing. If bubbles come exploding to the surface, ignore them. According to one source, the lobster should die within fifteen seconds.

*Old wives axiom:* If a lobster's lost a claw, before poaching or boiling, plug up the hole with kneaded dough or bread to keep the water from getting in.

A scientific study comparing these two methods was conducted at Jersey Marine Biological Laboratory at the request of the SPCA. With the lobster placed in cold water and the boiler put on the fire, there was no evidence of discomfort nor was there any attempt by the lobster to emerge from the water until the temperature reached 158° F (70° C) shortly after which the lobster collapsed and fell over on its side. At 176° F (80° C) all movement ceased; it was the conclusion of those watching that the lobster was dead.

*Cooking Tips:* Some cooks let the lobster cool down in the water, which not only keeps them juicier but gives the cook the beginnings of a court bouillion. Others say such meat is merely waterlogged. I remove my lobsters from the pot when done, laying them on their backs to cool and to keep the juices from flowing out.

On the other hand, with the lobster plunged alive into boiling water, there were violent attempts to emerge, and life was apparent for fifty-eight seconds; slight movements, probably reflex, continued up to 70 seconds. (In both cases reddening of the shell occurred before death.)

The theory behind the cold water method is that as the temperature rises gradually, the warmth penetrates slowly and destroys the sensitive nervous system gradually and painlessly. Those who've cooked them both ways, however, say that lobsters lose flavor when brought slowly to the boil.

To salt or not to salt the water is another question. One expert recommends using boiling water salted to the point where the brine will float an egg. For an average aged egg, that works out to four to five ounces of salt per one and three-quarters pint or one liter of water. Other experts shudder and note that salted water toughens the flesh.

The cowardly method is to put an inch or two of boiling water in the bottom of a large pot. Stick your lobsters inside head first and immediately cover with a lid, pushing any wayward legs or antennae callously underneath. Turn the heat down a bit, ignore any jigglings of pot and lid, and steam until cooked—about fifteen minutes per pound.

*Lexicon of lobster parts:*

The small white sac between the lobster's eyes is the stomach, called the "lady," and contains the lobster's teeth. Once thought poisonous, it isn't, but neither is it good to eat—it's terribly crunchy.

The green matter in the body is considered a delicacy and is called the tomalley. Though some mistake it for the liver, it's actually the hepatopancreas (the first stop for chewed food to get digested).

The salmon-colored sacs are the females ovaries, full of roe.

Blackish-green matter is diseased and should be discarded; wash hands and surrounding lobster meat thoroughly.

Gray, light blue, orange, green, or light pink fluids are lobster blood. When cooked, they're colorless and are called juices.

Our tender nerves are especially challenged by the recipes that call for uncooked lobster, but you *can* cheat and boil the lobster for two minutes (it should die in this time), then remove it and use its flesh as if uncooked.

You may read that the best way to get a dead raw lobster is to stab it in the space where its tail and carapace meet. Unfortunately, that won't do it. Your blow may paralyze, but it does not kill. The lobster has no cortex, brain, or spinal column—only a long nerve cord with various swellings or ganglia along its course. Therefore, it cannot be killed instantly by a knife thrust. Only those who can split a lobster in two down the middle line in one blow can claim to kill it instantly.

When you've handled the question of how to kill your crustacean, choose a recipe that will make all your efforts worthwhile. Among the world's great recipes are three lobster dishes: *homard Thermidor*, lobster *à l'Americaine*, and lobster Newberg. Besides their common ingredient the three share the distinction of having the most disputatious names in cuisine—everybody has a theory as to their origins.

Consider *homard Thermidor*, for instance. One book authoritatively states that this dish was created during Napoleon's time. A second disagrees, claiming it was first served at Maire, a restaurant on boulevard Saint-Denis, on January 24, 1894, upon the occasion of the premiere of Victorien Sardou's drama *Thermidor*, at la Comédie-Francaise. A third book acknowledges that it was named in honor of Sardou's play but insists it was created at a different restaurant, the Café de Paris, by Chef Leopold Mourier. A fourth concurs about the Café de Paris but insists it was during the reign of Mourier's successor, Tony Girod, in which case it was created long after the premiere of Sardou's play.

A fifth source, perhaps less romantic but more pragmatic, takes the dish at face value, translating its name as "lobster July–August." This because Thermidor was the eleventh month in the French Revolutionary calendar, extending from July 19 to August 17 and coinciding with the period when lobsters begin to molt. As the lobster grows a new shell within the old, its flesh, though sweet, becomes watery and stringy. The claw meat contracts so that it will pass from the old claw shell through the much smaller knuckle. In other words, this is not the ideal lobster to serve plainly broiled, baked, or steamed. Combined with a rich sauce and topped with cheese, however, as it is in lobster Thermidor, the flesh becomes more than acceptable.

By the way, deviled lobster, that first cousin to deviled crab, is a twin to lobster Thermidor and can be found in American cookbooks dating back to the early nineteenth century.

Talk about controversy over origins, more has been written about the origin of lobster *à l'Americaine* than Newberg and Thermidor combined. The controversy centers not around the dish itself but around its name. Some authorities insist that the recipe did not originate in America and that the name is a misspelling of l'Armorica, the former name of the French province of Brittany. Escoffier, on the other hand, believed that the dish was first served in Europe at Le Restaurant Français in Nice in the 1850s as *langouste de la Méditerranée*. Shortly thereafter, it traveled to America via Chef Pierre Fraysse from Sete in Languedoc. Unable to obtain *langoustes*, he substituted lobsters in the dish, which he diplomatically renamed in honor of his new country. Fleeing the Civil War, the chef returned to France and opened Noel et Peters restaurant in Paris in 1860. From the moment he served the dish, it was an instant success. Note the use of pimento, tomato, and olive oil in the dish—indicative of Provence on the Mediterranean, not Brittany.

Lobster *a l'Americaine* can't take all the prizes for intrigue—lobster Newberg has its share as well. Note the spelling of Newberg with an *e*, not a *u*; and what a difference the change in a single letter makes. The first change took place at Delmonico's where the dish originated. It was supposedly invented by Ben Wenberg, a sea captain, who discovered a South American sauce that screamed to go with lobster. Charles Ranhofer, Delmonico's master chef, agreed and named the dish after him. Then came a not-so-gentlemanly brawl—in the crowded restaurant, no less. In a huff, the W and N were transposed and the name changed from à la Wenberg to à la Newberg, an anagram, and was included in Ranhofer's *The Epicurean*, published in 1893, as *Lobster à la Newberg ou Delmonico*. The second change in the spelling took place in the index of *The Epicurean*. Although within the

**New enlistees to the English army were called "lobsters" because when sworn in and given their red coats they turned red. During the American Revolution, the colonists called all British soldiers "lobsterbacks" because of their uniforms.**

book Ranhofer consistently spelled his recipes for lobster, oyster crabs, and terrapin à la Newberg, two out of three are spelled with a *u* in the index. American cookbook authors, such as James Beard, Irma Rombauer of *Joy of Cooking* fame, and Fannie Farmer (alias Marion Cunningham), picked up Newburg. The wrong spelling stuck and became part of our food mythology. And sent many another cookbook author on a wild goose chase to find the true story of lobster à la Newburg (with a *u*).

One author, for example, found a 1927 cookbook by Madame Saint-Ange in which there is a recipe for "lobster à la Newburg or Van Der Bilt." From this came the conclusion that the dish's name was misspelled—it should have been "Newburgh" with an h. Newburgh was a stop on the Hudson River for the New York Central Railroad owned by Commodore Cornelius Vanderbilt.

That wasn't the only confusion. Census checkers, working with the erroneous spelling, thought they had demolished the myth by reporting that no Ben Wenburg, sea captain, showed up in the census rolls of the period. They were right. But if they had checked Wenberg, they would have found a different story.

In truth there was indeed a Benjamin J. Wenberg—with an *e* not a *u*. Born in 1835 in Portland, Maine, the son of a well-to-do shipmaster, he and his brother, Louis, came to Manhattan while still young and went into business at No. 101 Water Street. They prospered as shipping merchants, lived on Fifth Avenue, and were prominent club and society men, especially as both were bachelors. Evidently, in 1883 the two had a falling out, and Louis withdrew from the firm, moving to 101 Park-Place, Brooklyn. In 1885 the two died within days of one another: Louis from consumption on Thursday, Benjamin from pneumonia on Saturday. The two were interred together at Greenwood Cemetery. Neither headstone reads "Here lies the creator of lobster Wenberg alias Newberg," but the facts fit.

# Homard Thermidor
# à la Café de Paris

*The Café de Paris may or may not have been the birthplace of lobster Thermidor, but it undoubtedly has provided one of the best recipes for this dish. This version is based on one that appears in* Larousse Gastronomique II.

Split 2 small (1¼-pound) or one large (2-pound) live lobsters in two lengthwise. Crack the claws. Season the halves with salt, sprinkle with oil, and roast in a preheated 350° F oven for 15–20 minutes. Remove the lobster from the shell (reserve the shell for serving) and dice the tail and claw meat. Can use boiled lobster(s) if you wish; split them after cooking and do the dish in a casserole. This is not so fancy a service but much easier on the cook.

Cook 1 tablespoon of chopped shallots in a tablespoon of butter until tender. Add ½ cup fish stock (can use clam juice) and ½ cup white wine, plus a sprig of tarragon and some chervil. Reduce by boiling until it barely coats the bottom of the pan. Stir in thick béchamel sauce (see recipe below) to which one adds 1 teaspoon Dijon mustard. Return just to a boil and incorporate, tablespoon by tablespoon, 4 ounces (1 stick) of room-temperature butter. Taste for seasoning. If too thick, dilute with sherry. Pour a little of the sauce into the half-shells. Heap the shells with the lobster meat and nap, covering completely, with the sauce. Sprinkle with grated Parmesan or Gruyère cheese, dribble melted butter on top, then brown in a very hot oven or under the broiler. Serves two hearty eaters or four moderate ones.

## *Béchamel Sauce*

Melt 2 tablespoons butter and stir in 2 tablespoons flour. Cook for a few minutes, stirring constantly, to get rid of the raw flour taste. Gradually stir in 1½ cups of milk or, even better, heavy cream. Cook, stirring constantly until mixture becomes as thick as mayonnaise.

# Lobster à l'Americaine

*T his is essentially the classic recipe as per Escoffier, who had made a a study of the subject.*

Take a hen lobster and cut in even pieces. Reserve the coral and water of the lobster. Cook the lobster pieces in hot olive oil. Add salt, pepper, 1 pimento (chopped), 2 small or 1 large, peeled and quartered, ripe tomatoes. Add 1 tablespoon chopped onions. Cover with 2 cups dry white wine. Simmer gently for 20 minutes. Remove the pieces of lobster and keep in a warm place. Bring the cooking liquid to a rolling boil and reduce by half. Mash 1 stick (4 ounces) of room-temperature unsalted butter and blend in the coral and lobster water. Thicken the sauce with this butter. Optionally, add some lemon juice, chopped parsley, and tarragon. Pour the sauce over the lobster pieces and serve immediately.

# Lobster à la Newberg

*T his recipe is taken from Charles Ranhofer's* The Epicurean (1893), *in which it appears under the title* Homard à la Newberg ou à la Delmonico.

*At the time this dish was created, only whole lobsters were available. Today you can purchase 2 to 2½ pounds of lobster tails and eliminate the first step.*

*What makes the dish special is its sauce, which takes its flavor from the Madeira wine used in it. This rich, white or amber fortified wine, made in the Madeira Islands off the northwest coast of Africa, is often replaced with sherry today.*

Cook 6 lobsters each weighing about 2 pounds in boiling salted water for 25 minutes. Twelve pounds of live lobster when cooked yield from 2 to 2½ pounds of meat and 3 to 4 ounces of lobster coral [reserve for another use or for garniture]. When cold detach the bodies from the tails and cut the latter into slices, put them into a *sautoir* [frying pan], each piece lying flat and add hot clarified butter. Season with salt and fry lightly on both sides without coloring; moisten to their height with good raw cream [just cover the meat with heavy cream]; reduce quickly to half and then add 2 or 3 spoonfuls of Madeira wine; boil the liquid once more only, then remove and thicken with a thickening of egg yolks and cream [beat 2 to 3 egg yolks with same number of tablespoons of cream, slowly add approximately ⅓ cup of hot sauce to egg yolks to heat them and prevent their cooking when added to the liquid in pan]. Cook without boiling, incorporating a little cayenne and butter; warm it up again without boiling, tossing the lobster lightly, then arrange the pieces in a vegetable dish and pour the sauce over.

# M
## is for Mock

It's a verb, it's a noun, it's an adjective, it's an adverb, it's super word! It imitates, it counterfeits, it's not what it seems, and, in food, it's superabundant! For example, we have such mock berries as the strawberry, which, botanically speaking, is a rose. Conversely, the banana is no fruit; it is a berry and grows on the tallest herb in the world. The sweet potato mocks a potato in appearance and even during cooking, but it's a morning glory. Those aromatic bulbs of onion and garlic, those tender stalks of asparagus—what could be more vegetative? Almost anything, in fact, because these, too, are flowers—lilies, to be exact. And the deadly nightshade and the narcotic mandrake, on the other hand, are members of some venomous family, right? Wrong. They're botanical cousins to the eggplant and chili pepper.

All of these are what I call "mock" mock foods—travesties and aberrations in the plant kingdom, which authors love to list but only botanists can appreciate.

Out of need, man has created many a mock version of food. It is a venerable practice dating back to Apicius, that fellow from the first century A.D. who wrote the first cookbook and spent nearly $90 million on food before he was twenty-three years old. In his book, Apicius gives as his third recipe the methodology of making mock rose wine without rose leaves, substituting citron leaves and palm leaves and sweetening with honey. His fourth recipe is for making a mock expensive oil from a cheap one: Use inexpensive Spanish oil, add spices, stir frequently for three days, and then let stand. "Everybody will believe it is Liburnium oil," Apicius assures us—in Latin, of course. Finally, his fifth recipe, to make a mock white wine out of red: Add bonemeal or three egg whites or the white ashes of the vine to the flask—all of which will bleach the wine, giving it the look of white wine, but no guarantees on the taste.

Why would Apicius resort to such substitutions? Certainly not for lack of money. More likely he experimented when such ingredients or foods were needed out of season or at a time, for example, when Rome and Liburnia near Dalmatia were at war. In fact, when one examines the history of mock foods, one usually uncovers strong motivations for their development. Unavailability of ingredients is typical.

For example, Britain's green sea turtle soup is considered one of the world's great delicacies, the aristocrat of soups. Here in colonial times, when turtles were readily available at any fish market or wharf, the American housewife began her turtle recipe by buying a live sixty-pounder that she took home in a wheelbarrow or wagon and dumped near the chopping block. She then began the soup by chopping off his head, a task not often performed easily. Retractable heads have a tendency in strange surroundings to stay retracted. If the head could be enticed out of the shell, it took a quick whack with an axe or a 2-by-4 between the jaws to keep the head extended. Remember, 60-pound turtles have jaws that can crush a human arm. Obviously, making turtle soup was for neither the fainthearted nor the weak. And I'm not sure but that women secretly welcomed the news that it was becoming more and more difficult to get sea turtles.

Unfazed, the British came up with a mock turtle soup made from the liver, heart, and head of a calf, which, when cooked and cut up, has a gelatinous, meaty texture and a flavor that tastes deceptively like turtle meat. Tackling the original mock turtle soup recipe, while a major improvement on chopping off turtle heads, was no simple endeavor itself, taking two days to make.

For example, one late nineteenth-century cookbook tells the reader to have the butcher disjoint the jaws and take out the brains. (Using the ears is optional.) Now wash the head well through several cold water changes, pour boiling water through the throat and nasal passages, then wash it all again in cold water. Cover the head with more cold water and bring to a boil. Skim any froth from the pot frequently. Simmer a couple of hours or until the meat on the head is tender. Remove the meat and tongue and return the bones to the pot to simmer some more. Then, cool everything and place in a cold storage spot.

The famous green sea turtle isn't green at all, but brown. Its fat, when cooked, turns a lovely green. The sea turtle has been known to attain a weight of 1,000 pounds but averages 400 pounds. Smaller, younger turtles are most desired for soup. Commercial exploitation has severely depleted their numbers, and it is only through the efforts of ecologists that the species exists at all.

On the second day, bring the bones back up to the boil. Chop (rather finely) the meat from the head, including the tongue. Add spices, herbs, pot greens (like celery, scallion tops, and carrots), as well as ham, veal, and mushrooms if available.

Usually this dedicated nineteenth-century cook was also encouraged to strain and thicken this concoction, then garnish it with pieces of calf's head and tongue and chopped hard-boiled eggs. A last-minute addition might be some wine: Madeira, or port in Europe, sherry in the United States.

Just for the work alone, it deserves inclusion in the list of the 100 best dishes in the world, but since mock turtle soup is truly delectable, it rates its position on the basis of taste alone.

In Madagascar, turtles are bred for eating, but soup is considered only worthwhile for leftovers. Instead, body meat is cut into steaks to be marinated and broiled. Whole turtles are barbecued. The head, legs, tail, intestines, and flippers go into fricassees and stews and even turtle à la King.

Unfortunately, even today real, authentic mock turtle soup requires a calf's head, not the easiest item in the world to find. (In fact, I know of no supermarket that stocks calf's heads regularly or, for that matter, on any basis.) Therefore, because of unavailability of a crucial ingredient, we now have *mock* mock turtle soup made with meaty veal bones instead of the calf's head.

**Turtle meat and soup have enjoyed centuries of popularity partly because the turtle was classified as a fish by the Roman Catholic Church and could thus be eaten on days of abstinence.**

Unavailability of ingredients was, in particular, a problem. Prior to widespread canning and freezing and our modern distribution system, people ate foods strictly in season in the local area or else came up with a reasonable facsimile of it. For example, mock coconut pies were made with potatoes, and mock cherry pies were created from raisins and cranberries. In fact, the older and the more inclusive the cookbook, the more numerous the mock recipes. Mrs. Beeton's 1859 book on cookery and household management, for example, includes more than a half dozen such recipes, including how to make a mock goose out of one ox heart or two calves' hearts.

During wartimes mock cookery was a necessity. Butter, for example, was almost nonexistent and sugar hard to come by during the Second World War. Mothers saved up their sugar ration coupons to treat their youngsters to mock fudge made with mashed potatoes.

Furthermore, if one happened into the butcher's shop on a day when a lot of one particular meat was available, one bought one's ration's worth, then tried to invent ways to serve the same meat day after day without repeating the same taste. Recipes circulated for mock chicken legs and mock creamed chicken, both made from tough, tough beef. Mock chili was heavy on the beans but so light on meat that a single sausage might suffice for the whole pot.

Cost has always been a rationale for making do with a mock version of the real thing. During the Great Depression, men made their living selling apples on the street corners, but just as many couldn't even afford those apples. When faced with a special occasion, many's the family that feasted on a mock apple pie made with Ritz Crackers or a mock pound cake, made with less butter and fewer eggs than in regular pound cake. Many a family settled for mock plum pudding at Christmastime. And how about that mincemeat pie? Once upon a time, mincemeat meant exactly that: minced meat. But in hard times when meat was too expensive or impossible to get, mock mincemeat saved the day. In fact, finding a recipe using genuine mincemeat has become difficult to do. Many's the version of mincemeat in modern cookbooks that's really a mock mincemeat, often created from unlikely combinations such as raisins, currants, and lemons; crackers, molasses, and the liquid from a sweet pickle jar, whole oranges, currants, and vinegar; or dried apples, chopped lemons, and gingerbread spices.

Generations ago one of the luxury desserts in early America was a pie made from dried figs from Spain or Italy. Too expensive for most families, homemakers came up with a mock fig pie made from what are now very, very expensive sun-dried apples.

Today, with caviar costing $185 a pound and more, poor man's caviar sounds mighty appetizing. It isn't caviar, but it looks like caviar and often fools those not in the know. In fact, those who don't like real caviar often relish the mock version, which is made from eggplant.

Many mock versions come about because the original recipes are too difficult or temperamental for the inexperienced cook to prepare. Leading the list of such dishes must be hollandaise sauce. (I don't know a cookbook worth its salt that doesn't follow its hollandaise recipe with instructions on how to salvage a failed attempt.) Because of the high rate of failure, mock hollandaise sauces proliferate. There are no-cook hollandaise sauces based on store-bought mayonnaise, ones made from whole eggs or sour cream or even béchamel sauce (a white sauce made with flour and milk). You'll find *all* of these in two of the best-selling general cookbooks in America. Is it any wonder that among the best-selling dry sauce mixes in the country is hollandaise?

Angel food cake is a cake that tests a cook's skill—or used to in the days before electric mixers. But adding baking powder to the original recipe guarantees a high, if mock, angel food cake. One mock angel food cake recipe that touts itself as foolproof begins with flour and boiling water and uses not only cream of tartar but baking powder as well.

Does your cheesecake crack and sink and generally look poorly made? (Most cheesecakes crack because they are overcooked—the center should still jiggle when the cheesecake is done.) If you have little success with the real thing, try a mock cheesecake. Made with egg whites, it's a lighter, more stable product and holds up without cracking.

There is still a fourth reason—that of health consciousness—for substituting some ersatz product for the real thing, and Postum is one result. It's a coffee substitute made of wheat, bran, and molasses invented (actually, it was stolen) by Charles W. Post while a patient at the Battle Creek Sanitarium run by Dr. Kellogg.

The final and perhaps best reason for using a mock product instead of the real McCoy is a variation on unavailability. I refer to products available in other countries but not in ours. The perfect example of this is *crème fraîche*, which dozens, maybe hundreds, of French recipes call for but for which there is no comparable product in the United States. In France, *crème fraîche* is made with raw, fresh cream; it is neither a whipping cream nor a sour cream. Professional chefs love it because it has such a high butterfat content that it will thicken sauces easily without danger of curdling. Since it is not pasteurized, the bacteria in it change its taste from sweet to slightly tangy over a period of a couple days. In this country, because we can't get raw cream, we counterfeit *crème fraîche* by mixing buttermilk with heavy cream.

For whatever reason, these total impostors or merely convenient substitutes have become a permanent part of our cookery repertoire. Saving us money, time, and trouble, they demonstrate anew the ingenuity and resourcefulness of generations of clever cooks.

# Mock Turtle Soup

W*hat was once an ersatz version of the real thing has now become accepted in its own right as a gourmet classic. The following is an original English recipe in a simplified version. If you can't get a calf's head, make mock mock-turtle soup, substituting 2 pounds of veal bones with meat on them.*

1 calf's head

handful of coarsely chopped carrot, celery, onion, and/or turnip

1 sprig of parsley

1 teaspoon salt

4 tablespoons butter

½ cup (¼ pound) julienned ham strips

1 onion, diced

1 carrot, diced

2 ribs celery, sliced diagonally

4 tablespoons flour

3–4 ounces Madeira or sherry

1 tablespoon lemon juice

salt and pepper

1 small can mushrooms, drained and cut in halves

Put calf's head into a saucepan with coarsely chopped vegetables and parsley. Add salt and cover with water. Bring to a boil and then cook until meat falls off bone. Set head and meat aside to cool. Strain the broth.

Melt butter in skillet. Add ham, onion, carrot, and celery. Blend in flour and strained broth. Cook, stirring frequently, until mixture comes to a boil. Lower heat and cook until mixture begins to thicken (about 10 minutes). Stir in wine and lemon juice. Season to taste with salt and pepper. Remove meat from calf's head and cut into strips; add meat and mushroom halves to soup mixture. Cook over low heat about 5 minutes or until meat is warmed through. Serves 4.

# Mock Coconut Pie

*I*t is amazing what potatoes can simulate, such as in this recipe that dates back to World War I.

3 medium-size peeled and grated white potatoes

2 cups milk

3 eggs, well beaten

1 teaspoon grated nutmeg

½ cup sugar

1 9-inch pie shell, prebaked for 10 minutes in 450° F oven

Preheat oven to 350° F. Wash potatoes in a sieve under cold water to remove starch and drain dry. Measure 1 full-packed cupful. Cook milk, eggs, nutmeg, and sugar over low heat until mixture thickens slightly and coats a spoon. Add potato and stir well. Pour into 9-inch pie shell. Bake 30 minutes or until lightly browned and knife inserted near center of custard comes out clean.

# Mock Cheesecake

*T*his no-bake cheesecake relies on gelatin to hold it together and egg whites to lighten it.

## Crust

1¼ cups crushed vanilla or chocolate wafers

¼ cup granulated sugar or firm-packed light brown sugar

6 tablespoons (¾ stick) butter or margarine, melted

Combine crumbs, butter, and sugar. Press firmly into the bottom of a 9-inch springform pan. (If you wish, reserve ¼ cup of mixture for topping.) Chill until needed.

## Filling

3 envelopes unflavored gelatin

1 cup milk

2 eggs, separated

3 cups (24 ounces) creamed cottage cheese

1 6-ounce can frozen lemonade concentrate, thawed

¼ cup granulated sugar

1 cup heavy cream

Sprinkle gelatin onto milk in a large saucepan, and let stand until gelatin swells up and dissolves. Add egg yolks and mix well. Bring mixture slowly to a simmer, then remove from heat and pour into a large mixing bowl.

Process cottage cheese in a food processor or beat in a small bowl with an electric mixer until smooth and creamy. (Can also force it through a sieve.) Add lemonade and combine well. Stir mixture into the gelatin.

Using clean beaters and bowl, beat egg whites until they hold stiff peaks. Add sugar in four increments, beating after each one until mixture is not gritty. Fold into the gelatin-cheese mixture until mixture is lightened and no large blobs of egg white show.

Using a chilled bowl and beaters, beat whipping cream until thickened. Fold into the rest but do not overdo.

Pour mixture into crust and top with reserved crumbs if desired (make a border around top if you wish). Chill for about 2 hours. Serves 8 generously, 12 more modestly.

# N
## is for Napoleon

Not that luscious dessert with layers of flaky puff pastry, interspersed with even thicker layers of melt-in-your-mouth, custardy *crème chantilly*, and topped with an icing of vanilla fondant piped with chocolate.

No, I refer to Napoleon Bonaparte, the Corsican-born Frenchman, general made emperor. You know, the shortish fellow with the black hair that he combed forward to hide his bald spot, always shown in uniform with his left hand tucked within his tunic, full-cheeked, gently potbellied—obviously well and maybe even overfed. At least so he is pictured, based on the famous bronze statue done by Seurre in 1833 after Bonaparte's death. Actually, his contemporaries universally describe him as being very thin. A thin ruler was uncommonly rare in

When referring to the pastry, napoleon is a misnomer, having nothing to do with the man. It isn't even French. Instead, it's of Italian extraction. The horizontal layering is typical of Naples, and its name is a corruption of Neapolitan.

countries where multicourse meals, lasting for hours on end, were the rule. In this, like everything else, Napoleon Bonaparte was a rule unto himself. He had but two meals a day, allocated a mere fifteen minutes for any meal, and usually ate standing up. He had the world's greatest chefs in his kitchens, but he preferred the same fare every day and favored Italian olive oil–based dishes to French butter-based ones. He refused to be kept waiting, so his kitchens were run like an army's, like clockwork. He insisted, for instance, that his breakfast be served punctually at 10 A.M., three hours after he arose.

Interesting, you say, but what does this man have to do with culinary history? Lots.

It was Napoleon, while ruler of France, who decided to make her independent, at least food-wise, of other countries and colonies, in order to foil England's blockade of her ports. To this end he announced enormous financial incentives to anyone who could find substitutes for imported cane sugar, tea, coffee, and a dozen other necessities. One award went to Antoine Delessert who found the secret of extracting sugar from beets among the papers of a Prussian chemist; he claimed the reward, was given a medal, and soon had a sugar-beet factory operating in France. Unfortunately for him the blockade was soon lifted, sugar from cane became available again, and his factory went bust. Years later the extraction of beet sugar resumed and today accounts for about 40 percent of the sucrose used in the world.

Every time you open a can of anything, you can thank Napoleon for it. One of his awards went to Nicholas Appert in 1810 for his experiments in preserving foods (usually meat) by sealing them in a container while heating it—shades of Spam®.

"Canned meat 114 years old," writes Harold McGee in *On Food and Cooking*, "has been eaten without distaste if not exactly pleasure."

On the military front, Napoleon is credited with the aphorism, "An army marches on its belly." There is some question as to whether he really said it, but none that he practiced it. The armies of France were among the best fed in Europe—except, of course, on the retreat from Russia.

According to Napoleon's biographers, unlike other European armies that scavenged for supplies, his army received provisions from supply trains.

In an effort to ensure that his army's bread supply was not only adequate but remained fresh and palatable, Napoleon introduced into France longer-keeping pumpernickel bread from Westphalia. It came to his army's rescue at the Hospice of Saint Bernard as the French forces crossed the Alps to battle Austria for control of France's Italian territories.

There, on the bloody battlefield at Marengo, Italy, the story of the best-known chicken dish in the world has its origins. Let us begin with the version that appears in most cookbooks.

Allow me to set the stage. The time is 1800. France is under a military dictatorship masquerading as a Republic and led by Bonaparte as First Consul. The combatants are France versus England and Austria. The Austrian army invades France's Italian territories and besieges the vastly outnumbered French force at Genoa. In late spring Napoleon raises a ragtag army of thirty-five to forty thousand men and leads them through the dreaded great St. Bernard pass in the Alps in hopes of launching a surprise attack on the Austrians.

According to his American biographer, John Abbott, nothing that planning might forestall has been left to chance. Immense magazines of wheat, biscuit, and oats line the route to the pass, and each man carries rations for several days. Awaiting the men at the Hospice of St. Bernard on the summit is fresh pumpernickel bread, cheese, and wine.

Despite the plentiful provisions, many die in the snow during the crossing, and Napoleon and the remaining 22,000 men are surprised at Marengo early on June 14 by the Austrian forces, who have been forewarned of Napoleon's approach.

By late afternoon, the outnumbered French are in retreat and Austrian victory seems so eminent that the Austrian commander, leaving his second in command, retires to his tent to dispatch couriers throughout Europe announcing "Napoleon has been defeated." Unexpectedly, however, two of Napoleon's commanders, Desaix and Kellerman, disobey his orders—and come to his rescue. Desaix's troops charge the Austrian vanguard, stopping their advance, and Kellerman's cavalry not only turns the Austrian cavalry but captures Austria's acting commander. Defeat has been turned into victory. Napoleon Bonaparte himself writes the official report, stating that the twelve-hour battle has gone exactly as planned.

Night falls, and the thousands of dead are left in command of the field. Napoleon makes his inspection and visits the wounded, leaving until last the dressing of his own wound where a cannonball has taken away part of his left boot. The flush of victory is replaced by exhaustion and hunger. Napoleon, whose weak stomach prevents him from eating the day of battle, is famished and wants to eat. And here begins the fabled story of chicken Marengo, as passed on from cookbook author to cookbook author.

**Napoleon's greatest admirer was his opponent at the battle of Waterloo, Arthur Wellesley, the duke of Wellington, who said of him, "He was a general whose presence on the field of battle made the difference of forty thousand men."**

Napoleon's French chef, Dunand the Younger, hearing the battle has been won, comes forward only to find Napoleon's headquarters—and his kitchen equipment—ransacked by the Austrians. Desperate—remember, Napoleon wants what he wants when he wants it—Dunand sends men out to forage in the dark for provisions. They return, according to the *Larousse Gastronomique*, "with three eggs, four tomatoes, six crayfish [common in mountain streams], a small hen, a little garlic, some oil and a saucepan." The story continues with the chef, a resourceful man, drawing his own saber to disjoint the hen. He browns the pieces in oil flavored with garlic, fries the eggs in the same oil, adds the tomatoes and some brandy filched from Napoleon's own flask, and puts the crayfish on top to steam.

Dunand serves the dish on a tin plate, surrounding the chicken with the eggs and crayfish and pouring the sauce on top. Napoleon is so pleased with the dish that he is reported to have said, "You must feed me like this after every battle."

Dunand, however, is dissatisfied with the improvised dish and seeks to improve it. On the eve of the next battle, Dunand adds white wine and uses mushrooms instead of the crayfish.

But, the story continues, Napoleon, being very superstitious, refuses to eat it. Though not ordinarily observant of food, he notices the absence of the crayfish—perhaps because, as one gourmet put it, they went so badly with the rest. In any event, Napoleon orders the crayfish returned to the dish, accusing Dunand of trying to jinx him. Dunand has no choice but to comply, and the composition of the dish is fixed for all eternity.

Thus, for almost two hundred years has the story of chicken Marengo been passed on from one generation of chefs to another until it has achieved near mythic quality.

Unfortunately, that is exactly what it is: a myth.

"Not so," say some. "Look at the use of fried eggs served as garnish to a dinner entrée. This must have been an improvisation."

Not so, say I and other food historians. The practice of serving eggs not at breakfast but at dinner dates back to the sixteenth century.

Let us not argue over trifles. Instead, we shall consult an authority on Napoleon Bonaparte. The memoirs of Louis Constant, first *valet de chambre* to Napoleon, written after Marengo, recount a typical day in Napoleon's life *before* the invasion of Italy. Constant states that Bonaparte rose each morning at seven and breakfasted at ten. "The repast was exceedingly simple. He ate almost every morning some chicken, dressed with oil and onions. This dish was then, I believe, called *poulet à la provençale;* but our restaurateurs have since conferred upon it the more ambitious name of *poulet à la Marengo.*"

Where, then, did that dish come from on the night of June 14, 1800? Louis Antoine Fauvelet de Bourrienne, Napoleon's private secretary, says in his memoirs,

*Supper sent from the Convent del Bosco . . . Whether Kellerman did or did not give the crown of France to the First Consul, it is very certain that on the evening of the battle of Marengo he gave him a supper, of which his famishing staff*

*and the rest of us partook. This was no inconsiderable service in the destitute condition in which we were. We thought ourselves exceedingly fortunate in profiting by the precaution of Kellerman, who had procured provisions from one of those pious retreats which were always well supplied, and which soldiers are very glad to fall in with when campaigning. It was the Convent del Bosco which on this occasion was laid under contribution; and in return for the abundance of good provisions and wine with which they supplied the commander of the heavy cavalry, the holy fathers were allowed a guard to protect them against pillage and the other disastrous concomitants of war.*

**Clutching his stomach in pain, Napoleon died a British detainee on the island of Saint Helena, four months short of his fifty-second birthday in 1821. Some say he committted suicide; others blame nameless others for deliberate food-poisoning. Some historians contend it was stomach cancer like that which had killed his father. Still others blame gastric ulcers caused by a lifetime of improper eating habits, aggravated by improper medical treatment at the hands of the British.**

As for the chef who is credited with improvising chicken Marengo, he was not French but Swiss and had inherited the post of *chef de cuisine* to the Prince of Conde. He followed the prince into exile in 1793 and remained in his service for twelve years. He did not return to France nor enter the service of Napoleon until 1805, five years after the battle of Marengo.

Ah, well, it makes a great story—an improvised dish served to a general who used much forethought to care for his army but forgot himself. As to the identity of the original chef whose *poulet à la provençale* was served to Napoleon daily, of that, too, we are uncertain. But one might hazard a guess that her name was Letizia Ramolino Buonaparte—his mother.

# Chicken à la Provençale

According to cuisine legend, Napoleon's chefs devised a no-lose method of guaranteeing that they would have dinner ready for him whenever he got around to ordering it. They started preparing this dish an hour before his expected time to dine. Then, every 15 minutes, they started another one. You can imagine the waste, only partially alleviated by having everyone below stairs and in service eat, as Napoleon did, chicken Provençale day after day. This, by the way, may be plain home-cooking, but it makes for delicious eating.

1 cut-up chicken, or use all thighs or all breasts
2 tablespoons olive oil
2 tablespoons butter
1 large onion, halved and sliced
1 large bell pepper, seeded and cut into strips
4 ounces large mushrooms, halved and sliced
2 cloves garlic, crushed
½ cup white wine or sherry
1 teaspoon salt
½ teaspoon crushed peppercorns

Fry chicken pieces in olive oil and butter, turning frequently to make sure they are brown all over and done evenly. Remove from frying pan and keep warm.

In same skillet, adding more olive oil/butter if necessary, fry onions and green peppers until onions are transparent and peppers are lightly browned. Add mushrooms and garlic and fry a few minutes more until mushrooms and garlic soften. Deglaze pan by adding white wine. Season to taste with salt and pepper. Return chicken to pan, cover, and simmer for about 30 minutes, or until it is done.

# Chicken Marengo

Sometimes it seems as if there are as many versions of the Chicken Marengo recipe as there are of the story of its creation. For the most elaborate, containing a garniture of tomatoes, mushrooms, crayfish or shrimp, black olives, fried croutons, and french fried eggs, I refer you to From Julia Child's Kitchen, in which three pages are devoted to Chicken Marengo. The following is Escoffier's simplified version. (I have taken the liberty of separating out the ingredients.)

1 chicken, cut in halves or pieces

3 tablespoons olive oil

3 tablespoons white wine

1 small clove garlic, crushed

2 peeled, seeded, and sliced tomatoes or 1½ tablespoons tomato puree
    [or 1 teaspoon tomato paste]

10 small mushrooms, sliced stem and all

10 slices of truffle [can omit]

4 crayfish or 1 lobster, cooked [can substitute shrimp]

2 eggs, fried in butter

4 slices of bread, heart-shaped and fried in butter

¼ teaspoon chopped parsley

Sauté the chicken in oil [until browned and tender]. Swirl the saucepan with white wine, add 2 peeled and chopped tomatoes, or 1½ tablespoons of tomato puree, a bit of crushed garlic, 10 small mushrooms, and 10 slices of truffle.

Put [chicken] on a dish; cover it with sauce and garnish; surround it with heart-shaped croutons, fried in butter; small, fried eggs, and trussed crayfish cooked in court-bouillon [seasoned stock] and sprinkle the whole with a pinch of chopped parsley.

# O
## is for Opera

The oft-quoted phrase, "the opera isn't over until the fat lady sings" aptly sums up the relationship between opera and food: Those who sing the former relish the latter, and it shows. To be thin in the operatic world indicates one is either a beginner or a failure, wanting the wherewithal to eat. During the height of opera's popularity, not infrequently one's talent was measured by one's size—the bigger the better. Divas were "majestic" or "statuesque," but never "fat." Nor were they lacking admirers, especially among their fellow idolators of food, the great chefs of their day. Thus do we find some of our most famous and extravagant dishes dedicated to and named for prima donnas (tenors also got their share).

Take, for example, Luisa Tetrazzini (1874–1940), a grand Italian coloratura soprano in every way. She debuted in 1865 as Inez in the posthumous premier of Giacomo Meyerbeer's *L'Africaine*. So great was her success that dozens of dishes were named in her honor—not after her, but after the vehicle of her success. Although

*L'Africaine* enjoyed enormous acclaim in its day, later generations considered it super-ficial. To this day, however, you will find *à l'Africaine* on menus, referring not to native African food but to an opera-inspired gar-niture of olive-sized ovals of buttered potatoes and similar globes of cucumber, eggplant, or zucchini.

**"The opera isn't over until the fat lady sings" is not a Yogi Berra-ism; he said, "It isn't over until it's over." The fat lady quote appeared in a column written by Dan Cook in the *Washington Post* on June 13, 1978.**

Tetrazzini also had more than her share of dishes named directly for her. Chicken Tetrazzini, which James Beard believed originated in San Francisco, the city Luisa visited most frequently, is a voluptuous pasta dish of spaghetti topped with strips of boneless chicken breast in a calorie-rich sherry and cream sauce generously sprinkled with grated Parmesan cheese and cooked until lightly browned and bubbly. *Bellissimo!*

Whether the dish is American or not, no one knows. It is more a matter of attribu-tion by default: No French or Italian authority acknowledges it. Louis P. De Gouy, however, a French master chef who presided over ten world-famous hotel kitchens in Europe and America, includes not only a chicken recipe but one for shirred eggs Tetrazzini and another for turkey Tetrazzini-style in his 1947 *The Gold Cook Book*.

**One of the few prima donnas to go on a diet while pursuing her career was Maria Callas. She did it for her lover, Aristotle Onassis. Not only did she lose weight, she eventually lost Onassis—to Jacqueline Kennedy. What's more, as her waistline shrank, so did her register.**

Luisa would have devoured all three with gusto and asked for seconds. "She was," said James Beard, no anorexic he, "a woman of astounding girth." One restaurateur, reminiscing about her, described the composure of the staff of the Savoy Hotel in London. He noted none flinched when, in her cups and with much inebriat-ed help, Tetrazzini clambered up on a chair to sing "Home Sweet Home." Sturdy chairs they have there at the Savoy.

Hotels seem to take in stride the foibles of operatic stars. For example, New

York's Plaza once had as a guest Enrico Caruso (1873–1921), the robust leading tenor of the Metropolitan Opera. The whirring of an electric clock so disturbed his sleep that he ripped it out of the wall, thereby putting all the 224 other electric clocks in the hotel out of commission. The hotel's reaction was to send him a note of abject apology for disturbing his sleep along with a magnum of champagne to accompany his beloved spaghetti.

Like Tetrazzini, Caruso loved his pasta. He ate it tossed with a little bit of butter and some grated Parmesan; vegetarian style with tomato sauce, a dash of cheese, and fried zucchini; or in combination with almost any other food.

Chefs, knowing of his predilection, took pleasure in dreaming up new variations for him. *Spaghetti alla Caruso* was created and prepared just for him in the small ninth-floor kitchen of the old Knickerbocker Hotel by chef De Gouy. He combined sliced Virginia ham and diced bacon with three pounds of beef plus a veal knuckle, added one sliced medium-size truffle, half a pound of mushrooms, some diced celery, carrots, and leeks, a clove or two of garlic, and threw in a handful of herbs and a mountain of grated cheese. Beneath this was spaghetti made to Caruso's taste: not too tender, not too soft, a little crackly, a little chewy.

**De Gouy created the famous spaghetti Caruso, but Caruso himself created a second one. According to eyewitnesses, Caruso often wrapped an apron about his waist, clapped a chef's cap upon his head, commandeered a kitchen, and emerged proudly carrying a platter heaped high with spaghetti, tomato sauce, and chicken livers.**

The most famous opera-inspired dish was the work of a French chef at a London hotel in honor of an Australian soprano. It is also one of the few dishes for which we have the story of its creation in the words of its creator, Escoffier:

Madame Nellie Melba, the grand cantrice of Australia, sang at the Covent Garden in 1894. She stayed at the Savoy Hotel . . . at which time I was directing the kitchens of that establishment. One evening when Lohengrin was to be performed, Madame Melba gave me [tickets for] two seats. As you know, in *that opera, a swan appears. The following evening Madame Melba gave a petite souper for several friends . . . and to show her that I had profited agreeably from the seats she had graciously offered me, I sculpted from a block of ice a superb swan, and between the two wings I buried a silver bowl. I covered the bottom of the bowl with vanilla ice cream and on this bed of ice cream, I placed peaches soaked in a syrup of vanilla.*

He neglected to mention that working in the cold room (a walk-in icebox), just before serving the dish, he duplicated the soft pure white of the swan's plumage by coating his ice sculpture with confectioner's sugar. He then had just minutes to get the dish from kitchen to table, remove the domed lid, make the presentation, and serve the dish before the sugar began to melt. You can imagine the oohs and ahhs.

Noticeably absent from the initial presentation was the raspberry purée known as Melba sauce. It came later, in 1900, when Escoffier added peach Melba to the menu of the new Carlton Hotel at the juncture of the Haymarket and Pall Mall. It was here that he served, for the first time ever, *à la carte* meals. Shortly after the opening, he was serving 500 people at each seating on Sundays—the only day of the week Escoffier donned his chef's hat and jacket. Under the circumstances, hundreds of ice sculptures were impractical. But without the swan, the dish was simply a glorified, frozen version of another Frenchman's *pêches Madame Recamier*. The solution was the addition of a raspberry purée like that used in Escoffier's own *pêches cardinal* but without its garnish of slivered almonds.

It is interesting to note that Escoffier in his masterwork gives the recipe for peach Melba, including the sauce, but makes no mention of the ice swan. He also includes a recipe for *pêches aiglon*, which is identical to the Melba presentation except the swan is an eagle and the pêches are lightly dusted with crystallized violets. The question must be: Which came first, the swan or the eagle?

Among his fellow chefs, many felt his real masterpiece was *pêches Eugenie*, the recipe for which is lost. A description of it does exist, however. A masterpiece of simplicity, it included small peeled and pitted peaches about the size of an apricot, tiny wild strawberries, a sprinkling of sugar, some kirsch and maraschino. At the last minute, a laving of champagne-flavored sabayon was added to complete this symphony of colors and flavors.

The antithesis of such a blending of flavors is plain old melba toast, which was named for Nellie Melba but not created for her.

It seems that in the 1890s while Escoffier was working at the Savoy, he spent much of his free time with his soon-to-be partner, Cesar Ritz (as in "putting on the ritz," ritzy, and such Ritz hotels as the Paris Ritz and the Ritz-Carlton). One day Madame Ritz, Cesar's wife, complained that toast was never thin enough for her. To please her, Escoffier and Ritz toasted a slice of white bread, cut it in half, and toasted the white sides of the halves. She was delighted with the toast, and the men proposed christening it toast Marie. She demurred, saying she was not famous enough to have a dish named for her. The toast went without a name until Dame Nellie Melba returned ill from a successful tour of America and was put on a diet of milk and toast. Escoffier had an idea, and, voilà, melba toast.

*Pêches Madame Recamier* was a dish devised by Chevrier, an illustrious maitre d'hotel in Paris, when Madame Jeanne Francoise Julie Adelaide Recamier (1777–1849), wife to the French banker, had lost all interest in food. Seeing she was fading away, he said to himself, ". . . She likes peaches—I'll serve her some in my own way. And I put one, the best I could find, to cook in a bain-maire [water-bath]; I smothered it with exquisite sugar syrup, poured some cream over it" (*The Master Chefs*, St. Martin's, 1971). And there it was, *Pêches Madame Recamier,* which we know as peaches and cream.

In addition to peaches, sauce, and toast, Melba is the name of a garnish of small tomatoes stuffed with creamed chicken, truffles, and mushrooms bound with véloute sauce. In fact, more dishes may have been named for Nellie Melba than any other operatic personality, with the possible exception of composer Gioacchino Rossini.

Rossini (1792–1868), the Italian composer of *The Barber of Seville*, loved cooking more than composing. It was he who created omelet Rossini, salad dressing Rossini, roast chicken Rossini, scrambled eggs Rossini (all prepared with foie gras and truffles), and, his most famous dish, tournedos Rossini.

In restaurants, Rossini was in the habit of ordering, like Richard D'Oyly Carte, whatever he wanted. Sometimes, hang the menu. One day, at the Café Anglais in Paris, he called the chef out of the kitchen and described the dish he wanted. It was to have sliced truffles and sautéed foie gras atop a medallion of filet mignon.

*À la Carte* is a contraction for à la Richard D'Oyly Carte (1844–1901). The producer of Gilbert and Sullivan's *H.M.S. Pinafore,* he owned five touring opera companies, arranged Oscar Wilde's American lecture tour, and built the Savoy theater, the first public building in England lighted by electricity. Known for his objection to the use of a fixed menu, he demanded to be allowed to choose among all the dishes. Like Rossini, he got his way—and his name on millions of menus.

This much is evidently fact. The rest—well, judge for yourself. The headwaiter, fearing that others would order this dish that used the best, most expensive, and scarcest ingredients in the kitchen, served it *en retard les dos* (behind the back) so other patrons couldn't see it. This may be a bit far-fetched, but it fits the dictionary version: from the French *tourner,* to turn, and *dos,* the back.

The occasion of the opening of an opera always inspired chefs to new creative heights. For example, Puccini's *La Tosca,* a clever condensation of Sardou's famous drama, premiered in 1900 and is supposed to have inspired Escoffier to create a salad Tosca. If so, Escoffier either lost the recipe or judged it not up to his standards—it is not in his cookbook.

Jacques Offenbach, the creator of the light, burlesque, French comic operetta, inspired many a dish in 1865 when he produced his most famous one, *La Belle Helene*. Restaurants in Paris vied among themselves to take advantage of Offenbach's success. Among the dishes created were grilled tournedos, chicken supremes, even roasts—all Belle-Helene. The most famous was *poires Belle-Helene,* those chocolate-sauced pyramids of poached pears sometimes mistakenly credited to Escoffier. (His version, poires

Helene, included crystallized violets and was dedicated to Helene, the duchess d'Aosta and sister of the duc d'Orleans.)

The most famous of the operetta singers was an American, Helen Louis Leonard (1861–1922), more commonly known as Lillian Russell. Her appetite for music and men was exceeded only by her appetite for food (see chapter E), which she often enjoyed in the company of "Diamond Jim" Brady. Although during their lifetimes both had many dishes named for them by restaurateurs desiring to curry favor, only two of these survive, both created by that master of name-dropping, Henri Charpentier: for Lillian Russell, a pear-filled pancake drowning in brandy and for Diamond Jim a teetotaler, a not-quite-apropos sherried and brandied baked chicken.

## Pêches Melba

*T his recipe is based on the version that appears in Escoffier's* Le Guide Culinaire, Aide-Memoir de Cuisine Pratique, *published in France in 1903 and meant for professional cooks. In his* Ma Cuisine, *translated into English in 1965, the poaching is omitted and the peaches are served raw but sugared.*

Poach peeled, stoned peaches in vanilla-flavored syrup. Make the syrup by boiling 1 cup of sugar and 2 cups of water with a whole vanilla bean to 232° F or thread stage. Peaches should be cooked until they are tender enough to be pierced by a knife. Put them in a chilled metal dish upon a layer of vanilla ice cream and nap [coat] with a raspberry purée made by cooking raspberries with sugar and some water until thick, then putting through strainer and allowing to cool.

Elsewhere in his book he recommends making a raspberry sauce by melting down raspberry jelly or preserves. If the latter, the sauce must be strained before it is cooled.

To approximate the original swanlike serving, take two plain vanilla wafers and place in ice cream as if wings.

# Chicken Tetrazzini

Most modern cooks look upon this as the perfect dish in which to use leftover chicken. And it can easily be made by substituting cream of mushroom soup for the white sauce. Furthermore, it can be gussied up by adding chopped celery, bell peppers, onions, pimento, almonds—you name it—all of which help to stretch it when serving it as a casserole or buffet dish.

Making it from scratch is slightly more complicated, but once you taste it, you will understand why Tetrazzini was mad for it.

**3 pounds chicken pieces, preferably breasts, with skins and bones**

**1 teaspoon salt**

**boiling water to cover**

**½–¾ pound spaghetti**

**½ teaspoon salt**

**1 tablespoon oil**

**½ pound mushrooms, sliced**

**6 tablespoons butter (¾ stick), divided**

**6 tablespoons flour**

**1 cup heavy cream, scalded**

**⅓ cup dry sherry**

**½ cup grated cheese (Parmesan, Swiss, or half of each)**

Poach chicken pieces until tender in salted boiling water to cover. Let cool in broth until easy to handle. Remove meat from bones in large pieces, if possible. Return skins and bones to water. Cover, return to boil, and simmer for about an hour. Remove cover and large bones, and reduce broth to 2 cups. Strain and reserve.

While broth is cooking, cut chicken into large chunks (should have about 3 cups).

Cook spaghetti in salted and oiled water until *al dente* (or until it can be cut with the side of a spoon). Drain spaghetti well in a colander.

Preheat oven to 350° F.

Sauté mushrooms in large sauté or medium-size saucepan in 3 tablespoons butter. Using a slotted spoon, transfer them to a separate dish and melt remaining butter in the juices in the saucepan. Add as much flour as there is butter in pan (about 6 tablespoons) and stir well without letting flour brown. Add strained broth and cook over low heat, stirring constantly, until mixture is very thick. Stir in cream and sherry. Divide the sauce in half. To one half add spaghetti and mushrooms, to the other the chicken pieces.

Arrange spaghetti and mushroom mixture in large flat baking dish, banking it up the sides and making well in center. Put chicken in the middle. Sprinkle cheese over top and place in oven until lightly browned and heated through, about 15–20 minutes. Serve from baking dish. Serves 6–8.

# P
## is for Pepper

I don't mean bell peppers—red, yellow, green, and tangy-sweet—nor chili or cayenne peppers, so eye-watering hot. I refer not to pepperroot or peppergrass, which are very "in" but part of the mustard family, nor to peppermint, an herb cultivated for centuries for its aromatic oil. No, this is P for plain old ordinary pepper, as in salt and pepper.

Of course, pepper has never been ordinary. From Roman times on and particularly during the Middle Ages it served as currency, being literally worth its weight in gold. In fact, it was worth more than gold. Debasing of precious metal coinage with base metals was a common event in a time when every sovereign, even the head of a city, struck his own currency. To make matters worse and the currency worth less, "clipping" of coins was common. Each owner scraped or chipped a little gold or silver off the coins as the money passed from hand to hand.

Peppercorns, on the other hand, were a "stable" currency and recognized as such. In A.D. 408, Rome bought itself two years of freedom from sacking by paying off Alaric the Visigoth with a tribute that included 3,000 pounds of pepper. Unfortunately, that only whetted his appetite. Two years later he was back for more. This time he took not only the city's entire supply of pepper, he took the city. Four decades later Attilla the Hun was bought off by the Eastern Roman emperor, Theodosius II, with presents that included large quantities of pepper. Attilla died before he could come back for more.

During the middle ages one could accomplish much if one owned peppercorns. One could buy land, pay fines (even for such crimes as attempted assassination), dower a sister or daughter, and pay tithes, taxes, and customs duties—all with peppercorns. Serfs in France could buy their freedom with a pound of peppercorns. Hired hands in England took their wages in peppercorns. (Dockworkers in England during the reign of Queen Elizabeth I had to wear pocketless uniforms when unloading pepper, lest they be tempted to pilfer.) Pirates and marauders searched for peppercorns as they sacked cities. Heirs to large fortunes converted coins into peppercorns. And at all times and under all occasions, peppercorns made a highly acceptable bribe to judges, mayors, kings, and popes. In fact, during the Middle Ages the use of peppercorns as a measure of wealth was so pervasive that a man's wealth was no longer determined by the amount of land in his estate

*Peppercorn rent* is a term still used in legal documents in England to signify a nominal payment that does not represent the real value of the use of the property involved but constitutes simply a legal acknowledgment by the tenant that the premises he is occupying or exploiting remain the property of the landlord. For example, the Ritz Hotel in London rents its garden from Queen Elizabeth II, who owns the land, for a yearly fee of one peppercorn. In the same way, in November 1973, her son Prince Charles of England crossed the Tamar River and entered Cornwall, of which Queen Elizabeth had named him duke. For this honor he had to pay a feudal rent—a load of firewood, a pair of gilt spurs, a hunting bow, two greyhounds, and a pound of peppercorns.

but by the amount of pepper in his pantry. To say a man lacked pepper was to condemn him as poverty-stricken.

**Nobles who married commoners for their money were nicknamed "pepper bags" by the Saxon aristocracy. It is even reported that some of these traitors to their class were waylaid and forced to swallow such inordinate quantities of pepper that it killed them—an expensive, agonizing form of murder.**

Just exactly when India-grown peppercorns began trickling into the Mediterranean world, carried by small Arab caravans, is uncertain. By around 550 B.C. pepper was fairly common in Greece, although it was used more for medicine than cookery. Its gastronomic merits, however, were soon recognized. Pepper is that rare spice that is not a flavoring agent per se but a seasoning or blending agent. (One writer compared it to the ideal mate: both stimulating and soothingly sweet.) In conjunction with other flavors it increases the body of flavor, providing not bite but a pleasant taste and adding to the aroma. So popular did pepper become that it began to be added to almost all Roman dishes. (Unfortunately, it was most often used to mask the overpowering taste of gamey meats.) The Romans even added it to desserts, as did the Germans a thousand years later with their *pfefferkuchen* (literally pepper cake), a combination gingerbread and fruitcake, only better. Whenever wars abounded or hard times were at hand, however, the expensive pepper had to be eliminated from the cake, to be restored only during the good years. Eventually, the pepper

**The world's most popular spice, pepper manages to be both hot and sweet since, in the mouth, it stimulates the "hot" receptors while soothing the sweet buds.**

was totally eliminated except in the name. (A shame. You'd be surprised at the difference adding ½ teaspoon pepper makes in any standard gingerbread, chocolate cake, or yellow cake recipe. Try it—you'll like it.)

Pepper became so important to world cuisine that whoever controlled the pepper trade could influence world events. When the Crusades began, Venice hired out her ships at exorbitant rentals to carry fighting men to the Holy Land, then doubled and tripled her profits by bringing back those same ships loaded with pepper and spice from Alexandria. Venice was the pepper capital of Europe at a time when Europe was consuming 6.6 million pounds annually. When the Portuguese reached the Spice Islands, the monopoly passed to them. For much of the age of exploration, including the trips of Columbus, the pepper plant (*Piper nigrum*), a vine equipped with tendrils that climb any convenient tree, was a highly coveted discovery.

**The pepper capital of the United States was Salem, Massachusetts. In 1791 the United States imported, processed, and then exported only 500 pounds of pepper to other parts of the world. In 1805, thanks to Salem, it exported 7.5 million pounds, 15,000 times as much.**

The pepper plant produces berrylike grains, no more than a quarter-inch across when full-grown. Like most fruits, they are at first green; then they become a yellowish red and, finally, brown—not black—as they ripen.

Green peppercorns are the youngest and the smallest and are green in every sense: in color and in being unripe. If sold fresh—not packed in brine or pickled or freeze-dried—they are soft enough to be mashed into a paste for cooking. In taste they are less pungent and more fruity than you'd expect from pepper.

The peppercorns that are used to make our familiar black pepper are picked at a slightly later stage than the green, when the corns are still unripe but have not yet begun to redden. The corns are then dried (traditionally in the sun) and in a few days turn black through and through.

White pepper is simply black pepper soaked in water to loosen the outer husk, which is rubbed off in salt water. Again, the peppercorns are dried, but without their outer skin, the cores do not darken. Because they are minus their husks, more white peppercorns are needed to make an ounce, thus white pepper is slightly more expensive than black. The expense is justified, however, for use in white sauces or dishes where black specks might be undesirable. In addition, the white peppercorn is less spicy than its black counterpart.

Pink peppercorns are the berry almost completely ripened. (Entirely ripened whole red peppercorns are sold dried and are very strong and pungent.) Because of their color, they are in favor with chefs—they look chichi! On occasion, however, a lookalike berry is substituted for pink peppercorns.

**The most expensive peppercorns are the ripest, pink ones at approximately $6 an ounce. Green comes next at $4.75 per ounce. White is really quite cheap at less than $1.50 per ounce, while black costs just a little over $1.00 an ounce. These are whole-peppercorn 1990 prices, not ground varieties.**

These berries come from an unrelated weed, informally called the Florida holly, that has rosy pink berries about the size of black peppercorns. The taste is not at all the same, and the berries have been known to cause allergic reactions.

Substitution and/or adulteration of peppercorns isn't new; even the Romans did it. They added juniper berries to their peppercorn supply (maybe *that's* why Alaric came back). Today, buying the whole bean is the only way to avoid possible substitutes and impurities. Pepper in ground form may contain such ersatz ingredients as mixtures of ground "grains of paradise" (*Amomom cardamomum*) and inert additions such as ground date stones. Ground pepper is also likely to lose its flavor and aroma quickly as its volatile oils evaporate, so it's much more economical (and tasty) to buy whole peppercorns. When buying them, look for solid, compact corns of uniform color; they should be almost impossible to crumble.

The peppercorn-laced dish probably most familiar to us is *bifteck au poivre*, or steak with peppercorns, but you'll also find veal, chicken, and even fish *au poivre*. Sometimes *bifteck au poivre* is served with cracked black peppercorns, other times with whole green or pink ones. You'd think the whole ones would be more potent, but they aren't—the cracked black ones carry more kick. The dish originated in the Middle Ages as a roast, not a single portion, and was a symbol of conspicuous consumption. (How better to advertise one's wealth than to coat one's food with expensive pepper?) In the process, however, it was discovered that pepper acts as a preservative. Thus, genuine Smithfield hams, to this day, come coated with coarse cracked pepper. Although nothing should be simpler to do than broil a steak and serve it *au poivre*, you'd be aghast at how frequently this dish is ruined—by restaurants and home cooks alike. Inexperienced chefs do as the cookbooks tell them: They press the peppercorns into the meat before broiling. Unfortunately, pepper burns and becomes bitter if exposed directly to high heat; therefore, the professional way to handle *bifteck au poivre* is to put the pepper on the meat after it is cooked. One of the best ways to do this is to make a *poivrade* sauce, which once meant peppery, but now means only piquant.

Of course, many supposedly peppery foods aren't. Pepperpot, a Philadelphia soup-stew, is not peppery, but then neither are peppernuts, the cookies. They contain neither pepper nor nuts—they only look like they do. But you better believe peppered pecans are the real McCoy. They're sweet, they're salty, they're peppery, and they're addictive.

The idea of combining sweet and salt and pepper is an old one, but you haven't lived until you've tried two dishes: One is a pepper-poached pear. It is, as one food writer called it, a gastronomic adventure only improved upon by the addition of ice cream (he recommends caramel) and a slice of pound cake, or for the less adventuresome, a dish of chocolate sauce on the side.

The other dish is a pepper spread/sauce named Jezebel that, like its namesake, is bold and flaunts it. It's also very deceptive. Looking at the ingredients one would think this is volcanic stuff. It isn't. The pepper calms everything down and soothes the roughness out. It can be made ahead of time and kept refrigerated. I can't say how long it keeps—it's gobbled up fast at our house.

# Jezebel

No one who has ever tasted this sauce has failed to ask for the recipe. Although the exact origin is unknown, most concede the South gave birth to it. Some say the sauce was named not for the Biblical character, but for the Southern belle played by Bette Davis in the movie of the same name. Like her, it flaunts all your preconceptions.

It's not anywhere near as biting as you might think, nor is it too sweet and fruity. You should treat it like a fine cognac and let it mellow for at least a week in the refrigerator before serving. You can serve it cold, but it's better at room temperature.

To use it as an appetizer, pour it over cream cheese and serve with crackers. (Many people skip the cream cheese and serve it plain.) It also makes a delicious condiment for baked ham.

**2 jars (18–20 ounces) pineapple preserves or jelly**

**1 large jar (18–20 ounces) apple jelly**

**1 small can (1.12 ounces) dry mustard**

**1 tablespoon freshly ground pepper**

**1 small jar (4–5 ounces) fresh horseradish**

Cook the jellies over low heat until melted. Remove from heat and dump in other ingredients. Stir well. Let cool and refrigerate for at least a week before serving. In case of emergency, however, can make same day.

# Poivrade Sauce

*I* nstead of coating sides of raw meat with pepper, which will result in the pepper burning, grill your steak, then add this genuine pepper sauce.

- 2 tablespoons butter
- 2 tablespoons flour
- 1½ cups beef stock or chicken stock
- ¼ cup heavy cream
- 2 tablespoons red wine (white with chicken) or wine vinegar
- 2 tablespoons green or pink peppercorns (or half of each) or 1 tablespoon coarsely cracked black peppercorns
- ¼ teaspoon salt

Melt butter over medium heat in a medium-size saucepan, then add flour to make a roux and cook until lightly browned. Gradually add beef stock, stirring well (use a whisk) to prevent lumping. Bring to a boil, then reduce over low heat until quite thick, stirring constantly. Add cream, wine, peppercorns, and salt. Continue cooking until thick. Serve immediately. Makes 1 cup.

A classic *poivrade* is made with a *mirepoix* (1 each chopped onion, carrot, and celery rib), which is sweated for 15–20 minutes in butter. Flour is then added to form a roux to which, in turn, the stock is added. When the mixture thickens, force it through a strainer before adding cream, wine, peppercorns, and salt.

# Peppered Pecans

*T*his may seem like a lot of work, but once you see the reaction of others, you won't begrudge a moment of it.

**¼ cup sugar**

**1 teaspoon coarse kosher salt or sea salt**

**½–1 teaspoon freshly ground pepper or 1 teaspoon purchased ground pepper**

**1 cup (4 ounces) pecan halves**

Have a large jelly-roll pan handy. In a small bowl, combine sugar, salt, and pepper. (If you are really fond of pepper, use the large amount of freshly ground pepper for a spicier nut. If you choose to use purchased ground pepper, which loses strength during storage, you'll need at least 1 teaspoon.)

Heat a skillet until it is hot enough to vaporize a bead of water. Add pecans and stir about for approximately 1 minute. Sprinkle with half of sugar mixture. Shake pan and stir until sugar melts, about 1 minute. Repeat with balance of sugar. Immediately turn pecans out onto jelly-roll pan. Spread nuts apart with spatula. Be very careful, as they will be hot. Allow them to cool. Store in airtight tin or "zippered" plastic bag. Makes 1 cup. (If you have a large skillet, you can double the recipe.)

# Q is for Quiche

Pronounced "keesh," this delicious custard-based tart is deceptively named. Like French fries that are really Belgian, Creme Anglaise that is American, Swiss steak that is English, and sauerkraut that is Chinese, quiche is more German than its French name would lead us to believe. And it's all the fault of a Polish king.

It all started centuries ago in the formerly independent little duchy of Lothringia (now Lorraine), bordered on two sides by Germany, on one by Switzerland, and on the fourth by France. The Lothringens took the German *kuche* (cake) and transformed it into an ooh-la-la tart. They filled

The French word *quiche* reveals the dish's Austrian ancestry: It is derived from the German word *kuche,* and the diminutive of *kuchen,* or cake.

its butter-rich crust with tidbits of sliced bacon, some sautéed onions, and strips of cheese. Then they topped it off with egg-enriched cream, a little salt, and a little pepper and put it in the oven so the cheese could melt and the custard could set. Voilà—a dish fit for a king!

It was fit not for a *French* king, however, but a Polish ex-king: Stanislas Leczinski (1677–1766). Twice crowned king of Poland (1704, 1733) and twice deposed (1709, 1735), he had the good sense to marry his daughter Maria Leczinska to France's Louis XV in 1725. When Stanislas fled Poland, his son-in-law installed him as duke and ruler of the newly formed French protectorate, Lorraine. There Stanislas exercised his true renaissance proclivities, proving to Poland its error in ousting him. He transformed Nancy, the capital of Lorraine, into one of Europe's most palatial cities and a brilliant example of urban planning. He built an academy of science, a museum of the arts, a theater, and a military college. He renovated the palace of the Dukes of Lorraine (circa 1420), incorporating the latest technology, even in the kitchen, and building the reputation of his court for fine food and lavish banquets.

Upon his death, Lorraine was inherited by his daughter, Queen Maria, and promptly annexed by France. By doing so, the French also annexed quiche Lorraine, the madeleine, the macaroon, and the *Baba au rhum*—all dishes for which we have to thank Stanislas and his chefs.

From the Lorraine kitchens of Stanislas Leczinski came the miniature pound cake known as the madeleine. These butter-rich, slightly lemony flavored cakes, which were baked in scallop-shaped aspic molds, were introduced to Paris society by Stanislas in 1730 and became an immediate hit. In those

**Supposedly, real men don't eat quiche. Except it was the real men fighting in France during World War II that brought quiche to U.S. shores in the 1940s.**

**In Nancy, a traditional Quiche Lorraine is called a féouse and is made with pieces of smoked pork belly (the French equivalent of bacon). Other areas have their own versions of the dish: *quiche à l'Oignon,* the onion quiche of Alsace; *flamiche,* the leek quiche of Burgundy; and *pissaladiére,* the onion-anchovy quiche from Provence. The list of combinations goes on, including a quiche made of onions, cream cheese, and pumpkin.**

days the madeleine was known as the *tot-fait* ("quickly made") cake. Jean Avice, a nineteenth-century French pastry cook and master to the apprentice Carême, is credited with renaming the *tot-fait* madeleine. Why madeleine? Some say for a peasant by that name who had taken Avice's fancy; others say for a young lady named Madeleine Paumiers. (For more on madeleines, see W is for Writers.)

The macaroon, which derives its name from the fact that it is shaped like a "monk's navel," was a specialty of the Carmelite Sisters of Nancy. During the French Revolution two nuns from the convent went into hiding in the town, where they earned their keep by making the convent's specialty. Their nickname, "The Macaroon Sisters," was given in 1952 to the street where they'd worked. These small, round cakes, which today we think of as cookies, are made of almond paste, sugar, and egg whites. Today the most popular version is probably the one loaded with chewy shredded coconut.

Another of Stanislas's contributions to Lorraine and eventually French cookery was the *Baba au rhum*, which supposedly took its name from the tale of Ali Baba in *The Arabian Nights*. The name was soon shortened to *Baba*, and it refers to a sweet bread made from a yeast dough loaded with raisins and saturated with a rum-flavored sugar syrup.

Actually, it is simply a variation on the *kugelhopf*, which Stanislas had enjoyed first as a boy and then again during his exile in Wissembourg between his elections as king of Poland. The *kugelhopf* was the invention of Viennese bakers. In 1683, their city under siege by the Turks, they proved they were not cowed by the army outside nor lacking a sense of humor. Instead, working with a Turk's-head cake mold (so known because the swirled exterior duplicated a Turkish turban), they inserted a bulletlike tube down through the middle and created the shape we now associate with angel food and other "hole in the middle" cakes.

That same siege saw the development of what is now considered the quintessential French pastry—the *croissant*. When Vienna didn't immediately fall, the Turks dug tunnels under the city walls. The Viennese bakers, who started their work in the middle of the night, heard the noise and gave the alarm. The Turkish sappers were caught, and their tunnels were destroyed. The siege continued until an army of 20,000 Poles fell upon the Turks from the rear and drove them back to Raab. The Viennese bakers were rewarded with the monopoly on a flaky, buttery pastry that they invented and shaped in the form of the Turkish crescent. When the pastry eventually reached France, it became known as *le croissant*. So thoroughly have croissants become identified as French that a cookbook on the cuisine of Vienna notes that Demel's famed bakery "now offers croissants from France."

**You can't believe all you read: Some cookbooks attribute croissants to the besieged bakers of Budapest, not Vienna. History tells us that in 1683 neither the town of Buda nor Pest (united in 1873) were under siege. Both had been in the hands of the Turks since 1541 and were not liberated by the Christians until 1686.**

The French are also given credit for introducing coffee to European gourmands via cafés (coffeehouses)—but they shouldn't be. Again, the siege of Vienna was responsible. When the Viennese burned what they thought was camel fodder left behind by the retreating Turks, it turned out to be green coffee beans. A well-trained interpreter/courier/spy with the liberating Polish army took one whiff of the roasting beans, knew what they were, and had an idea that was to take the world by storm.

Franciszek Jerzy Kulczycki doused the fires and claimed the sacks of coffee beans from the city council as his just reward for leading the Polish army to the rescue of the city. Eventually, he opened Vienna's first coffeehouse, The Blue Bottle. Today there are more than 800 coffeehouses in the city. In 1983 a plaque honoring Kulczycki's role during the siege was hung at his Vienna home. Except for a new facade, his original coffeehouse looks much the same as it did 300 years ago, and the

**Substitute sugar for Kulczycki's honey, add a pinch of cinnamon, and you have Viennese cappuccino.**

dark, bitter Turkish coffee, sweetened with honey and lightened with milk, is still a favorite there.

Alas, there are still more non-French foods that by name or belief we wrongfully credit to the French. Take, for example, vichyssoise. The version of leek-and-potato soup we call by this name has an American birthplace. Chef Louis Diat, for forty-one years the culinary major domo at New York's Ritz Carlton Hotel, fiddled with the French recipe for hot leek and potato soup and had the good sense to serve it ice cold. (See Z is for Zuppa.) The New York birthplace of the soup notwithstanding, France is given the credit for vichyssoise.

Only in the case of French dressing do the French disabuse us of the notion that they invented it. Authentic French dressing is a light and simple mixture of oil, vinegar, salt, and pepper. Neither the French nor anyone else want to admit ownership of that red-hued, tomato-based dressing that is no more French than Russian dressing is Russian.

# Quiche Lorraine

O*ne of the cautions given with quiches is not to freeze them. That's not true of this classic one.*

1 9- or 10-inch pie crust

5 strips bacon

½ pound ham, julienned

1 medium onion, sliced

¼ pound Swiss cheese, cut in strips

1 cup light (half-and-half) cream

3 eggs

1 tablespoon flour

¼ teaspoon salt

pepper

1 tablespoon melted butter

Bake pie crust for 5 minutes at 450° F. Reduce heat to 375° F. Fry bacon until crisp, ham until lightly browned, and onions until limp and transparent. Place in pie shell along with cheese. Scald light cream and cool slightly. In medium-size bowl, beat eggs, flour, and seasonings. Add scalded cream and melted butter. Pour custard into pie shell. Bake 35–40 minutes at 375° F until brown.

Freeze baked quiche if desired. Thaw 30–45 minutes, then heat in 275° F oven for 45 minutes to 1 hour.

# R
## is for Recipes

S ome cooks love 'em. Some never use 'em. Some swear by them, some swear at
them. Some treat them like sacred writings, and some read them for entertainment. Recipes are a bane to some, a boon to others—it all depends on the cook
and the kind of cooking.

Like Gaul and Neapolitan ice cream, cookery is divided into three parts. The first
is cooking—the day-in/day-out meat-and-potatoes kind of meal preparation most of us
learn to do without recipes. The second is baking, or pâtisserie, for which most of us
promptly reach for a cookbook to make our cakes, pies, cookies, and breads. The third
is confectionery, which centuries ago incorporated baked goods but now refers strictly
to sweets like ice cream and candy. Again, most cooks who attempt confectionery
depend upon recipes to get them through this most temperamental area of cookery.

The cook, if experienced, rarely needs recipes for daily cooking, and then only as a guide. Cooking meat, potatoes, and vegetables is by its nature an inexact science. The baker, on the other hand, must know the proper proportions between dry ingredients and wet, between leavening and flour, between fat and sweetening. But again, those proportions need not be exact, and recipes reflect that. A recipe for bread, for example, will approximate the amount of flour needed as six and a half to seven cups.

**Weighing ingredients is more exact than measuring ingredients. For example, a pound of hard wheat flour can weigh as little as 3½ cups per pound and as much as 4½ cups. To this day professional cookbooks give measurements in pounds, ounces, and grams, not cups or tablespoons.**

The candy maker deals in exactitude, if such a characteristic can be said to exist in cookery. He or she must have exact quantities, exact procedures, and exact temperatures (which may need to be adjusted for fluctuations of humidity and such). The candy maker is, in a manner of speaking, a food chemist, whose recipes read more like scientific formulas.

In America past generations of home cooks have tried to master all the branches of cookery, relying upon recipes as needed. In France, on the other hand, homemakers leave the baking and sweet-making to the professionals and concentrate on what they do best—the cooking. No fudge making, no biscuit baking, no birthday cakes; they even buy their daily bread, daily! This approach is both practical and realistic, according to *célébrité de cuisine* Jules Gouffe (1807–1877). Master cook at age seventeen, student of the great Carême, and author of two master works, one on cookery and

**Although candy-making has existed since the first beehive was raided for honey, the scientific methods we are accustomed to today are relatively new to the cookery scene—a mere 200 years old.**

the other on pâtisserie, he wrote, "A good pastry chef easily becomes a capable cook while one never sees a cook become a great pastry chef."

The cook goes about the daily meal preparation adding a pinch of this and a handful of that, usually without benefit of recipes. Recipes are most helpful when they provide new ideas for flavor and/or texture combinations. The cook appreciates even the vague advice offered, for instance, in an Elizabethan recipe for humble pie that calls for "a good quantity of mutton sewet [suet] and halfe a handful of herbes."

Such imprecise measurements would spell disaster for a baker. Thus, it was baking, not cooking, that forced cookbooks to become exact and detailed.

To complicate matters, however, illiteracy was common. Enter mnemonics—recipe names that provided shorthand clues to ingredients and/or measurements.

The most famous of these mnemonics and the grandmother of most other cakes is the pound cake. Its recipe lives up to its name; it calls for a pound of sugar, a pound of flour, a pound of butter, and a pound of eggs (weighed in the shell, of course). A further refinement of the basic recipe was "A Pound and a Pinch," the pinch being of salt, lemon rind, and/or mace. The French version, *quatre quarts*, means four-fourths—four ingredients in equal weights; this is still the same old pound cake but can result in a cake of a much more manageable size.

A variation is 1-2-3-4 cake, which enjoyed a renewed popularity in the early 1970s when one of the cooking-oil companies promoted it as a cake made with a cup of oil instead of butter. Traditionally, one would measure 1 cup butter, 2 cups sugar, 3 cups flour, and 4 eggs, plus seasoning—the eggs were the only leavening. With the advent of baking powder, however, the recipe was amended to include as many teaspoons of baking powder as there were eggs. Its great advantage in the days of nonstandard measurements was that it was nearly foolproof: all measuring was done with the same cup! Of course, the cake varied in size depending on the cup you used.

Another of the early mnemonics was "cup cake," not to be confused with the

Yes, one really could eat humble pie. This sixteenth-century potpie was made from humbles, or the innards of deer. Some authorities take this to mean tripe (the stomach); others think of it more on the order of a very thick giblet mixture.

If you've mastered the pound cake, you also have conquered the Dolly Madison cake, England's Victoria sponge, Finland's *kermakakku,* and dozens of similar recipes. If you cut the butter and flour back by half, you can add the Robert E. Lee cake to your list of achievements.

miniature cakes baked in fluted paper cups. Cup cake goes together so fast it is also called lightning cake. To make it, measure out one cup of sugar and one cup of flour, put a quarter cup of melted butter and two whole eggs in a cup and add milk to fill, mix all ingredients together, pour the batter in your pan, and bake.

Also a mnemonic, but definitely misnamed, is the Jewish 44-ingredient cake. The "44" refers not to individual ingredients but to the total number of measurements, as in sixteen tablespoons flour and as many of sugar. Personally, I would find it devilishly hard to remember, but it does make for a snappy recipe and a real conversation piece—and the cake's good, too.

Bread, too, has its mnemonics, the most famous of which was "thirded bread." The thirding refers to the proportion of different flours used: one third Indian [corn] meal for sweetness and crunch, one third rye for flavor and body, and one third wheat for lightness and elevation. It appeared in many early cookbooks, but by 1896 Fannie Farmer had shortened its name to third bread, and within a score of years, it was appearing under various names from rye to Indian meal bread to just plain rye bread to anadama (with a New England final *a*, which sounds like *er*) bread. One explanation of the latter name is that Anna was good baker but a lousy wife and her husband named it that "Anna, damn her, bread."

Some mnemonics had nothing to do with the ingredients but everything with the cooking. For example, petit fours—the name translates to "low temperature" and, in professional bakeries, refers to small cakes baked when the oven is cooling down. That masterpiece of soup, bouillabaisse, has not a hint of fish nor soup in its name. Instead, it refers to the cooking instructions, "Quand ça commence a bouillir—baisse!" Translation: When it begins to boil, reduce the heat.

A real test of one's memory, not to mention your religious education, is famed scripture cake. Rare is the all-purpose cookbook that includes it and equally rare the spiral-bound local cookbook that doesn't. To make it, one must translate and/or memorize fourteen cryptic Biblical allusions in chapter and verse which, in turn, give you measurements, ingredients, and cooking instruction. Interestingly enough, among those cookbooks that include it, few add the translation. A true do-it-yourself recipe, this is a big hit at church bake sales.

Of all the gimmicks used to help one remember the recipe for a dish, my favorite is a recipe in rhyme for a New England steamed brown bread.

> One cup of sweet milk,
> One cup of sour,
> One cup of corn meal,
> One cup of flour,
> Teaspoon of soda,
> Molasses one cup;
> Steam for three hours
> Then eat it all up.

To which I add:

> Oh, no, the recipe has a fault:
> Forgot half a teaspoon full of salt!

# Pound Cake

*I*f you visit Colonial Williamsburg, tour the Governor's Palace. In the "kitchen/cook house," you will be treated to a lecture-demonstration of the cooking of the time. Frequently, the recipe used is an old-fashioned pound cake, which serves the demonstration purpose well because, when made authentically, it is a very time-consuming pursuit. A demonstrator can easily spend hours making this cake since everything is done by hand, with the exception of the egg whites, which may be beaten with that sixteenth-century version of the whisk, a bundle of twigs. Note that in the recipe, ingredients and key instructions are capitalized to catch your attention. Note also that I have included the use of optional milk in case the mixture is too thick. Butter in those days was not uniformly consistent and contained more moisture than today's homogenized product.

Work one Pound of Butter until soft [with your hands]. Cream with one Pound of Sugar [you can use a spoon]. Beat [with your hands until light and thick] the Yolks of Twelve Eggs [one pound], removing any strings [chalaza], then work in one Pound of Flour (sifted twice) [4½ cups]. [Add ¼ cup milk or rose water if necessary.] Combine Mixtures. Add [fold] stiffly beaten Whites. Pour into a well-greased and floured [Turk's head] Mold and bake in a moderate Oven [350°F]. The Secret of this Cake lies in careful Baking. [Use greased tube pan and bake 60–75 minutes.]

# 1-2-3-4 Cake

H ere's another easily remembered recipe, one that was adapted later into a chiffon cake whose recipe sold for $25,000. For ease of remembering, the ingredients are always listed in the order of the quantity used, rather than in the order you use them.

1 cup milk

1 cup butter or margarine

1 is to 2 (½) teaspoon salt

2 cups sugar

3 cups sifted cake flour along with

3 teaspoons baking powder*

3 times as much vanilla extract as salt (1½ teaspoons)

4 eggs

Preheat oven to 350° F. Prepare three 9-inch cake pans by cutting wax paper lining for bottom. Grease, line, grease again, and dust with flour.

Cream shortening and sugar along with salt. Add eggs one at a time and beat well. Add cake flour and baking powder, alternating with milk. Beat until smooth, then add vanilla. Bake for about 25 minutes or until cake is golden brown and pulls away from the sides.

* Note: In old days when baking powder was less potent, you would have used 4 teaspoons, as many as there were eggs.

# Scripture Cake

*This cake must have appeared in more community cookbooks than any other. Long before that, however, it was a fixture in England. Many of those chafing against the heavy strictures of the Puritan movement must have gotten a secret pleasure out of the instructions.*

| | |
|---|---|
| ½ cup Judges 5:25, last clause | ½ cup butter |
| 2 cups Jeremiah 6:20 | 2 cups sugar |
| 2 tablespoons I Samuel 14:25 | 2 tablespoons honey |
| 6 Jeremiah 17:11, separated | 6 eggs |
| 1½ cups I Kings 4:22, sifted | 1½ cups flour |
| 2 teaspoons Amos 4:5 | 2 teaspoons baking powder |
| II Chronicles 9:9, to taste | spices (see below)* |
| pinch of Leviticus 2:13 | ⅛ teaspoon salt |
| ½ cup Judges 4:19, last clause | ½ cup milk |
| 2 cups Nahum 3:12, chopped | 2 cups figs |
| 2 cups Numbers 17:8 | 2 cups almonds |
| 2 cups I Samuel 30:12, chopped | 2 cups raisins |

Preheat the oven to 300° F. Grease a 10-inch tube pan.

Whip the Judges, Jeremiah, and I Samuel until very light. Beat the 6 yolks of Jeremiah 17 and add along with Kings, Amos, Chronicles, and Leviticus, alternating with Judges. Fold in Nahum, Numbers, and Samuel. Beat Jeremiah 17's 6 whites until stiff and fold into the rest of the batter. Bake 2 hours.

*Possible combination of spices: 2 teaspoons cinnamon, 1 teaspoon nutmeg, ½ teaspoon ginger, ½ teaspoon cloves.

# S

## is for Suzette

Here is cookdom's version of the whodunit. Who was Suzette, as in crepes Suzette, probably the world's most famous dessert? Who invented the original version? Who named it? What was it made of?

The clues as to who inspired it: Suzette, although it sounds French, is also an English name and/or a diminutive. Thus it is possible that the Suzette in question was the young daughter of a gentleman-friend of Edward, Prince of Wales, the eldest son of Queen Victoria and the future King Edward VII. Another version proposes that Suzette was the French nickname of a German actress who never even knew "Bertie," as the Prince was known. Yet another story avers that she was a French princess who lived long before the time of England's Queen Victoria. There are even claims that there was no *real* Suzette—she was a fictional character in a French play.

For each explanation of the inspiration for the dish, there is a story of the origin of the dish—how it first received an orangey sauce, how the sauce became a blending of orange and other liqueurs, how the whole became a flaming triumph. As you might suspect, however, the accounts are contradictory.

**Read enough variations on the story of the origins of crepes Suzette and eventually you will come across one that more than hints that Prince Edward's Suzette was no child, but his friend, spelled** *demimonde.*

Did it, as an occasional dish will do, leap to life like a gastronomic Minerva, springing fully armed and with a tremendous battle cry from the brain of a single creator? Did it evolve slowly as successive cooks added to it and improved it? Was it an accident, the result of a cook's mistake? Could it have resulted from spontaneously combusting in several places at once—a case of great minds thinking alike? You be the judge.

Version One: In 1945 the last of the great name-a-dish-for-a-patron practitioners, Henri Charpentier (1880–1961), privately published a cookbook called *Food and Finesse, the Bride's Bible*. In it he told of his invention of crepes Suzette.

**"The one who tries to fool another is a great fool himself."**

**— HENRI CHARPENTIER**

According to him it happened in 1895 at the Café de Paris in Monte Carlo when he was fifteen and striving to hold his position as *commis des rangs*, a kind of assistant waiter. At that time a frequent visitor for lunch was the fifty-four-year-old Edward, Prince of Wales.

One day, through a series of what Charpentier calls "fortunate circumstances," he was serving the Prince of Wales, who inquired as to the afternoon's menu. Charpentier promptly promised the prince "a sweet never before served to anyone," and Edward agreed to sample it.

The dish Charpentier had in mind was a version of French pancakes, made with one egg and much flour, precooked in the kitchen, and then recooked in a chafing dish at tableside with thin strips of lemon and orange peel in a sugar syrup to which a selection of cordials were added at the last minute.

According to Charpentier, the unexpected happened. The cordials caught fire!

He thought the dish was ruined and that he would have to begin again. When the flames burned off, he tasted it. It was, he said, the most delicious melody of sweet flavors he'd ever tasted. The accidental flaming, instead of ruining the sauce, had brought all the flavors into harmony. Submerging the folded pancakes into the boiling sauce, he turned them and added two more ponies of a previously prepared blend of equal parts of maraschino, curaçao, and kirschwasser, which again burst into flame.

To make crepes princesse (alias crepes Suzette), according to De Gouy, one must "pour into it a mixture of two ponies of maraschino, curacao, and kirschwasser. These will catch fire." Sound familiar?

The prince ate the pancakes with a fork, but used a spoon to capture the remaining syrup. When asked the name of the dish, Charpentier said it was "crepes princesse." The prince noting the presence of a young lady at his table—supposedly the little daughter of one of his companions —asked, "Will you change the name from crepes princesse to crepes Suzette?" Charpentier agreed, and so testified in his book.

Another country heard from: According to the *Larousse Gastronomique*, new American edition, Leon Daudet in *Paris Vecu* (1929) speaks of pancakes called Suzette made in 1898 with jam and brandy, which were one of the specialties of Marie's Restaurant along with *oeufs Toupinel* and *entrecote bordelaise*.

Thus the story stood until Charpentier's death in 1961. Then brave naysayers came forward to question not only Charpentier's veracity but his expertise in the kitchen. They laughed at the thought that a fifteen-year-old assistant waiter had access to, much less conversation with, a prince. That the *maitre d'hotel* would have allowed this callow youth near the person of the prince with his chafing dish. That the *chef de cuisine* would have even allowed the lad into or out of his kitchen.

Version Two comes from Joseph Donon—one of the last private chefs in America—who wrote in *France-American* that, among others, the crepes were invented by another chef, Monsieur Joseph, for a German actress, Suzanne "Suzette" Reichenburg.

According to Donon, Monsieur Joseph first made the crepes in 1889 while working at the restaurant Paillard, at the rue de la Chaussee-d'Antin and the boulevard des Italiens. At this time, they were spread with an orange-sugar-butter sauce and remained nameless. When Monsieur Joseph opened his own restaurant, the Marivaux, he continued to make the crepes. Then, in 1897, a play opened at the Comedie Francaise, in which a character, a maid called Suzette, was to serve the principals some pancakes. It was arranged that these would be supplied, nightly, by Monsieur Joseph from his restaurant. So that the kitchen staff would know for whom the pancakes were intended, they were called simply the pancakes for Suzette or crepes Suzette. For the sake of the actors—eating cold pancakes is not particularly to be relished—just before rushing them across to the theater and on stage, Monsieur Joseph dipped them into a sizzling mixture of butter, sugar, and orange juice. "No multi-colored liqueurs in it, nothing but orange juice," concurs Andre L. Simon, the noted cookbook author. And, therefore, no alcohol and thus no flames. In which case, are these pancakes crepes Suzette or an entirely different dish with the same name?

We call as our next witness Louis P. De Gouy, a contemporary of, but five years senior to, Charpentier. De Gouy had worked at the Hotel de Paris in Monte Carlo, but as a chef; later, he had worked, as had Charpentier, at the Waldorf-Astoria here in America. He disagrees with all previous accounts and puts forth Version Three. He maintains crepes Suzette originally appeared in a cookbook published in 1674, title unknown, and compiled by "L.S.R." According to De Gouy, Jean Reboux is credited with creating the crepes, which were served with afternoon tea to Louis XV and fellow huntsmen in the forest of Fontainebleau by order of Princesse (Suzette) de Carignan, who was infatuated with the king. Was she, then, the source of both of Charpentier's names: first crepes princesse and then crepes Suzette?

Version Four is presented by still another authority, Robert Courtine, alias Savarin, who states that all these previous authorities are incorrect in that they specify using the essence of an orange captured on a sugar cube. Courtine says the true crepes Suzette were made with tangerines. Alas, tangerines, also known as mandarin oranges, were not introduced from China until the nineteenth century, so they could not have been used for crepes princesse. Further, the tangerine yields much less oil than any other orange, changing the recipe dramatically. Let us strike Monsieur Courtine's comments from the record.

And so one asks the question? In crepes Suzette, as we know them—delicate crepes served flambéed in an orange-flavored sauce—do we have one dish with two names or two dishes with the same name? Or even several different dishes with the same name? Our curiosity is tickled by the intriguing characters of these twisting tales, much as our taste buds are tickled by this liqueur-lavished, spectacularly flambéed delight.

# Crepes Suzette

*B*asically, this is the recipe the Prince of Wales liked so much. It not only eventually brought Charpentier fame but also and more immediately—like the following day, he said—brought the gift of a jeweled ring, a panama hat, and a cane from the prince.

## *Crepes*

2 eggs
2 tablespoons flour
3 tablespoons half and half
⅛ teaspoon salt
1–2 tablespoons butter, divided

Stir ingredients together until smooth and the consistency of heavy cream (it should be thinner than most pancake batters). Heat a crepe pan or small round-bottomed frying pan on medium-high heat; put in 1 teaspoon of butter. When the butter begins to bubble, pour in and swirl just enough batter to cover the bottom of the pan. When the

~~~~~~~~~~~~~~~~~~~~~~~~~~~~~~~~~~~~~~~~~~~~~~~~~~~~~~~~~~~~~~~~~~~~~~~~

batter begins to bubble up (approximately 1 minute) turn the pancake over. Continue sauteing until very lightly browned. It should be slightly underdone, since it will cook again in the sauce. Fold the circle in half and then in half again. Remove from pan and keep warm. Add butter to pan as necessary and continue making crepes until you have eight triangles.

## Sauce

peel and juice of 2 oranges
peel and juice of 1 lemon
¼ cup granulated sugar
1 teaspoon pure vanilla
4 tablespoons (½ stick) butter
¼ cup rum (light)
¼ cup white Curaçao
1 tablespoon maraschino
¼ cup kirschwasser

Remove the bitter white pith from the peel and julienne the peel. Mix with the sugar and vanilla and place in the top of a chafing dish. Add the strained citrus juices and butter. Let it come to a boil and then add the rum and liqueurs. When it returns to a boil, add the crepes. Flame and serve immediately, being sparing with the sauce. Any leftover sauce can be used over ice cream, puddings, or dessert omelets. Sauce will keep for months in the refrigerator without spoiling. In fact, in the words of Charpentier himself, "like good wine, it will improve with age." Serves 4.

Note: The original recipe called for an unspecified quantity of vanilla sugar because, according to Charpentier, "vanilla sugar is one of the requisites for a fine cuisine. Put three or four [whole] vanilla beans into a quart jar of granulated sugar. After several days [may take a month depending on quality of vanilla beans] the sugar will be delicately flavored by the vanilla in the beans." If you'd like to try the vanilla sugar version of the sauce, simply replace plain sugar with vanilla sugar and omit the teaspoonful of pure vanilla.

# T is for Thanksgiving

Once upon a time in the days before tin cans and frozen foods—and that wasn't so long ago—people's fear of winter's deprivations was all-consuming. Thus they welcomed spring with fertility rites and celebrated the bounties of the harvest with autumn feasts and festivals.

Most harvest feasts were folk festivals in which men and women celebrated the surcease of their labors and the success of their efforts. The English Harvest Home festival, for example, was also known as the Kern, Mell, or Horkey Supper and took place when the last load of the harvest was brought in. The farmer and his wife provided a hearty harvest supper for the reapers. As a rule, the meal was served in the barn, which had been specially decorated with garlands and branches, and the fruits of the summer's labor were shared by all. Said fruits, meat-wise, were usually of animals slaughtered in the fall for laying away for the winter, especially the pig, of whom it is rightly said all parts are useful except the squeal.

Not everyone had a pig to slaughter, however, so "the poor man's pig"—the goose—was often served instead. The goose is treasured because it eats anything, matures in about six months, lives anywhere, and reproduces prodigiously in the barnyard. Besides, like the pig, every part of it can be used—except the honk.

To this day, it is the goose that is traditionally served at such thanksgiving feasts in England as Michaelmas on September 29, when geese are plentiful and beautifully fattened. For England's Martinmas on November 11 and France's Feast of St. Martin, a goose is a must. According to legend St. Martin was so annoyed by a goose, he ordered it killed and served for his dinner. Henceforth on his feast day a goose was sacrificed in his honor.

The domestic goose would have been the bird of choice at the Pilgrims' thanksgiving festival in Massachusetts in November of 1621, the anniversary of their arrival on Martinmas the year before. Fortunately, wild geese were migrating through the region. These and other game birds, and venison, of course, made up the body of the feast proclaimed by Governor William Bradford to commemorate the survival of the colony through its first difficult year. Of the original 102

Autumnal harvest rites sometimes took bizarre twists to ensure fertility the following year. In Prussia, for instance, the last sheaf of wheat was called the "bastard;" a boy slipped inside it and the woman who bound it pretended she was in labor. An old woman served as midwife until the "birth" took place and the boy inside the sheaf squalled like a baby.

Some of the English harvest festivals, especially one in Lincolnshire, featured the appearance of the "Old Sow." Two men, disguised in sacking, wore a pig's head stuffed with evergreens, which were used to prick the other revelers. The meal included *frumenty*—a milk pudding made from wheat boiled in milk with raisins and currants and flavored with spices and sugar. In addition to or in place of this dish, there would be a roast and a plum pudding, all served with plenty of beer.

settlers who arrived at Plymouth on November 11, 1620, only 55 were still alive the next spring. In fact, the entire colony might have perished if not for the unwitting help of the Wampanoag Indians, who had stored caches of foods throughout the tribe's territory in case of future need. The settlers stumbled upon one of them. "A heap of sand . . . newly done, we could see how they [the Indians] had paddled it with their hands—which we digged up . . . and found a fine great basket full of fair Indian corn; and digged further, and found a fine great basket of very fair corn of this year, and with some six and thirty goodly ears of corn." Using these stores, the Pilgrims kept a little more than half of the colony alive.

**Michaelmas was one of the "quarter-days" in England—a day on which quarterly rents were due. It is said that tenants frequently gave geese as a good-graces gift to their landlords.**

The Pilgrim's first thanksgiving feast probably lasted several days. Attended by nearly one hundred Wampanoag braves, there were games, displays of arms, and general good will, as in English harvest festivals. The Wampanoags contributed to the feast, and, according to legend, the chief's brother, Quadequina, slipped into the woods at one point in the festivities and returned with a gift of special corn. At first popcorn was known as "parching corn," and "rice corn," and "popped corn." Only after 1820 did it become popcorn.

**Some historians give credit for the first American colonial Thanksgiving feast to the settlers at Jamestown, Virginia, because they celebrated the Harvest Home festival, a traditional English autumnal rite, a few years before the Pilgrims' feast at Plymouth.**

Exactly what was served at this feast is a matter of great dispute among historians. We can assume, however, that since the settlers' fields of Old-World grain had failed, the vegetable staples of the Wampanoag diet were included: corn or maize (from which the tradition of serving cornbread and/or corn pudding is traced), beans, and squash.

It is said (but cannot be verified) that at this feast oysters, eel, corn bread, venison, watercress, leeks, berries, and plums were eaten, all accompanied by sweet wine.

The only written record of the feast and what was served was a letter by Edward Winslow written on December 11, 1621: "Our Governor [William Bradford] sent four men out fowling that we might after a more special manner rejoice together. . . . They four in one day killed as much fowl as, with a little help beside, served the company almost a week." No mention of any turkey. If there had been turkey, it would not have been stuffed and roasted but cooked on a spit. Actually, it took nearly 200 years for the turkey to become well established as the feast's main course. Further, we know that the bird we think of today as a turkey is not our native American bird but a domesticated fowl imported by the colonists to North America from England. (They had originally been imported in the early 1500s to England via Spain from South America.) It was this domesticated European stock that became the ancestors of the modern "bronze turkey" variety that is the basis of the American turkey industry.

**So many people have so many problems with baking their Thanksgiving turkeys that every year the Butterball people provide an 800 hotline to help cooks solve them.**

By the time of the American Revolution, the turkey had become the bird of choice for feasting. Benjamin Franklin went so far as to nominate the turkey as the official United States bird, only to be deeply disappointed when the bald eagle got the nod instead. Writing to his daughter, Sarah Bache, on January 26, 1784, Franklin said, "I wish the bald eagle had not been chosen as the representative of our country. He is a bird of bad moral character; like those among men who live by sharping [swindling] and robbing, he is generally poor, and often very lousy. The turkey is a much more respectable bird and withal a true original native of America."

The next recorded thanksgiving feast in Plymouth Colony was held on July 30, 1623. At this feast pumpkin pie was supposedly served. *Pumpkin*, however, is a variation of *pumpion*, meaning "melon," and dates back to the 1640s not the 1620s. It is more likely that in 1623 it was squash that was made into a dessert. (There are many today who prefer squash pie to pumpkin as being more subtly flavored. Others can't tell the difference because of all the spices.)

Another staple of our modern feasts, the cranberry, was known to the Pequots of Cape Cod as *ibimi*, meaning "bitter berry," and was used to make pemmican, the Indian version of journey cake. The Wampanoags crushed the berries with stones, then combined them with dried venison and fat drippings into little cakes to be carried in their belt pouches as emergency provisions. Although the Indians shared the recipe with the European settlers, it is unlikely that cranberries in any form appeared at the second and midsummer thanksgiving since they are a fall-harvested berry.

When Thanksgiving resumed its place as a fall harvest feast, the settlers might well have incorporated cranberries into their breads or made them into a sauce, like the English piquant chutney usually served with game.

The inclusion of candied sweet potatoes in the Thanksgiving feast is a southern tradition, for the sweet potato was derived from Central America. But the candying of it through the use of maple syrup was a New England touch.

Between 1623 and 1789 many local thanksgivings were held in celebrations of bountiful harvests, an important concern to the nine out of ten Colonists involved in farming. Then, in 1789, President George Washington issued a general proclamation naming November 26 (a Wednesday) a day of national thanksgiving. Why November 26? No one knows. Furthermore, it was a one-shot deal, good for that year only, because Washington was deliberately avoiding setting precedents that would bind his successors.

During the next seventy-four years, presidents occasionally proclaimed a day of thanksgiving to celebrate a specific event, such as the end of the War of 1812, but the creation of an official national holiday had to wait until President Lincoln proclaimed it in 1863. It was the work of Sarah Josepha Hale, author of "Mary Had a Little Lamb" and editor of *Godey's Lady's Book*, an influential Philadelphia-based national magazine. She nearly single-handedly lobbied the government to make November 26 a permanent day of celebration.

The woman was relentless. No politician, no state representative, no president was safe from her efforts. She envisioned the holiday as a patriotic occasion as well as a day of personal thanksgiving by family and friends. She wrote letters to senators, representatives, and governors; she even petitioned the president. What finally did the trick was devoting the November 1862 issue of her magazine to the subject. At that point readers began writing to Washington, D.C. Finally, almost a year later, on October 3, 1863, Lincoln declared the last Thursday in November, which just happened to be November 26, a national holiday.

From then until 1939, every president, every year, proclaimed the fourth Thursday in November a day of celebration.

**The first big Thanksgiving Day Parade was held in Philadelphia in 1921, sponsored by Gimbels department store.**

Then, in 1939 and again in 1940 and 1941, President Franklin Delano Roosevelt, in an attempt to lengthen the Christmas selling season, moved Thanksgiving Day up a week. In December 1941, Congress passed a resolution moving the observation back to the original fourth Thursday in November and making it, by law, not presidential decree, a national day of celebration.

Even if turkey were not served at the Pilgrim's first thanksgiving feast in 1621, Americans have certainly made up for the lack in recent years. Nearly 250 million turkeys are produced annually in the United States, one for every man, woman, and child in the country. In 1990 each of us ate the equivalent of a sixteen-pound turkey. Sixty years ago we ate less than a pound and a half, total, in a year. Which all goes to show how centuries-old tradition can turn into a multimillion-dollar industry.

# Roast Turkey

*Only because we cook a turkey so infrequently and always in front of an expectant audience, do we run into such problems that every year at Thanksgiving time, the Butterball people man a toll-free hotline (the number changes from year to year) to help people solve their turkey problems. Here are some tips just in case you can't get through to them.*

1. What do you do if the turkey doesn't fit the pan . . . or worse, the oven? The only solution: Do the turkey in segments. In which case, start the drumsticks first.

2. Must I check both cavities for innards? Yes. Usually the neck is stuffed inside the breast while the heart, liver, and kidneys are in a bag in the abdominal cavity. If you wish to make giblet gravy, don't use the turkey liver, as it's bitter.

3. How do you keep the wing points from burning? Cut them off before roasting or cover them with foil.

4. Isn't there an easier way to make stuffing besides chopping and frying the onions, the celery, and the bread? Absolutely. Forget the frying. Use roughly chopped plain bread or packaged croutons. Add the seasoning of your choice—usually sage—to some melted butter or broth, pour it over the dry ingredients, mix well, then stuff away just before you start roasting the turkey.

5. How does one truss the opening between the legs to keep the stuffing from coming out? Stuff the heel of a loaf of bread in the opening, and forget pins and twine and interlacings.

6. The charts say to bake it for X number of hours, so how come the pop-up gizmo hasn't popped up? Pop-up gizmos don't always work, so don't rely on them. When the turkey is done, an instant, microwave thermometer inserted in the upper thigh area should register 170–175° F and the juices should flow clear from the spot where the thermometer punctures the skin.

7. How can one keep the breast from overcooking, overbrowning, and tasting dried out? Option #1: Baste it with broth every 15 to 20 minutes throughout its cooking. Option #2: Begin its roasting upside down. Soak a doubled piece of cheesecloth, twice the width of the roasting pan, in oil of any kind—use butter if you can afford it, price-wise or cholesterol-wise. Drape it across your pan on top of the roasting rack. Place the turkey upside down on top of the cheesecloth. This way, through the laws of gravity, the juices will be flowing downward into the breast. Halfway through the cooking, enlist a helper—equipped with oven mitts—to help you grab the cheesecloth and turn the bird over. Finish roasting as per schedule, but baste the bird every twenty minutes or so from now on. If it starts browning too fast, put a tent of aluminum foil over the bird to help keep it from getting too dark.

8. Why should I remove the turkey from the oven before I'm ready to serve it? Won't it get cold? To answer your last question first, not unless you put it in a cold place. Removing it from the oven about twenty minutes before serving allows the meat to stiffen, which makes carving easier. Besides, you can then make your gravy in the roasting pan and save an extra pan to wash.

# Pumpkin Pie

*A*lthough pumpkin pies have long been a staple of New England cooks, who were known to make them by the dozen every fall, once Amelia Simmons published this custardy version in 1796, it quickly became the standard. (If you choose to be even more authentic and make this pie with squash, use much smaller amounts of the spices.)

One quart [of cut-up pumpkin or squash], stewed and strained [put through Foley food mill or grinder, then pressed through sieve], 3 pints cream [light or heavy], 9 beaten [whole] eggs, [brown] sugar [start with ½ cup and continue adding more to taste], mace [most modern cooks would substitute cinnamon], nutmeg, and ginger [normal proportions are 2 cinnamon to 1 nutmeg to ½ ginger or cloves—begin with a tablespoon and continue, to taste, by ½ teaspoons], laid into paste [see apple pie crust recipe but triple it and place it in all three pie plates before proceeding]; and with a dough spur [dough-crimping wheel that looks like the trowel at the end of a cowboy's spur] cross and chequer it [with strips of dough] and baked in dishes three quarters of an hour [at 450° F for ten minutes, then 350° F for 40 minutes or until pumpkin is set in the center.]

# Cranberry Sauce

*Nothing could be simpler than making cranberry sauce, which is just one in a centuries-long line of tart-sweet meat accompaniments. If using fresh cranberries, wash them in a large pot of water, discarding any that don't float.*

**2 cups (1 pint) fresh or frozen whole cranberries**

**1 cup water**

**1 cup sugar**

Place the berries in an enamel or stainless steel pan. Add water and cover. Simmer gently (checking every now and then) until the cranberries have burst. Add sugar and stir until it is dissolved. Simmer approximately 20 minutes without stirring until mixture thickens. Remove from heat and let cool in same pot.

*Variations:* Some cooks like to substitute ⅓ cup orange juice for some of the water. Others, concerned that the mixture won't candy properly, mix the orange juice with 1 tablespoon cornstarch and add it after the mixture has cooked 10 minutes. Then they continue to cook until thickened.

# U is for Upside Down

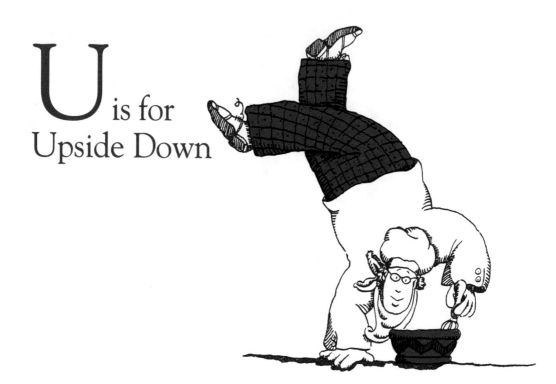

Let's face it—upside down is not the most positive of concepts. In fact, it conjures up images of disaster, such as a slice of bread falling to the floor, jelly side down. One's first thought might be that something turned topsy-turvy can only be an accident, but in food preparation upside down is a legitimate technique, equally as sound as right side up. In fact, some of the most famous dishes in the world start out right side up, only to be presented to the diner upside down.

One such dish that comes quickly to mind is pineapple upside-down cake. Dating back to the 1930s, it is a relative newcomer to the cake scene and, most likely, a case of disaster-turned-success. Pineapple, especially raw pineapple, is so heavy that slices starting out on top are soon enveloped by rising batter and disappear from view. The only way to end up with visible pineapple is to put it on the bottom to begin with, then serve the cake upside down. We don't know who actually invented the cake, but it started a trend—seven upside-down cakes were winners in the first twenty-five years of the Pillsbury Bake-Off® contest.

The most popular winner ever of Pillsbury's contest is the Tunnel of Fudge Cake, which in 1966 won for its creator, Ella Helfrich of Houston, Texas, second prize and $5,000 in the seventeenth Bake-Off. Originally the recipe called for five ingredients and a box of chocolate frosting mix. Mixed together properly, they produced a cake with a moist, fudgelike center—a cake that was served, angel-food style, upside down.

**For an entry blank for the Pillsbury Bake-Off, which is held every other year, write to The Pillsbury Company, 2866 Pillsbury Center, Minneapolis, MN 55402-1464.**

The cake made an overnight success of a twenty-year-old tube-type cake pan that had been brought from Germany to the United States by a Mrs. Abrahms. In the mid-1940s she asked Dave Dalquist, owner of a small Minneapolis foundry, to duplicate her pan so it could be used in fund-raising for the local Hadassah. The pan was so popular that other Hadassahs started ordering it and Dalquist kept it in his line for twenty years. In 1966, with the popularity of the Tunnel of Fudge cake, Pillsbury and Dalquist found themselves with runaway hits on their hands. Later Pillsbury came up with a line of Bundt® cake mixes, each of which sold for 89 cents, and offered, as a premium for $2.00, Dalquist's Bundt® pan. The public responded by ordering 1,152,000 units in ten days. Many cooks refused to wait for their premium to arrive, and housewares departments sold out of the pan overnight.

**Mrs. Abrahms had a heavy German accent and pronounced *bund* (meaning "bundle") as if it ended with a *t*. It took Dalquist more than three years to convince the United States copyright office to register the name.**

Pillsbury and Dalquist's Bundt® cake mixes remained a classic tale of success until well into the seventies. Then prices of ingredients soared, Pillsbury could no longer afford to underwrite the cost of the pan, and the Bundt cake was no longer seen at every bake sale in the land.

Today, one can buy Bundt® pans almost anywhere. It's the cake that's hard to duplicate. The box of chocolate frosting mix specified in the original recipe is no longer available. Pillsbury instead offered a Tunnel of Fudge package mix, but die-hard fans of the cake still wanted to make it the original way. So, Pillsbury was flooded with requests for a from-scratch version. (Recipe follows.)

Another contest winner and upside-down dish is Perfection Salad. Long before Pillsbury started its Bake-Off, Charles Knox was running cooking contests. In 1905, with Fannie Farmer as a judge, the winner of the third-place prize—a $100 sewing machine—was Mrs. John E. Cooke of New Castle, Pennsylvania. Her entry, Perfection Salad, later became a fixture in advertisements for Knox gelatin. To author Laura Shapiro it also was the epitome of the culinary reform movement toward "scientific cookery" of the early 1900s. Shapiro, writing in *Perfection Salad, Women and Cooking at the Turn of the Century* in 1986, says, "Shortly after the turn of the century there emerged a gelatin salad that . . . captured, confined and molded raw vegetables themselves. This was the Perfection Salad, a mixture of cabbage, celery, and red peppers all chopped fine and bound by a plain aspic. . . . [it was] the very image of a salad at last in control of itself."

Although Shapiro does not give the original recipe, she maintains that unlike other salads, such as the Waldorf, the Perfection Salad changed little over the decades. Not so. In a perfect example of how one recipe can multiply like rabbits, the salad has taken on various names and forms. In some versions it is made with tomato juice instead of a clear beef-broth jelly; other versions call for lemon-flavored gelatin. Pimentos are substituted for peppers, cooked beets for the pimentos, raw carrots for the beets. On occasion diced raw peeled cucumbers and/or cooked green peas are added.

Of course, like most molded gelatin salads, Perfection is made to be flipped over, much to many a cook's dismay. Put a molded salad on the menu, and you know eventually there comes that moment of truth when one shall have to take the chilled mold, cover it with a service plate, turn it upside down, and, with a dexterous, well-practiced, downward yank of the hands, spring that salad from its mold. Unfortunately, sometimes it sticks like glue. Of course, that's not as bad as when it falls free in pieces, the remainder staying stubbornly in place. Still, if you get it right, the color it adds to a table makes the nightmare worthwhile.

**To release a molded salad easily, oil or, if it is nongelatin or spicy, butter the mold. If using gelatin wet the mold. You can also line the mold with plastic wrap before you fill it (wrinkles show and will need to be hidden). When ready to flip, loosen the sides of the mold with a knife (using your finger works well with gelatin molds).**

One of the most famous molded—and therefore upside down—dishes is the charlotte, which originally was served hot and made in a heavily buttered mold lined with slices of buttered bread. It was a point of pride to cut the bread to fit the bottom perfectly and in a quiltlike pattern so that when the dish was unmolded and inverted the golden brown topside drew *ooh's* and *aah's* from the guests.

Invented in England by Carême, circa 1800, its name has been gallantly ascribed to Queen Charlotte and Princess Charlotte, mother and daughter, respectively, of George IV (1762–1830). The truth is probably less diplomatically political. According to some historians Carême, who was just learning English and had a thick French accent, said, when asked the name of the dish *schaleth*, the name of a Jewish apple pudding that it greatly resembles.

Carême was also responsible for creating a cold version of the dish, which is now the most famous charlotte of all. Cold charlottes are lined with lady fingers or slices of cake rather than bread and are filled with gelatin-based *Bavarois* or mousses that hold their shapes when turned upside down.

**These days hot charlottes may be desserts of the fruit variety, savory vegetable side dishes, or even entrées made with fish or meat.**

The charlotte Russe began life as charlotte à la Parisienne but was changed by Carême when he served as Czar Alexander I's temporary chef. Culinary histories report that the dish was not what Carême intended. Ordered to prepare a victory celebration of the Czar's final defeat of Napoleon, a reluctant

Carême planned to serve a gelatin-based cold charlotte. Though he was short of gelatin, he made the dish anyway. It collapsed. He packed it in ice and semifroze it. When the guests, unaware of the disaster, raved about the dish, Carême promptly changed its name to charlotte Russe, either as a subtle touch of Gallic contempt for the undiscerning Russians or to reflect a change in serving styles instituted by the Russian ambassador to France. Count Kurakine liked his food to be served as hot or as ice cold as intended by the cook. The French tradition of setting all dishes out at once made a great show but effectively cooled off the hot dishes and warmed up the cold ones. Therefore, Count Kurakine insisted dishes be served in courses, which came to be known as Russian style.

Another upside-down dish is an easier, practically foolproof version of that *crème de la crème* of desserts: *crème brûlée*, mentioned some twenty chapters ago. Forget scorching your *brûlée* by cooking it too long or too close to the flame. Ignore the possibility of an undercooked plain sugar crust instead of a crisp caramel one. With *crème renversée* the caramel goes in the bottom of the individual dishes and the custard on top.

Whether their origins lie in deliberate artistry, like the charlotte, or have arisen out of necessity, like the pineapple upside-down cake, bottom-side up dishes have become such a part of our culinary heritage that no one thinks twice about them. But you should the next time something doesn't come out right; just flip it upside down and smile knowingly when it garners compliments.

# Perfection Salad

*T*his is an updated version of the recipe that began appearing in Knox Sparkling Gelatine advertisements back in the early part of the century.

2 envelopes Knox Unflavored Gelatine
1 cup cold water
1½ cups boiling water
½ cup sugar
½ cup vinegar
2 tablespoons lemon juice
1 teaspoon salt
1½ cups finely shredded cabbage
1½ cups chopped celery
¼ cup chopped green pepper
¼ cup chopped pimientos

In large bowl sprinkle unflavored gelatine over cold water; let stand 1 minute. Add boiling water and stir until gelatine is completely dissolved, about 5 minutes. Stir in sugar, vinegar, lemon juice, and salt. Chill, stirring occasionally, until mixture is consistency of unbeaten egg whites, about 50 minutes. Fold in remaining ingredients. Turn into 6-cup mold or bowl; chill until firm, about 3 hours. To serve, unmold onto serving platter and garnish, if desired, with salad greens. Makes about 6 servings.

# Tunnel of Fudge Cake

## *Cake*

1¾ cups margarine or butter, softened

1¾ cups granulated sugar

6 eggs

2 cups powdered sugar

2¼ cups Pillsbury BEST® All Purpose Flour

¾ cup cocoa

2 cups chopped walnuts*

Heat oven to 350° F. Grease and flour 12-cup fluted tube pan or 10-inch angel food tube pan. In large bowl beat margarine and granulated sugar until light and fluffy. Add eggs, one at a time, beating well after each addition. Gradually add powdered sugar; blend well. By hand, stir in remaining cake ingredients until well blended. Spoon batter into prepared pan; spread evenly. Bake at 350° F for 58 to 62 minutes. Cool upright in pan on cooling rack 1 hour; invert onto serving plate. Cool completely.

## *Glaze*

¾ cup powdered sugar

¼ cup cocoa

1½ to 2 tablespoons milk

In a small bowl combine glaze ingredients until well blended. Spoon over top of cake, allowing some to run down sides. Store tightly covered. Serves 16.

*Nuts are essential for the success of the recipe.

# V
## is for Vinegar

V is also for Versatile and Valuable and Various—all of which describe vinegar to a V. A ripe 10,000 years old (give or take a century or two), vinegar is the world's first manufactured condiment. Though other condiments followed, only vinegar heightens other flavors, stimulates the appetite, aids digestion, and acts as a preservative (as in pickling).

To be honest, humans can't take total credit for creating vinegar. As everyone knows who has had a bottle of wine go bad, vinegar occurs naturally whenever wild yeast cells have access to wine. In fact, it is from the French *vin aigre*, or sour wine (either red or white) that the word *vinegar* derives. Vinegar is simply the natural end product of the fermentation process of wine. Or beer, for that matter.

**The French call the fungus growth that appears in opened, half-used wine bottles** *la mere ∂e vinaigre,* **or mother of vinegar.**

Probably the oldest vinegar came from fermented malt; it is still in use by the English on their fish and chips.

Today, cooks can choose from a full shelf of vinegars: fruit vinegars, such as the everyday apple-cider variety, as well as raspberry and plum; *vinaigres nouveau*, which include balsamic, rosemary, garlic, thyme, and tarragon varieties; and even walnut vinegar. These are just a few of the vinegars that bring tang to our kitchens.

All vinegars are made essentially the same way. Natural sugars ferment first to alcohol and then, with the help of bacteria, turn to vinegar. All commercial vinegars have a minimum 4 percent acidity. Some manufacturers express this in grains by multiplying the percentage by ten; thus labels say 40-grain vinegar. The stronger the acidity the better, or more accurately, the quicker for pickling and marinating. Many people, however, find such acidity unpleasant. Though very few cooks taste their vinegar straight, they are surprisingly selective in their choice of vinegar. Some prefer their vinegars simple, not much more than a wine gone slightly sour, others demand a full, herb-strong variety.

What are the characteristics of a good vinegar? It should be clear and transparent, colorless if made from white wine, pinkish if made from red (never as red as the parent red wine). The taste must be frankly acid; the aroma reminiscent of the wine from which it came. An apple-cider vinegar should be lighter colored than cider but have at least a hint of apple fragrance.

**Through the centuries vinegar has been produced from many food products, including molasses, sorghum, fruits, berries, melons, coconut, honey, beer, maple syrup, potatoes, beets, malts, grains, and whey. New to the United States is rice wine vinegar, made from the residue of sake, the traditional rice wine of Japan. The residue is the soft pulp that remains after the clear beverage has been drawn off. Preparation of rice vinegar does not differ from that of any other vinegar, and it can be used in any salad dressing calling for vinegar.**

The best-selling vinegar of all, white vinegar, isn't really a vinegar but a distillation of grains into ethyl alcohol. It's very useful for unclogging drains and cleaning up puppy piddles, but to eat it is to miss realizing the properties of a true vinegar.

# V is for Vinegar

Imagine the reaction of the first person to open a flask, or worse, a whole cask of wine, and find a thick, gelatinlike skin on the surface of the brew. Was the first response to throw the whole mess out? Probably, but when it happened again and again, someone must have decided to taste the stuff and make a good thing out of bad, for, by the time of the writing of the Bible, vinegar is mentioned almost as often as wine. In the Book of Ruth, for example, Boaz begins his courtship of Ruth by saying to her, "At mealtime come thou hither and eat of the bread and dip thy morsel in the vinegar." The practice of bread-dipping in vinegar (buttering wasn't known then) had become so common by Roman times that bowls of vinegar were set out as a matter of course on dining tables.

**Most of the energies of ancient brewmasters were devoted to preventing the formation of vinegar. To this end, they floated oil on top of wine to serve as a barrier to yeast. They used beeswax to seal and reseal bottles, and they put their wines and casks deep underground to keep them cool. Best of all, they encouraged their customers to drink the brew while it was still fresh, which their patrons were only too happy to do.**

Up until a couple of centuries ago, meats were frequently served on the spoiled side and required cooking in a sweet and sour mixture of honey and vinegar to disguise the underlying putrid flavor. Just as they often are today, tough cuts and, in particular, dried meats were marinated in spiced and herbed vinegars before they were boiled tender but tasteless. To make them palatable, they were served with a thick goop, such as a yellow sauce made with ginger and saffron, or a variation on our *sauce verte*, loaded with ginger, cloves, cardamom, and green herbs. Most popular of all was *cameline sauce*, which was made of wine-soaked ground bread crumbs flavored with cinnamon and other spices, then diluted with vinegar. It became so omnipresent that chefs were chastised by cooking authorities as taking the easy way out by serving cameline sauce instead of going to the trouble of making a proper sauce such as a pepper-based *poivrade*.

It wasn't until the seventeenth century that Pierre Francois de la Varenne (1618–1678) elevated vinegar to the gourmet level. Disapproving of heavy spices and thick sauce mixtures, he recommended sauces based on meat drippings combined with a mere touch of vinegar, lemon juice (a luxury item at the time), or verjuice (juice of sour grapes or crab apples).

Vinegar did service not only as an ingredient but also as a beverage. The Spartans, for example, were famous for their black vinegar broth, combining pork blood, stock, vinegar, and salt. One sybarite who tasted it announced he'd discovered the secret of the Spartan willingness to fight to the death: Who wouldn't rather die than drink that stuff? On the other hand, the practical, pragmatic Roman legionnaires found it faster and easier to make forced marches when carrying small casks of vinegar to be diluted with local water. There were no complaints in the ranks about the lack of wine; they found vinegar-water invigorating. Nearly two thousand years later, the Victorians felt the same about strawberry vinegar. They diluted it and other fruit vinegars with water as a refreshing drink in the summer and as a tonic during the winter.

The oldest and most common use of vinegar is as a preservative. Without vinegar there would be no relishes and no pickles (sweet, kosher, dill, or any other kind). That's today. Two, three, four hundred years ago, cooks pickled almost everything: vegetables such as peppers, onions, cabbage, beets, beans, and broccoli stalks; fruit, including peaches, pears, apricots, and cherries; and seafood such as oysters, cockles, mussels, pike, flounder, sole, sprats, and eels. Pickled walnuts? Why not? They were even making vinegar pies, taffies, and candies.

And, of course, vinegar was appearing on the table in the form we know it best: as a dressing for a salad. Cookbooks of Queen Elizabeth I's time give recipes for "sallets," "served simply without anything but a little Vinegar, Sallet oyle, and sugar." Even sallets meant for great feasts or the Queen's table were dressed in the same, simple way. Today, the classic French vinaigrette is not much different from the dressing served more than 400 years ago.

By the last half of the eighteenth century, cooks were even pickling salad makings, including various varieties of lettuce. Flowers, such as roses and marigolds, considered to have a medicinal quality, were also pickled.

# *V is for Vinegar*

~~~~~~~~~~~~~~~~~~~~~~~~~~~~~~~~~~~~~~~~~~~~~~~~~~~~~~~~~~~~~~~~~~~~~~~~~~~~

In addition to dressing salads and pickling, vinegar has many other uses in the kitchen. Diluted with an equal amount of water and brushed on bread, vinegar gives a beautiful sheen to the crust. Added straight to egg whites (¼ teaspoon per white), it makes meringues fluffier and more stable. It cuts excess sweetness or saltiness. Most important, it tenderizes tough meat.

Vinegar's medicinal virtues also have been known for centuries. Hippocrates prescribed it in 400 B.C., and the Bible refers to its soothing and healing properties. During the seventeenth and eighteenth centuries, well-bred people protected themselves from the stink of open sewers by breathing through vinegar-soaked sponges kept in little silver boxes called, like the dressing, vinaigrettes. During the American Civil War, large doses of vinegar combatted scurvy. As recently as World War I, physicians cleansed wounds with vinegar. Today it is recommended for the treatment of rashes, bites, and other minor ailments.

Anthropologists estimate vinegar to have been in use for 10,000 years in a thousand ways. The most unusual, bizarre, and fascinating instances are the three dealing, respectively, a general, a queen, and four thieves.

Hannibal, the general, according to a history of Rome written by Livy (59 B.C. to A.D. 17), used vinegar to clear his army's way through the snowy Alps:

> *T*he soldiers were . . . set to work to construct a road across the cliff—their only possible way. Since they had to cut through the rock, they felled some huge trees that grew near at hand, and lopping off their branches, made an enormous pile of logs. This they set on fire, as soon as the wind blew fresh enough to make it burn, and pouring vinegar over the glowing rocks, caused them to crumble. After thus heating the crag with fire, they opened a way in it with iron tools and relieved the steepness of the slope with zigzags of an easy gradient, so that not only the baggage animals but even the elephants could be led down.

Even in Livy's time, this tale was considered fable, mostly by those who assumed, erroneously, that the vinegar was used to dissolve rocks or melt snow and make the way less slippery. Geologists are not so quick to laugh, knowing that heating the stones and pouring liquid on them would cause cleavage by the expansion of the liquid when it came in contact with the heat in the fissures of the rock. Those who argued for the accuracy of the account, however, were rebuked with the sheer impracticality of hauling vinegar to the summit, especially when there were tons of snow to melt into liquid. Christopher Wren, Bishop of Windsor and father of the great architect of the same name, disagreed. He thought Hannibal could have achieved his goal with but a few hogsheads of vinegar. He compared Hannibal's feat to the process of making flint, in which stone is burnt, then quenched in a small quantity of vinegar, causing the stone to cleave asunder. It would seem, then, that vinegar indeed played a role in Hannibal's amazing march.

An Egyptian queen stars in another vinegar tale. According to *Natural History* by Pliny the Elder, Cleopatra used a pearl to win a wager with Mark Antony that she could spend ten million sesterces (about 9 million dollars) on a single banquet. As an army of slaves brought the food into the banquet room, Cleopatra was handed a gold goblet of vinegar. Toying with her earrings, she removed one of a matched pair of the largest pearls in the world. Daintily, according to accounts, she dropped the pearl into the vessel of vinegar, swirled it about, watching the pearl dissolve, then drank to Antony's health. Plancus, chosen to judge the proceedings, immediately pronounced the queen winner of the wager and convinced her not to dissolve the second pearl earring.

Pure food-fiction, some historians claim, and yet . . . pearls are carbonates, consisting of 91.7 percent calcium carbonate, 6 percent organic matter, and 2.3 percent water. As such they should dissolve in vinegar containing 6 or 7 percent acetic acid. Of course, because of their great hardness, pearls, especially large ones, would dissolve in such vinegar very slowly. An average-size pearl would take at least three to four hours to dissolve in very strong vinegar. Therefore, if Pliny's account is correct, the Egyptian queen either waited a very long time for the pearl to dissolve or she used vinegar of such great strength she could not have drunk it without serious injury. Perhaps, instead of dropping it daintily in the goblet, she pulverized it first; then the pearl would readily dissolve and even effervesce mildly. In fact, in Pliny's account he does say that the Egyptian queen prepared the most expensive carbonated drink in history.

Now allow me to introduce you to four thieves who lived in the seventeenth century. Four nameless French men with no redeeming qualities, they preyed on rich and poor alike. Fortunately for them, when they were caught, Marseilles was in the grip of the influenza plague.

Instead of losing their hands (the normal sentence for thievery) or receiving a life sentence to prison, the four criminals were sentenced to bury plague-victims. Surprisingly, the thieves did not contract the deadly disease that ravaged the city. The explanation? They drank a curative-preventative made from a mixture of garlic and wine vinegar. The story is merely legend—there is no certainty that the vinegar made the difference or even that there actually *were* four thieves—but for hundreds of years "Four Thieves vinegar" has been touted as the most potent of remedies, capable of curing most anything, including influenza.

**Use vinegar to cut grease, remove soap film, polish stainless steel, unclog drains, relieve itches, wash windows streak-free, rinse hair without bleaching, soften fabrics, and more. Many environment-friendly guides provide enough ideas to put vinegar on your grocery list on a regular basis.**

Miracle cure or not, vinegar is unlikely to soon disappear from the pantry shelf, either as food, medicine, or preservative. In fact, publicity for its myriad uses has increased in recent years as environmentalists tout it as a natural, versatile, and economical household helper. Rescued from its centuries-ago reputation as a wine-barrel nuisance, vinegar wins high honors in culinary history.

# Vinaigrette

Dissolve salt in one part vinegar to three parts of oil—for example, ½ teaspoon salt, ¼ cup vinegar, and ¾ cup oil. Then add seasonings to taste: freshly ground pepper and/or any herbs, ½ teaspoon dry or 1 tablespoon prepared mustard, and a clove of minced garlic or 1 tablespoon garlic juice. Shake in a jar or stir vigorously until an emulsion forms.

# Marinade

(For a quick marinade, use any bottled or packaged salad dressing.) Beginning with the vinaigrette recipe, increase the salt to 1 teaspoon, the vinegar to ⅓ cup, and the oil to 1 cup. Add seasonings. You can also add a classic *mirepoix* consisting of a chopped medium onion, a chopped large carrot, and a chopped large celery rib including leaves. Unless a marinade is made with a protein-digesting enzyme such as papain, it treats only the outside of the meat. Therefore, the tougher the meat, the smaller the pieces into which it should be cut and the longer it should marinate. If all of the meat is covered with marinade, do it the night before and refrigerate overnight. Otherwise, do it in the morning and let sit on the counter for several hours, turning the cubes at hourly intervals.

When you remove the meat from the marinade, reserve the *mirepoix* and brown it in a small amount of oil, then add to the meat. You can also dilute the marinade liquid with water to use as a braising liquid. After the meat has cooked to fork-tender, strain out the vegetables and process in a food processor, then add to the cooking liquid to give you a lovely, brown, vegetable-based gravy.

# W
## is for Writers

In search of verisimilitude, many writers of fiction describe the meals and eating habits of their characters—so many, in fact, that books have been written about books that showcase food, even if only in bits and pieces. To my knowledge, however, only one author has ever named a book for a dish. The author was Owen Wister (1860–1938). Who? Well, at the turn of the twentieth century, he was the country's combination Louis L'Amour and Danielle Steel.

A sickly boy and a sickly man, Wister went West for his health, and from his experiences there came a novel in 1902. It was the first modern western, with its hero the forerunner of Gary Cooper and John Wayne—a quiet man's man, larger than life, and untouched by lust. *The Virginian: A Horseman of the Plains* was a best-seller. Made into a play, it ran for four months in New York and went on the road for more than a decade. Eventually, it was made not once nor twice but four times into a movie, and finally, into a television series. The country's seemingly insatiable appetite for *The Virginian* led Wister's publishers to press for a second novel.

That next book, a romance, was called *Lady Baltimore,* and despite articles and rumors to the contrary, it had nothing whatsoever to do with the real Lord and Lady Baltimore of Maryland's Calvert family. It had to do, as you guessed, with Lady Baltimore the *cake,* and it was so titled because, as Wister said, "The cake had begun it, the cake had continued it, the cake had brought them together. . . ."

The Lady Baltimore in question was of a type well known in the South: a Lady Cake. Recipes for these date back to the early 1800s; one version, identical to the Lady Baltimore in everything but leavening, was brought to the White House in 1829 by President Andrew Jackson.

In the 1800s cakes had begun to take their names from the person to whom you'd serve it. Expensiveness of the ingredients had much to do with the ranking of a cake. Thus a king's or Imperial cake called for expensive fruits, nuts, and spices and was the most time-consuming to make. One step down was Queen Cake, which not only called for a pound of butter and ten eggs but a wineglass of wine and brandy, rose-water, mace, cinnamon, and nutmeg. Next lower on the list was Lady Cake, also a butter cake and of the pound cake family.

Within this group were Lady Cakes Tennessee–style and North Carolina–style, etc. The names were a necessity since without them one couldn't tell what was beneath the icing. In the case of Lady Baltimore (or Lady Cake, Baltimore-style), it was the candylike cooked filling made with walnuts that made it distinctive. (Baltimore, at the time, had made itself a reputation for its candy-making; you will recall it was the birthplace of fudge.)

Over the years, however, Charlestonians contracted the cake's name in a

**Unlike many cookbook authors, Wister in his novel always refers accurately to the cake as simply Lady Baltimore, never Lady Baltimore cake. (The latter would have been redundant since the "cake" was understood, as is camera in Polaroid, tissue in Kleenex, and margarine in Oleo.)**

gourmet ellipsis from Lady Cake Baltimore–style to the more simple Lady Baltimore.

Back to Wister. *Lady Baltimore* was published in April of 1906 and became an instant hit. Eliza, the heroine, noble but poor, rolls up her sleeves and works hard in the Women's Exchange; there she serves the narrator slices of Lady Baltimore and wins the heart of the hero despite the maneuvers of a sophisticated gold digger. A feminine Horatio Alger, young Eliza.

**Southerners speak knowingly of a real Eliza. She was, they say, Alicia Rhett Mayberry, citing as proof her contribution of the original Lady Baltimore recipe to the Charleston cookbook. The question is, *which* Alicia Rhett Mayberry, for there were two. The first was a Mrs. Ed F. Mayberry, born in June 1873, and the mother of a daughter, also Alicia Rhett Mayberry, who was two years old in 1898 when Wister first visited Charleston and six years old when he returned to write his book. It was the younger Alicia who supplied the original recipe to the cookbook, but nowhere does she say it was her mother's. Nor does Blanche Rhett, her relative and editor of the cookbook, stake any familiar claim to the recipe.**

The public believed *Lady Baltimore* provided the true inside dope on Southern society, and that the story was a true-life version of Cinderella marrying the prince—in this case, Lord Baltimore. Wister slyly encouraged the public's perception, first, by describing and having illustrations done of genuine Charleston landmarks (even though the novel's locus was the fictitious Kings Port), and second, by refusing to deny that there was a real Eliza. He only smiled enigmatically on his way to the bank.

Smart move—Owen Wister had reaped enormous publicity from his refusal to name the living prototype of the Virginian, and the trick worked again with *Lady Baltimore*. The *Gone with the Wind* of its day, within two months it was the most popular book in the land and, shame of all shames, in the following months vied with *The Jungle* by Upton Sinclair for literary awards. The excellent writer Sinclair won the prizes; the natural publicist Wister earned the royalties—$11,250 the first year.

Whatever else it did, the book made the cake famous. In Charleston the "Owen

Wister Lady Baltimore" became a thriving industry. Each year at Christmastime, hundreds of tall, round, fragile cakes were sent from Charleston to all parts of the country. Indeed, several Charleston ladies made an excellent living baking these famous cakes. In Boston the Lady's Exchange had so many orders for the Owen Wister Lady Baltimore that they could not fill them. The Okemo Cake Kitchen Company in Newton Center, Massachusetts, added three cakes to its price list: the Lady Baltimore, the Round Owen Wister, and the Square Owen Wister.

Even Wister found himself overwhelmed by the cake. On his last visit to Charleston, he had to clamber over piles of boxes blocking his hotel corridor—boxes containing Lady Baltimores. Of course, in a way, he asked for it, considering how he ended his book:

> And so my portrait of Kings Port is finished . . . and if Miss Josephine St. Michael [spinster aunt who raised the hero] should be pleased with any of it, I could wish that she might indicate this by sending me a Lady Baltimore; we have no cake here that approaches it."

What is strange is that little is said about the cake in the book to prompt such excitement. Only twice does Wister even hint at a description, and thus cooks and pastry chefs have been granted complete freedom to do with this cake as they would. In *Two Hundred Years of Charleston Cooking*, three recipes for Lady Baltimore are given, one of which is identified as the original. It is also the only one of the three to fit the meager description Wister gave us: It is a soft layer cake containing nuts and a candylike filling and frosting; it easily doubles or triples for use as a wedding cake; and it can be made the day before the wedding. Most important of all, it stays amazingly fresh and moist for a long time. Oh, one detail more: it is, as Owen Wister wrote, delightfully, surprisingly delicious. It is easy to understand when one tastes it why Americans would demand more of this mouth-watering wonder. Today, the novel languishes in libraries, but the cake—by word of mouth—continues!

Lady Baltimore was a large cake that begat an insignificant book. A magnum opus, on the other hand, began with a small cake, a tea cake, a *madeleine*—correction, a crumb of that cake. When Proust dunked a madeleine in a cup of lime tea, the taste of a lime-tea–saturated crumb triggered his memory and prompted him to write his semi–autobiographical *A la recherche du temps perdu. Remembrance of Things Past* eventually grew into a book in seven parts published in sixteen volumes. One hates to speculate on what an entire bite might have prompted and shudders at the literary consequences of his devouring the whole thing. I venture a guess that more cooks have actually made madeleines—delicate butter cakes baked in special scallop-shaped pans—than have tasted lime tea or read any one of these seven volumes.

**Some time, somewhere, some clever pastry chef decided the Lady Baltimore deserved a male counterpart. He justified it by claiming that the Lord Baltimore utilized the yolks of the eggs left over from making Lady Baltimore. The only trouble is, there usually weren't any yolks. Most Lady cakes, and all three of the Charleston Lady Baltimores, called for whole eggs. Still, so logical seemed the concept of a Lord Baltimore that even James Beard, one of the most accurate of food writers, endorsed the heresy in 1972 in *James Beard's American Cookery*.**

The second most famous Madeleine in the world must be a little girl who lived in a Paris hotel and whose tale was told in a book of the same name in 1939 by Ludwig Bemelmans (1862–1962). Besides writing *Madeleine* and more than half a dozen adult novels, he is most lionized and anthologized for a piece he wrote in 1937 entitled "The Elephant Cutlet."

The posthumous editors of Ludwig Bemelmans work, *La Bonne Table*, assigned "The Elephant Cutlet" to the section called Fancies, or fiction. The story, however, was actually based on fact, with one exception: The heroine in the story is a distinguished lady, a countess. In real life there were two protagonists, Ludwig Bemelmans and the equally noted food writer, Roy Andries de Groot.

It seems that one day in pre-World War II Vienna, Bemelmans found a restaurant with a name so obviously dishonest that it made him seethe. It was called Chops from Every Animal in the World.

He called the restaurant and made dinner reservations for himself and his friend, de Groot—and used their real names. The call threw the restaurateur into a panic. He told the chef, who then called the owner at his home, who hurriedly threw on his dinner jacket and headed for the restaurant, arriving just as the famous guests did. He greeted them in the lobby with a deep bow. Bemelmans was seething even more, having just seen again the five-foot-high floodlighted letters in the restaurant's sign across the front of the building.

The respected diners were seated at the best table. As the owner approached with menus, Bemelmans waved him away, saying they already had made up their minds and would each have an elephant chop. The owner blanched but, steeling himself, asked how they would like the chops prepared. Bemelmans is reported to have asked for them sautéed, rare, in butter, à la Milanaise, served with a covering of risotto and topped with crossed anchovy fillets and a black olive in the middle of the cross.

The owner bowed his way out of the dining room and ran into the kitchen. Meanwhile, the two diners sipped their aperitifs and chuckled at the thought of the owner feuding with the chef, the commotion, the hand-wringing, the blaming.

Shortly the chef himself approached their table, bowed, and asked if they had ordered elephant chops. Hearing their reply in the affirmative, he asked if ladies would be joining them for dinner, to which they replied no. The chef then asked if they wished just one elephant chop apiece, and the answer was yes.

**Food is the universal language of all writing. It serves as simile (brown as toast, milk-white, pea-green); metaphor (the world is his oyster; he ate humble pie); and maxim (take the fat with the lean; an apple a day keeps the doctor away).**

At this point, Bemelmans lost his cool and asked in a loud voice why they were being subjected to such impudent questions. Whereupon the chef drew himself up to his full height and said, "I am sorry, monsieur. For only two chops we will not cut up our elephant."

Did they settle for less exotic chops and enjoy their meal? Did they stomp out in mock anger? Or did they laugh and applaud the chef's savoir faire? De Groot in his account of the adventure never says, and neither did Bemelmans in his short story.

William Shakespeare's food-inspired metaphors speak such basic truth that for nearly four centuries they have been quoted so frequently as to be part of our cultural lexicon. Queen Elizabeth II, addressing the British Parliament, received a roar of approval when she said, " 'In our salad days when we were green in judgment. . . .' " (Cleopatra, *Antony and Cleopatra* I,v, 73). These, too, are all Shakespeare's: He has eaten me out of house and home. A dish fit for the gods. Unquiet meals make ill digestions. The ripest fruit first falls. Falser than vows made in wine.

Whether memory-nudger or enigmatic title, food often provides inspiration for authors. Its role can range from an entire plot, as in the invisible meal served to test a man in *The Arabian Nights*, to a simple device, such as the leg of lamb that serves as a murder weapon in an O. Henry short story, or the bombe (frozen dessert), ticking away bomblike, in the movie and book *Who's Killing the Great Chefs of Europe?*

In most fiction, especially contemporary works, however, food serves simply to enhance the realism of the setting. Unfortunately, most writers fail to dish out prose that makes your mouth water. Instead, they serve up a list of dishes like a blackboard menu and ask your imagination to do the rest. Of course, our imaginations are well equipped for this task, but the description of food is a criterion by which readers can separate the merely competent or decidedly incompetent from the truly gifted.

# The Original Lady Baltimore

*T*he second of three recipes for such a cake, this is the one contributed by Alicia Rhett Mayberry to 200 Years of Charleston Cooking (Random House, 1930). "It was this recipe which was used at the Woman's Exchange when Owen Wister wrote Lady Baltimore." Although salt was called for in the original recipe, it was left out of the directions. It's use may be optional. If you decide to add it, put it in with the flour.

½ cup butter [at room temperature]

1½ cups [granulated] sugar

2 eggs [at room temperature], separated

1 cup [whole] milk

2 cups [cake] flour

1 teaspoon baking powder

½ teaspoon salt

Cream the butter and sugar, add the beaten egg yolks and beat well. Mix and sift the flour and baking powder twice, then sift slowly into the first mixture, adding the milk gradually. Fold in the beaten egg whites last of all. Bake in three well-buttered [and floured, with bottoms lined with wax paper] layer cake pans [8-inch] in a moderately hot oven (375°F) for about 25 minutes.

When the layers are baked, pour the soft filling given below on each layer before you put on the hard filling. It is this filling with the indefinite flavor that makes this cake so distinctive.

## Lady Baltimore Soft Filling

1 cup [granulated] sugar

1 cup walnut meats [coarsely chopped]

¼ cup water

1 teaspoon vanilla

1 teaspoon almond extract

Put the sugar, walnut meats and water into a saucepan and cook to the very soft ball stage [230–234°F. In ice water, the mixture will form a ball that softens immediately upon removal from the water.] Remove from the heat and let cool until lukewarm (110°F). Add the flavorings and beat until slightly thickened before pouring on cake.

## Lady Baltimore Hard Filling

2 cups sugar

½ cup water

2 egg whites

1 teaspoon vanilla

1 teaspoon almond extract

juice of ½ lemon

1 cup chopped raisins

1 cup chopped walnuts

Bring the sugar and water to the boiling point and cook until it will form a firm ball [244–248°F]. Pour slowly over the stiffly beaten egg whites, beating constantly, and continue beating until cool, adding the raisins, nuts, flavoring, and lemon juice as it begins to harden. [Spread quickly.]

# Madeleines

*To duplicate Proust's memory-jogging experience, serve lime sherbet with these madeleines—a no-fail recipe that is best made on a cool, not-too-humid day. You will need two large-size (12 per) madeleine pans.*

2 eggs

1 cup granulated sugar

1 cup cake flour, sifted

¾ cup (6 ounces or 1½ sticks) butter, melted and cooled

1 teaspoon rum or pure vanilla extract

powdered sugar

Preheat oven to 450° F. Place eggs and sugar in top of double boiler and cook until lukewarm. Beat until fluffy and set aside to cool. Add cake flour to egg mixture and incorporate melted butter. Add flavoring. Fill madeleine pans two-thirds full with batter. Bake for about 8 minutes or until edges are just brown. This is important because they should not get overbaked as you want them moist inside. Cool and remove from pan and place on wax paper. Dust both sides with powdered sugar.

# X

## is for Xavier

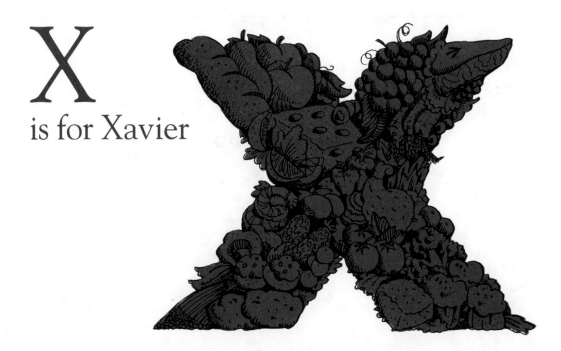

I t's a terrible letter, the X. So few words begin with it that compilers of food dictionaries must come to an exasperating halt to begin an extensive search for an exemplary X-word. In other words, there are simply not enough words, particularly pertaining to food, beginning with the letter X.

Some, such as Craig Claiborne, Len Deighton, and Simon Howe, to name just a few, explore no further. Feeling they have exhausted all possibilities and needing no other excuse, they exhibit great savoir faire and skip X completely.

But there is one exception. One exultant soul in need of a recipe beginning with X came up with exactly one example: Xavier soup. And therein lies its creation story. Until now it was exhibited in exactly one food dictionary; now it is in two. And my guess is it will soon find its way into many more. Especially since Xavier soup not only solves the X problem but is an extraordinarily delicious soup, bearing a striking resemblance to *Hwa Ton*, or egg drop soup.

# Xavier Soup

Thicken chicken broth with cornstarch (1 tablespoon of cornstarch to 2 cups of broth). Take one beaten egg per 2 cups of soup and pour through a strainer into the gently boiling soup while stirring vigorously. (This keeps the eggs in shreds.) Add diced ham or scallions for garnish and extra color.

# Y
## is for Yorkshire Pudding

Taking its name from the county in England, Yorkshire Pudding dates back to at least the seventeenth century and is a pudding in the sense of being an "open-faced pie." Originally the batter, very like a pancake batter, was put in a pan directly under the roast of beef turning on its spit. The bottom would cook up solid, like a crust, while above would be a filling of delicious beef cooking juices. Today the procedure is reversed. The juices are collected first and put in the bottom of the pan with the batter poured over them. The result is a pastry baked on top and fried on the bottom. Like a soufflé and a popover, Yorkshire pudding must be served before it collapses.

# Yorkshire Pudding

*T*his dish can be made in individual gem or cupcake pans provided they are greased and then filled ¼ inch deep with fatty roast beef juices. Most recipes do not require that the eggs be separated, but so doing ensures a lighter, crisper pudding.

**3–4 eggs, separated**
**1 cup bread flour**
**⅓ teaspoon salt**
**1 cup cold milk**

Beat egg whites until stiff. Add flour and salt to egg yolks and make a thick paste; thin down with milk until consistency of cream and beat well. Incorporate whites until no big globs of white show.

Pour batter into large roasting pan at least ¼ inch, preferably ½ inch, full of pan juices and roast in preheated 400° F oven for 10 minutes; then reduce heat to 350° F and continue baking, about 20–30 minutes or until puffed and golden brown. Serve at once.

If you wish to make pudding in roasting pan along with roast, make a half recipe using 2 eggs and pour around roast. Bake about 15 minutes or until golden brown.

# Z
## is for Zuppa

Italian for soup, except that in Italian, *zuppa* is not a generic term like the English word *soup*. It refers instead to a specific type of soup—one that is thick but not creamy, free of pasta or rice but ladled over toasted bread. Of course, definitions are not always definitive. Just to confuse the facts, neither of the two most famous zuppas fit that description.

The most famous zuppa of all, like so many other dishes, has a martial background. The hero of the story is Admiral Lord Horatio Nelson (1758–1805) whose victories for England cost him nearly everything. At the taking of Corsica in 1794, he was wounded in the right eye and suffered impaired sight. Three years later in a battle for Santa Cruz de Tenerife, the largest of the Canary Islands, he was shot in the elbow and lost most of his right arm in a bungled amputation. A year later, during the Battle of the Nile, a blow to the head put him in a coma from which it was feared he might never recover. He did, only to suffer a worse blow, one delivered to his heart, at the victory celebration, by Emma, Lady Hamilton, a lady in name only.

The wife of Sir William Hamilton, ambassador to the Court of Naples, Emma was a great favorite of Queen Maria Carolina of Naples and the two Sicilies. After Nelson's victory in 1798 at the Battle of the Nile, the Queen of Naples gave him a dukedom and a country palace and arranged a celebratory banquet in his honor. The pièce de résistance was a dessert created especially for Nelson. An Italian chef's attempt to make a traditional English trifle or pudding, it was a bit on the soupy side and became known as *zuppa Inglese*. Needless to say, this is no traditional *zuppa*. Yes, it is thick, but a thick *creamy* custard. Yes, it is free of rice and pasta, but instead of toast points, it is ladled over cake.

As for Emma and Horatio, their mutual contact with the court brought them together, and she enslaved him just as she had her husband. The three had the most famous ménage à trois in Europe. When Hamilton was recalled to England in 1800, Nelson accompanied them, and his daughter by Emma was born in 1801. When Hamilton died in 1803, Nelson didn't marry Emma—the first time he had refused her anything—and two years later in the battle of Trafalgar, he was killed even as victory was complete and the French fleet annihilated. Remembered generously in Nelson's will, Emma's gambling and extravagance put her in debtor's prison for a year, and she died broke in Calais in 1815. No happy endings for these two, but they left us a culinarly legacy in *zuppa Inglese* that many claim to be the best marriage of custard and cake in existence.

**Zuppa Inglese differs from place to place in Italy. In some areas it is a true trifle; in others, an Italian rum cake. Sometimes it's a meringue-topped custard; other times it's a soft, runny custard.**

The second soup, *zuppa alla pavese*, is the result of another of those king-defeated-in-battle-takes-refuge-in-farmhouse-is-fed-common-peasant-food-loves-it-and-demands-recipe stories. The king in this story was Francis I of France, and the battle was that of

Pavia in 1525, in which Francis was not only defeated but eventually captured. The farmhouse is unknown as is the farm wife, but the soup became famous.

In her best and maybe only bowl, the anonymous wife placed a slice of fried stale bread. Atop that she broke two newly laid eggs. Over that she slowly ladled the ubiquitous stock found simmering in every peasant's kitchen. The egg whites obligingly cooked slightly while the yolks remained runny. To complete the dish, she added a grating of quick-melting *grana padano*—a cheese similar to parmigiana but less expensive.

The king was so impressed he demanded that the recipe be given to one of his servants. Evidently the servant miswrote it or lost it, for there is no comparable soup in French cuisine. And just in case you didn't notice, unlike a proper zuppa, it was not a thick soup but a broth with poached eggs in it.

Another peasant soup is the now soignée French vichysoisse, whose name comes from the town of Vichy, about 225 miles southeast of Paris and famous for its hot and cold alkaline springs. Known to the Romans as *Vicus Calidus*, it was considered a sovereign remedy for hepatic conditions and was enjoyed by the French nobility from the seventeenth century onward. Its waters, when used to cook *carrots à la Vichy* (plain boiled carrots) and other foods, were supposed to help the liver and figured as well in the making of a peasant soup of potatoes and leeks.

Imagine yourself at the opening of the Ritz-Carlton's roof garden restaurant in New York. The year is 1917. The maitre d'hotel has convinced you to try a brand new soup created for the occasion by Louis Diat. A white-gloved, tuxedo-clad waiter places before you a tall, hoar-frosted, sterling silver, footed tureen (like the modern, stainless steel shrimp cocktail dish, only much fancier). With a flourish, the maitre d'hotel removes the lid. There, nestled in ice, a soupçon of chopped chives floating on top, is your first dish of vichyssoise. The staff watches you take that first reverent sip and nod your approval. The chef, Louis Diat himself, peering from behind the serving door, permits himself a small smile. He has done it again. Pulled a fast one on the Americans. For what sits so nobly in that dish is plain, old, cold *potage bonne femme*, the leek and potato soup known in every French household. The only element Diat has added—or subtracted, if you will—is its serving temperature, inspired by the *Cold* Springs of Vichy. Serving the soup ice cold, in the manner of the finest beluga caviar, made Diat's reputation in culinary histories.

He would, however, be horrified to see what passes for vichyssoise today in this country. Diat's original recipe has been bastardized by American cooks to include onions instead of leeks, chicken stock instead of water, and, like zuppa, rich milk but no cream—not even sour cream or yogurt.

Another French soup, French onion, has had a checkered existence. It began magnificently enough as the fourteenth-century creation of Guillaume Tirel, France's first great chef and author of the first cookbook written in French. By the seventeenth century, however, the soup had fallen on hard times. It was ignored at court and considered fit only for peasants. That was until Stanislas Leczinski, former king of Poland, gave it his imprimatur. Culinary legend has it that he was on his way to Versailles to visit his daughter, Maria, queen of France, when he stopped at an inn at Châlons. His choice of food was limited and only the onion soup was hot, so he and his party ordered it. They were so taken by this hearty broth with the huge crouton and melted cheese on top that Stanislas insisted on staying until he learned how to prepare it. The next morning he was in the kitchen in his robe, tears streaming down his face as he peeled onions for a huge crock of onion soup.

Unfortunately, only the chef at the Châlons inn, Stanislas himself, and his own chef knew how to make the soup, which, upon being served to his royal daughter and son-in-law, immediately received royal favor. Thus, a variety of recipes were concoct-

**The belief that soup has healing properties is a view shared by many cultures. Hence jokes that chicken soup, for instance, is the Jewish penicillin. Nika Hazelton, cookbook author and tell-as-it-is, notes that in this conviction the Italians are leaders, since they firmly believe in what can only be called the grail-like qualities of *il brodo* (broth) as the healer of all bodily and mental distress.**

ed in European cities, and authenticity went out with the dishwater. Some onion soups were made with broth, some with water, some with white wine. Some were bound with egg yolks, some with milk but no cheese. Some had a touch of Armagnac, some port, some vinegar. Some topped their crouton with Gruyère, Conte, or Parmesan; others used Camembert, Brie, or Roquefort.

Today you can find as many recipes for onion soup as you have cookbooks. Anything goes, as long as you use onions. You can top a steaming crock with chopped raw onions, sliced black olives, bread crumbs, slivered almonds, or you name it. All because Stanislas made onion soup a dish fit for a king.

In like manner, the French bouillabaisse is never prepared authentically in this country—or in any other country for that matter. Even in Marseilles, the city of its origin, it varies. That, surprisingly enough, is what makes it authentic. A soup so thick it is almost a stew, its antecedents have been traced to Pliny. Most authorities agree it began as a means for the fisher folk of Marseilles to cook their unsalable catch. Since then recipes have been unanimous in only one respect: They all include the *rascasse*, or scorpion fish (an unattractive fish with poisonous spines that can only be obtained at Marseilles). Some recipes call for saffron, some orange peel, some both. Some include tomatoes, others denounce them. Some say yes to adding wine, others say no.

**In the port of Les-Saintes-Maries-de-la-Mer in the Camargue, every year at the end of May, bouillabaisse stars in the celebration of the arrival of the Marys. According to legend, St. Mary Magdalene, St. Mary Jacob, St. Mary Salome, St. Mary of Bathsheba, and St. Martha, among others, escaped from the Holy Land after the crucifixion and supposedly set sail for Marseilles. Shipwrecked during a terrible storm, they washed ashore on the Camargue, where fishermen, watching over great cauldrons of this stew, succored them.**

Because there is so much difference from one soup pot to the next, seventeen Marseilles restaurateurs established a charter in 1980 defining the authentic contents of—but not the recipe for—bouillabaisse. The charter specified that at least four from a list of approved species of fish must be included in the soup-stew for it to be considered "authentic." Of course, hundreds of other restaurateurs immediately disagreed and continued making and serving their own pet recipes.

Some say the real attraction of a bowl of bouillabaisse is that it's always different. Others say it is the freshness of the ingredients, not the ingredients themselves, that determines the quality of the soup. Farm-fresh or store-bought, authentic or bastardized, peasant or patrician, soup in any language is one of the most satisfying creations to come from the kitchen. Savory or sweet, hot or cold, the blend of fine and simple ingredients in our most famous soups is a tribute to the inventiveness of the world's great cooks.

# Vichyssoise

*This recipe is based on that of Chef Louis Diat of the Ritz-Carlton Hotel in New York. Unlike other chefs, Diat never seemed to appreciate the significance of this soup—maybe because he was all too aware of its peasant origins.*

4 leeks, white part only, cleaned and finely sliced

1 medium onion, finely sliced

4 tablespoons (½ stick) sweet butter

5 medium uncooked potatoes, peeled and finely sliced

4 cups water or chicken broth

1 tablespoon salt

2 cups milk

2 cups light cream

salt and white pepper to taste

1 cup heavy or whipping cream

Sauté leeks and onion in butter until limp and transparent. Add potatoes, water or broth, and the tablespoon of salt. Bring to a boil and cook 35–40 minutes or until potatoes are mushy. Drain and purée in a Foley food mill or food processor. Return to heat and add milk and cream. Season to taste and bring to a boil. Cool and [to be really swish!] put though a strainer. Be sure it's cold before adding the heavy cream. Chill thoroughly until ready to serve. Serves 8.

# French Onion Soup

*I wish I could say this was the authentic, the one and only and original French onion, but I can't! That one is lost. This, however, meets all the descriptive criteria of the legendary one. You might, however, like it better with Swiss or mozzarella cheese.*

3 medium-size onions, thinly sliced

2 tablespoons butter

1 tablespoon flour

2 cups consommé

4 cups water

salt and pepper to taste

¼ cup scalded milk

6 slices stale French bread, lightly toasted

2 tablespoons melted butter

¼ pound grated Gruyère cheese

Cook onions until golden brown in butter. Sprinkle flour over them and stir until it is incorporated and free of lumps. Add consommé and water. Cover and cook gently for 20 minutes. Add milk, the secret ingredient. Put a slice of buttered bread in the bottom of a heatproof soup bowl, pour soup on top, and sprinkle with cheese. Place in 450° F oven until cheese is melted. Serves 8.

# Bouillabaisse

*Since one can't get the real thing—unless you're willing and able to fly in rascasse—this bouillabaisse is all things to all people. Any ingredient you don't like, simply eliminate.*

1 small lobster or crab (optional)

5 pounds fish fillets (4 pounds if using optional shellfish)*

1 large onion, chopped

1 large tomato, peeled, seeded, and chopped

3 cloves garlic, chopped

1 bay leaf

1–2 sprigs parsley

1 small twig fennel

1 small piece orange peel

½ cup olive oil

1 teaspoon salt

½ teaspoon pepper

several sprigs saffron

2 cooked and peeled potatoes (optional), kept warm

chopped parsley

stale French bread, dried or toasted (can be rubbed with garlic)

If using shellfish, poach it separately. When it turns red, reserve the cooking liquid and discard all shells but those of the lobster.

In a heatproof casserole with cover, place onion, tomato, garlic, parsley, fennel, orange peel, poached shellfish, and the firm-fleshed fish. Moisten with olive oil and add salt, pepper, and saffron. Let marinate covered, in a cool place for several hours.

Add sufficient boiling water (or the reserved shellfish cooking liquid) to casserole to cover the fish. Bring to a boil. Cook for approximately 7 minutes. Then add tender-fleshed fish and continue boiling for another 7–10 minutes or until all the fish is cooked but not falling apart.

Traditionally, the soup and the fish are served separately. Transfer fish with a slotted spoon to a serving dish along with optional potatoes. Put the sliced French bread in a tureen and pour soup stock over it (through a sieve if you want to be fancy). Garnish with chopped parsley. Use lobster shells to garnish the soup tureen. (In the old days, when eating out of the pot, the shell was used as a spoon.) Serves 6–8.

* Ask fishmonger for half firm-fleshed and half tender-fleshed fish (keep separated). It's best to use at least four different kinds, such as sea bass, haddock, white, cod, halibut, red or gray snapper, conger eel, etc.

# Bibliography

What follows is, admittedly, an incomplete list of all the books I consulted over the many years that I researched this book. A complete listing would number close to a thousand and go on for page after page after page. Such a list, although enriching the typesetter, could do serious damage to my publisher's bottom line. Therefore, I culled vigorously, eliminating, for example, the many biographies of Catherine de Medici that proved inconclusive. To the authors of the following, my thanks for all your help in helping me sort out the facts, fictions, and fables that came to be known as *The Cook's Tales!*

Apicius. *The Roman Cookery Book.* Translated by Barbara Flower and Elisabeth Rosenbaum. Great Britain: George G. Harrap & Co., Ltd., 1958. Translated by Joseph D. Vehling. New York: Dover, 1977.

Aresty, Esther B. *The Delectable Past.* New York: Simon & Schuster, 1964.

———. *The Exquisite Table, a History of French Cuisine.* New York: Bobbs-Merrill Company, 1980.

Beard, James. *Beard on Food.* New York: Alfred A. Knopf, 1974.

———. *James Beard's American Cookery.* Boston: Little, Brown & Company, 1972.

Beebe, Ruth Anne. *Sallets, Humbles & Shrewsbery Cakes.* Boston: David R. Godine, 1976.

Beer, Gretel. *Austrian Cooking.* Great Britain: Andre Drutsch Limited, 1954.

Beeton, Isabella. *Mrs. Beeton's Cookery and Household Management.* Revised and edited by Maggie Black and Susan Dixon. Great Britain: Ward Lock Limited, 1980.

# Bibliography

Benson, Elizabeth. Ali-Bab, *Encyclopedia of Practical Gastronomy*. Philadelphia: McGraw Hill Book Company, 1974.

Benson, Evelyn Abraham, ed. *Penn Family Recipes, Cooking Recipes of William Penn's Wife, Gulielma*. York, Pa: George Shumway, 1966.

*Better Homes and Gardens Heritage Cookbook*. Des Moines: Meredith Corporation, 1975.

Bliss, Mrs. *The Practical Cook Book Containing Upwards of One Thousand Receipts*. Philadelphia: David McKay, 1890.

Blue, Anthony Dias, and Kathryn K. Blue. *Thanksgiving Dinner, Recipes, Techniques, and Tips for America's Favorite Celebration*. New York: Harper Collins, 1990.

Brillat-Savarin, Jean Athelme. *The Physiology of Taste*. France, 1825. Translated and annotated by M.F.K. Fisher. New York: The Heritage Press, 1949. Translated and published by Peter Davia Limited: Dover Reprint, 1960.

Cannon, Poppy, and Patricia Brooks. *The President's Cookbook*. New York: Bonanza Books, 1968.

Carley, Eliane Ame-Leroy. *Classics from a French Kitchen*. New York: Crown Publishers, 1983.

Carr, Bessie, and Phyllis Oberman. *The Gourmet's Guide to Jewish Cooking*. London: Octopus Books Limited, 1973.

Carson, Jane. *Colonial Virginia Cookery, Procedures, Equipment, and Ingredients in Colonial Cooking*. Williamsburg: The Colonial Williamsburg Foundation, 1985.

*Cassell's Dictionary of Cookery*. Circa 1890.

Child, Julia. *Julia Child's Kitchen*. New York: Alfred A. Knopf, 1975.

Child, Mrs. *The American Frugal Housewife*. Boston: Carter, Hendee, and Co., 1878.

Claiborne, Craig. *Craig Claiborne's The New York Times Food Encyclopedia*. New York: Times Books, 1985.

Clayton, Bernard, Jr. *The Complete Book of Breads*. New York: Simon & Schuster, 1973.

———. *The Complete Book of Pastry, Sweet & Savory*. New York: Simon & Schuster, 1981.

Cosman, Madeleine Pelner. *Fabulous Feasts, Medieval Cookery and Ceremony*. New York: George Braziller, 1976

Courtine, Robert. *The Hundred Glories of French Cooking*. Translated by Derek Coltman. New York: Farrar, Straus and Giroux, 1971, 1973.

Coyle, L. Patrick, Jr. *Cook's Books*. New York: Facts on File Publications, 1985.

Day, Avanelle, and Lillie Stuckey. *The Spice Cookbook*. New York: David White Company, 1964.

De Gouy, Louis. *The Gold Cook Book*. rev. ed. Philadelphia: Chilton Company—Book Division, 1948.

de Bourrienne, Louis Antoine Fauvelet. *Memoirs of Napoleon Bonaparte by his Private Secretary. . . .* Edited by R.W. Phipps. New York: Charles Scribners & Sons, 1871.

de Groot, Roy Andries. *In Search of the Perfect Meal*. New York: St. Martin's Press, 1986.

de Temmerman, Genevieve, and Didier Chedorge. *L'ABC de la Gastronomie Francaise*. Paris: Editions Scribo, 1988.

Deighton, Len. *ABC of French Food*. New York: Bantam Books, 1989.

Del Conte, Anna. *Gastronomy of Italy*. New York: Prentice Hall Press, 1987.

Diat, Louis. *Cooking a la Ritz*. Philadelphia: J.B. Lippincott Company, 1941.

# Bibliography

Digby, John, and Joan Digby, eds. *Food for Thought*. New York: William Morrow & Company, 1987.

Dueland, Joy V. *The Book of the Lobster*. Somersworthy, N.H.: New Hampshire Publishing Company, 1973.

Dumas, Alexandre *(pere)*. *Alexandre Dumas' Dictionary of Cuisine*. Translated, abridged, and edited by Louis Colman. New York: Simon & Schuster, 1958.

Escoffier, Auguste. *La Guide Culinaire (Escoffier Cook Book)*. New York: Crown Publishing Company, 1941.

———. *Ma Cuisine*. Translated by Vyvyan Holland. London: The Hamlyn Publishing Group Limited, 1965.

Farmer, Fannie. *The Boston Cooking School Cookbook, 1896*. Facsimile edition. New York: Weathervane Books.

Ferrary, Jeannette, and Louise Fiszer. *California American Cookbook*. New York: Simon & Schuster, 1985.

Field, Carol. *Celebrating Italy*. New York: William Morrow and Company, Inc., 1990.

Field, Michael. *All Manner of Food*. New York: Alfred A. Knopf, 1970.

Fisher, Mary Frances Kennedy. *The Art of Eating*. New York: The Macmillan Company, 1971.

FitzGibbon, Theodora. *The Art of British Cooking*. Garden City, NY: Doubleday & Company, Inc., 1965.

Fussell, Betty. *I Hear America Cooking*. New York: Viking Penguin, Inc., 1986.

———. *Masters of American Cookery*. New York: Times Books, 1983.

Glasse, Hannah. *The Compleat Housewife.* 1774.

Glenn, Camille. *The Heritage of Southern Cooking.* New York: Workman Publishing, 1986.

Goock. Roland. *The World's 100 Best Recipes.* Melrose Park, Ill.: Culinary Arts Institute, 1971.

Gorman, Judy. *The Culinary Craft.* Dublin, N.H.: Yankee Publishing Incorporated, 1984.

Grigson, Jane. *British Cookery.* New York: Atheneum, 1980.

Guidroz, Myriam. *Adventures in French Cooking.* New York: The Macmillan Company, 1970.

Hazan, Marcella. *The Classic Italian Cook Book.* New York: Harper's Magazine Press, 1973.

Hazelton, Nika. *From Nika Hazelton's Kitchen.* New York: Viking, 1985.

Herbst, Sharon Tyler. *Food Lover's Companion.* New York: Barron's Educational Series, Inc., 1990.

Hill, Janet McKenzie. *The Whys of Cooking.* Cincinnati: Proctor & Gamble, 1922.

Hillman, Howard. *Kitchen Science.* Boston: Houghton Mifflin Company, 1989.

Hume, Audrey Noel. *Food.* Colonial Williamsburg Archaeological Series, no. 9. Williamsburg: The Colonial Williamsburg Foundation, 1978.

Jacobs, Jay. *Gastronomy.* New York: McGraw Hill, 1978.

Kimball, Marie. *Thomas Jefferson's Cook Book.* Charlottesville, Va.: University Press of Virginia, 1976.

Knox, Ann. *Cooking the Austrian Way.* London: Spring Books, 1958.

# Bibliography

Kolatch, Alfred J. *The Jewish Book of Why*. New York: Jonathan David Publishers, Inc., 1981.

——. *The Second Jewish Book of Why*. New York: Jonathan David Publishers, Inc., 1985.

Lang, George. *Lang's Compendium of Culinary Nonsense and Trivia*. New York: Clarkson N. Potter, Inc., 1980.

Lang, Jenifer Harvey, ed. *Larousse Gastronomique*. Hamlyn Publishing Group, Ltd., New York: Crown Publishers, Inc., 1988.

——. *Tastings, The Best from Ketchup to Caviar*. New York: Crown Publishers, Inc., 1986.

Langseth-Christensen, Lillian. *A Basic Recipe Book for Epicures*. New York: Funk & Wagnalls, 1969.

Lorwin, Madge. *Dining with Shakespeare*. New York: Atheneum, 1976.

Marshall, Agnes B. *The Book of Ices*. Reprinted as *Ices, Plain and Fancy* by the Metropolitan Museum of Art. New York: Charles Scribner's Sons London, 1976.

*Martha Washington's Booke of Cookery*. Transcribed by Karen Hess. New York: Columbia University Press, 1981.

McCully, Helen. *American Heritage Cookbook and Illustrated History of American Eating & Drinking*. New York: American Heritage Publishing Co., Inc., 1964.

McGee, Harold. *On Food and Cooking*. New York: Charles Scribner's Sons, 1984.

Merinoff, Lina. *Gingerbread*. New York: Simon & Schuster, 1989.

*Mrs. Beeton's Cookery*. London: Ward, Lock & Co., Limited, n.d.

Page, Edward B., and P.W. Kingsford. *The Master Chefs: A History of Haute Cuisine*. New York: St. Martin's Press, 1971.

Panichas, George A. *Epicurus*. New York: Twayne Publisher, Inc., 1967.

*Practical Housekeeping, a Careful Compilation of Tried and Approved Recipes*. Minneapolis: Buckeye Publishing, 1886.

Prudhomme, Paul. *Chef Paul Prudhomme's Louisiana Kitchen*. New York: William Morrow and Company, Inc., 1984.

Randolph, Mary. *The Virginia House-wife*. Columbia, S.C.: University of South Carolina Press, 1984.

Randolph, Sarah N. *The Domestic Life of Thomas Jefferson*. New York: Frederick Ungar Publishing, 1976.

Ranhofer, Charles. *The Epicurean, a Complete Treatise of Analytical and Practical Studies on the Culinary Art*. 1893. Dover Reprint, 1971.

Rhett, Blanche, Lettie Gay and Helen Woodward, eds. *Two Hundred Years of Charleston Cooking*. New York: Random House, 1934.

Root, Waverly, and Richard de Rochemont. *Eating in America, A History*. New York: William Morrow & Company, 1976.

Root, Waverly. *Food*. New York: Simon & Schuster, 1980.

———. *The Food of France*. New York: Alfred A. Knopf, 1958.

Rorer, Sarah Tyson. *Mrs. Rorer's Philadelphia Cook Book*. Philadelphia: Arnold and Company, 1886.

Schulz, Phillip Stephen. *As American as Apple Pie*. New York: Simon & Schuster, 1990.

*Seventy-Five Receipts for Pastry, Cakes and Sweetmeats*. Boston: Munroe and Francis, 1828.

Shapiro, Laura. *Perfection Salad*. New York: Farrar, Straus, and Giroux, 1986.

Sharman, Fay. *The Taste of France, A Dictionary of French Food & Wine*. Edited by Brian Chadwick and Klaus Boehm. New York: Macmillan, 1982.

Shute, Miss T. S. *The American Housewife Cook Book, Parts I and II*. Philadelphia: George T. Lewis and Menzies Co., 1880.

Simmons, Amelia. *American Cookery*. 1796.

Simon, Andre L. *A Concise Encyclopedia of Gastronomy*. New York: Harcourt, Brace and Company, 1982.

Simon, Andre L., and Robin Howe. *Dictionary of Gastronomy*. London: Rainbird Reference Books Limited, 1970.

Solomon, Jon, and Julia Solomon. *Ancient Roman Feasts and Recipes*. Miami: E.A. Seemann Publishing, Inc., 1977.

Stern, Jane, and Michael Stern. *Real American Food*. New York: Alfred A. Knopf, Inc., 1986.

Tannahill, Reay. *Food in History*. New York: Stein and Day, 1973.

*The Williamsburg Art of Cookery, or, Accomplished Gentlewoman's Companion*. Compiled from books known to have been used in Virginia. Williamsburg: Colonial Williamsburg Foundation, 1938.

Time-Life Book Editors. Foods of the World series. New York: Time Inc. and Time-Life Books.

Trager, James. *The Food Book*. New York: Grossman Publishers, 1970.

Tschirky, Oscar. *The Cookbook of "Oscar" of the Waldorf*. Werner Company, 1896. Dover Reprint, 1973.

Turgeon, Charlotte, and Nina Froud, eds. *Larousse Gastronomique*. English Edition. New York: Crown Publishers, Inc., 1961.

Tyree, Marion Cabell. *Housekeeping in Old Virginia*. Louisville: John P. Morton and Company, 1879.

Weaver, William Woys. *The Christmas Cook, Three Centuries of American Yuletide Sweets*. New York: HarperCollins, 1990.

————. *A Quaker Woman's Cookbook, the Domestic Cookery of Elizabeth Ellicott Lea*. Philadelphia: University of Pennsylvania Press, 1982.

Wolfe, Linda, ed. *The Literary Gourmet*. New York: Random House, 1962.

Wood, Emma. *Antique Dinner Recipes*. Mount Vernon, NY: Constantia Books, 1987.

# Index

# Index

# *Index*

# *Index*

# About the Author

LEE EDWARDS BENNING is by education a home economist, by perseverance a gourmet cook, by instinct a researcher, by choice a writer, and by good fortune the wife of a supportive writer who has either edited or coauthored all of her books, including this one. By him she is the proud mother of a tall, handsome computer-engineer-to-be at Syracuse University.

Her literary output includes three cookbooks, one novel, and four nonfiction books, covering everything from an exposé of the pet industry to the 1992 publication of the definitive book on point-of-purchase advertising.

Currently, the president of Words, Inc., she also has been an award-winning radio-TV-print copywriter, a teacher of creative writing, and the CEO of Can Do Communications.

*Globe Pequot* has an enticing selection of cookbooks for all interests, from the latest bluefish recipes to gourmet delights for the calorie-conscious cook. Here are some other fine cookbooks that will pique your interest. Please check your local bookstore for other fine Globe Pequot Press titles, which include:

*The Sage Cottage Herb Garden Cookbook*, $12.95
*A Little Book for a Little Cook*, $8.95 HC
*Gourmet Light*, $10.95
*The Gourmet Light Menu Cookbook*, $10.95
*Substituting Ingredients*, $8.95
*The Bluefish Cookbook*, $8.95
*The Salmon Cookbook*, $8.95
*Old Sturbridge Village Cookbook*, $1095
*Secrets of Entertaining*, $13.95
*The North End Italian Cookbook*, $13.95
*Truly Unusual Soups*, $8.95
*Another Season Cookbook*, $24.95 (hardcover); $17.95 (paper)
*Canning and Preserving without Sugar*, $11.95
*Martha's Vineyard Cookbook*, $10.95
*Easy Microwave Preserving*, $10.95

To order any of these titles with MASTERCARD or VISA, call toll-free 1–800–243–0495; in Connecticut call 1–800–962–0973. Free shipping for orders of three or more books. Shipping charge of $3.00 per book for one or two books ordered. Connecticut residents add sales tax. Ask for your free catalogue of Globe Pequot's quality books on recreation, travel, nature, gardening, cooking, crafts, and more. Prices and availability subject to change.